THE ROUGH GUIDE to

Happiness

by

Dr Nick Baylis

ROUGH
GUIDES

www.roughguides.com

Credits

The Rough Guide to Happiness

Commissioning editor: Ruth Tidball
Picture research: Ruth Tidball and Nick Baylis
Typesetting and indexing: Ruth Tidball
Proofreading: Jason Freeman
Production: Rebecca Short

Rough Guides Reference

Editors: Kate Berens, Peter Buckley,
Tracy Hopkins, Matthew Milton,
Joe Staines, Ruth Tidball
Director: Andrew Lockett

Front cover image: Jens Lucking/Getty Images
Author photo: Dr Alejandra Gardiol
Inside front cover image: Roy McMahon/Corbis

Publishing information

Published April 2009 by
Rough Guides Ltd, 80 Strand, London WC2R 0RL
375 Hudson St, New York 10014, USA
Email: mail@roughguides.com

Distributed by the Penguin Group:
Penguin Books Ltd, 80 Strand, London WC2R 0RL
Penguin Group (USA), 375 Hudson Street, New York 10014, USA
Penguin Group (Australia), 250 Camberwell Road, Camberwell, Victoria 3124, Australia
Penguin Group (Canada), 90 Eglinton Avenue East, Suite 700, Toronto, Ontario, M4P 2Y3
Penguin Group (New Zealand), Cnr Rosedale and Airborne Roads, Albany, Auckland, New Zealand

Printed and bound in China

Typeset in American Typewriter, Optima and Myriad to an original design by Ruth Tidball

The publishers and author have done their best to ensure the accuracy and currency of
all information in *The Rough Guide to Happiness*; however, they can accept no
responsibility for any loss or inconvenience sustained by any reader as a result of its
information or advice.

336 pages; includes index

A catalogue record for this book is available from the British Library

ISBN 13: 978-1-84836-015-0

1 3 5 7 9 8 6 4 2

Contents

Author's acknowledgements

I gratefully acknowledge…

▶ my much-loved friends and family, who mean all the world to me.
▶ the literary agent Robert Kirby (founder of unitedagents.co.uk), who rode shotgun on the author's contract through some pretty rough country.
▶ Rough Guides' Development Editor, Ruth Tidball – thank you, Ruth, for making the journey such a welcome education. Through your good nature and expertise, working on this was a privilege for me, from our first thoughts to our final draft.

About the author

In the early 1990s, Nick graduated from the MA in creative writing at the University of East Anglia, and then The National Film and Television School. All the while he'd been moonlighting on an Open University diploma in criminology, and so became a creative writing tutor cum counsellor in Feltham high-security young offenders prison, founding in 1998 the Trailblazers mentorship programme for inmates, which still goes from strength to strength (see trail-blazers.org.uk).

Earning his PhD in developmental psychology from Cambridge University in 1999, Nick created YoungLivesUK.com and spent a year interviewing some of the most accomplished individuals of their generation in many walks of life, from students of dance, art and music through to Nick Hornby, Gary Lineker, Kate Adie and the Commander of the Special Air Service Sir Peter de la Billière. The fundamental question was this: "How do you achieve your goals in life, and how do you enjoy the journey?". Nick's first book, *Learning from Wonderful Lives*, reflects this research.

Nick went on to be Britain's first lecturer in Positive Psychology and the Science of Well-being, launching his course at Cambridge University in 2001 and co-organizing The Royal Society's three-day international conference on the Science of Well-being in 2003. Since these beginnings, his explorations have endeavoured to be far broader, embracing the arts and philosophies, therapies and physical activities that when woven together can help a life to thrive and flourish. In pursuit of this vocation, Nick has a home in Cambridge but enjoys accepting invitations to spend much of the year teaching and learning overseas. (Visit nickbaylis.com.)

Dedication

*For adventure-lovers and creative outlaws
wherever in the world you find one another.*

Wishing you bon voyage!

Nick Baylis

Preface

In cultures where elephants are conscripted into the human working world, it is common practice each night to tether the baby elephant to a wooden post from which the chubby little fella can't escape. It seems that even though the elephant grows much wiser and stronger in so many ways, they never again challenge the authority of that post. They've long since presumed it can't be done. But if only they knew what they were capable of, and explored the possibilities.

Rather like those elephants, it's all too easy for us to get stuck with one view of the world and be slow to challenge the accepted ways of doing things. Yet our lives, and the lives of those we care for, are just too valuable to be left to the scientists and so-called experts, the gurus and government officials. Their proclamations and decrees just don't cut it. Reason being that no two lives are the same, nor any situation, which means we can't rely on the off-the-shelf solutions that people try to sell us claiming "one size fits all!" And it's exactly because there are no silver

bullets, no cure-alls, nothing that *always* works, that we each of us have to find out for ourselves what fits best and when.

What does this Rough Guide mean by "happiness"?

In 1948, the founders of the World Health Organization defined the word "health" as meaning "physical, mental and social well-being, not merely the absence of disease or infirmity".

In the same spirit, this Rough Guide is about "happiness" in the very broadest sense of the word. These pages set out to investigate what principles and strategies, what skills and experiences, seem to foster a life that is profoundly healthy, highly adventurous, good-hearted and rich in creative partnerships. In other words, a life that is going well on all its major fronts – physical, psychological and social – not only for the individual but for the communities in which we live and work, and for the wider natural world.

Such a "wholesome" happiness requires that we thrive in the face of adversity (i.e. the setbacks and sadness, the loneliness and regret, the anger and shame) just as readily as we thrive in the sunshine of friendship, joy and success. By contrast, if this book only focused on happiness in the sense of pleasurable feelings, it would be quite useless to us – as useless as consuming vitamin C tablets as our only source of good nutrition. Why? Because vitamin C will only work properly when it's interacting with all the other vitamins, minerals, fats and fibres to be found in a well-rounded, well-balanced meal. The same goes for life – it likes to be lived in a full and natural form.

Why on earth do we need a guide?

"Things are better today than at any other time in human history": this is what many of the big-name psychologists, economists and politicians are all too keen to tell us.

Oh really? It's by no means clear that we humans have been able to shape all that Internet information into "greater wisdom", because we're still, self-evidently, not very good at living. Are we really convinced that school teaching in crowded classrooms is better than the one-to-one apprenticeships it replaced? Or that artificial air-conditioning is better than the warmth of a fireside or the cool waters of a river? Or that watching television is better than experiencing the world first-hand?

Possibly not.

Well-being is on our to-do list, but never gets prioritized. The good health of our body, mind and personal relationships too often gets left until the end of the working day. It's the last thing we get around to… and only if there's time. Oh, we all talk earnestly about well-being (we individuals, schools, universities, businesses, parents and politicians), but when push comes to shove, we tend to prioritize A-grades and income brackets along with our favourite TV shows and pizza toppings.

Part of the problem may be that well-being is so very close to home that it's just too hot to handle. Other than ourselves, do we know anyone who is not troubled deeply by certain aspects of everyday life? Our eyes tear up, our temper rises, or our stomach sinks with despair, all because of some trigger that seems to derail us. Either that or it feels as if we're driving around with the handbrake on: revving like mad but making damned little progress. What's wrong with us?

Whereas we might readily confide to a stranger that we have cancer or a heart problem, by contrast we sometimes can't tell even our closest friends that we're depressed or having panic attacks or relationship troubles. We are all too aware that these "secret problems" cost us dearly, but what's to be done about them?

This Rough Guide hopes, where it can, to come face-to-face with all that unspoken but extremely important stuff. It's written on the principle that life is a skill, just like swimming; and like swimming, it can go from being about sheer survival to feeling wonderful, all depending on how good we become at it. Good fortune plays a role, but even fortune favours the well-prepared.

Putting our lives back together

Too often at school and university, different subjects are taught in isolation from each other, and our world and its history can remain fragmented in our minds for the rest of our lives. In open defiance of this accidental tradition, this Rough Guide is an attempt to step back a couple of paces to see how things fit together. It's a sort of aerial photograph for reconnaissance purposes. After all, life is multi-dimensional and interwoven, and so is this handbook. Not just in its focus as explained above (i.e. happiness viewed in the broadest sense), but in the kaleidoscope of lenses it endeavours to look through. As well as collecting some of the most compelling science, philosophies, faiths and therapies that have something to say about living well, this

Rough Guide tries to give a good deal of space to the creative and performing arts. How have novels and films, poetry and paintings, songs and sculpture, dance and drama explored and expressed what it is to be alive? Western approaches are certainly not seen as the only way, and we'll read about Chinese and Indian approaches to everything from energy therapies to sexual practices. Life is full-colour, so why not our exploration of it?

Not narrowing down, but opening up

The bookshop shelves devoted to happiness and well-being are groaningly heavy with one-horse wonders that advocate their single silver bullet to solve the problems of modern life, their patented panacea that will put us all right. Happiness itself is often sold as the latest in a long line of cure-alls for stress, depression and our highly demanding lifestyles.

Taking a stand against all of that, this handbook is neither trying to get its arms around everything, nor to distil the essence; rather it endeavours to illustrate the richness of life. Unless you're a pompous professor with a book to sell, or a blabbering drunk (the two personalities are often indistinguishable), you'll appreciate that there are no right answers, just intriguing possibilities, many of which you'll devise for yourself en route as counter-arguments to what you read here.

If that's what happens, then it's all to the good.

This isn't an encyclopaedia of happiness you're holding, nor a satellite navigation device barking out orders. It's a chance to compare notes. These ideas aspire to start discussions rather than finish them. To be a fuel for debate rather than a defence against dissent. To prompt controversy rather than police it. They offer an antidote to all those bestselling books peddling their happiness hype and humbug, which give only one point of view of what works. As Voltaire said, "I honour the man who seeks truth, but despise the man who claims to have found it". In respect of this, these pages challenge the accepted wisdoms with some of the most compelling evidence that flies in the face of proclamations by the latest TV professors and government officials. More than occasionally you will hear an irreverent voice calling out "The Emperor's wearing no clothes!", because when it comes to life guidance, there have been some big lies and bad science. This book blows the whistle on all of that baloney. You might even say it's an elephant in sheep's clothing, because it's pulling at that post in the ground, to find out what's possible.

Vive la différence!

For every world-class specialist who points us in one direction, there's another equally convincing authority pointing us in quite another. Which is why the quotes and pictures you'll find in these pages are not there to win you over with the weight of their reputation – they are merely intended to illustrate the rich and various range of opinion and evidence on all of these topics. If ever a turn of phrase appears to be offering a definitive conclusion on a subject, then please forgive it as an accident of style or over-enthusiasm. Nothing in this handbook is claiming "here's how things really are"; it's simply proffered as a starting place, a catalyst for adventure, kindling for a fire that might light the way and drive the steam engine.

In short: this is *not* a know-it-all self-help book. Quite the opposite. It simply dares to suggest that no one really knows, so we'd better explore for ourselves! And we shouldn't be too embarrassed about feeling a bit flummoxed by things. Let's remember that our Planet Earth circles a sun that's part of a galaxy of billions of other stars burning brightly. What's more, there are billions of such galaxies in our universe, and this universe is being stretched outwards by something physicists rather dramatically call "dark energy" that they confess they simply don't understand… save to say that it may have something to do with the equally mysterious "dark matter" that's holding you, me and the whole caboodle together.

The point is that life, by its very nature, is awe-inspiring stuff and seemingly impossible.

This idea that there are no golden rules to rely on feels a tad frightening at first. Then we realize it's actually very liberating. In learning to fish for ourselves, we can experiment, play and partner up. In respect of which, these pages aren't a set of rules, they're simply some raw ingredients. It's entirely up to us what to make of them, and with whom to share the experience.

We're in with a good chance

It's good to hear that Professor George Vaillant, long-time director of the Harvard Study of Adult Development (see pp.194–195), suggests that our skills for coping, for enjoying and for doing good each have the capacity to improve greatly. As the professor puts it, even those of us from "spectacularly dysfunctional families" can go on to create

fabulous lives. Painful memories and personal scars can lessen and mend if we persevere with self-healing choices. The past may seem to stack the odds, but it can never dictate the next steps we take, or that providence provides. Life is far less predictable than we dare to believe.

If that all sounds rather too hopeful, let's bear in mind how we each of us have learned some pretty daunting tricks in the past: to run, to swim, to talk, to kiss (okay, maybe some of these still need a little fine-tuning...), and as with riding a bike, we never forget how to make such impressive leaps forward. Why not with life?

This, dear reader, is your *Rough Guide to Happiness*: a travelling companion for elephants everywhere, gently exploring what's possible.

Nick Baylis
Cambridge, August 2008

1

Foundations for a beautiful life

Foundations for a beautiful life

Here is the first of ten inter-related chapters that endeavour to honour in spirit the richly woven nature of life. From the arts and sciences, philosophies and faiths, education and therapies, they gather together some of the most compelling approaches and insights, both ancient and modern.

This opening chapter introduces three central propositions, three "themes" if you will, which will be developed throughout this Rough Guide:

▶ **Theme 1:** that prioritizing pleasure isn't a helpful goal in life. Ridden well, *all* of our emotions – painful as well as pleasurable – have the capacity to carry us forward.

▶ **Theme 2:** that a wholesome life, characterized by well-rounded, well-balanced well-being, is the most promising route to a profound sense of rapport with ourselves and the world around us.

▶ **Theme 3:** that, in pursuit of a wholesome life, we each of us could boldly explore for ourselves what works best and when. Such a dynamic and versatile strategy is highly recommended, not only because the one-size-fits-all, off-the-shelf solutions are so ineffective, but because the gurus, governments, experts and authorities who sell them are just too unreliable.

Theme 1: A life in progress

"I just want to be happy!" is the Western world's dominant mantra, and we tend to think ourselves rather enlightened and guru-like for putting this feeling firmly at the centre of life's bigger picture. Happy is the new rich, the new beautiful. Governments have picked up on this new trend, and are now officially "measuring our happiness" (more on this in Chapter 8), presumably so they can calculate how much they can tax us before we go hopping mad with misery and overthrow the state. Yet, for many of us, happiness seems elusive. We're either less happy than we feel we ought to be, or we feel it's always slipping through our fingers just as we think we're getting somewhere.

The problem is we've set ourselves on a wild goose chase. Across the centuries, philosophers, scientists and thinkers of all stripes have attempted to pin down what exactly we mean by "happiness", and they've tended to fall in behind a single slogan: lots of pleasure, and an absence of pain. The eighteenth-century thinker Jeremy Bentham was one of the first to attempt to systematically measure our happiness. His theory was simple: to find how much happiness is generated by an action, we should add up all the pleasure and subtract the pain. A century or so later, Freud summed up what was still the generally accepted definition of happiness: "an absence of pain and ... strong feelings of pleasure". And this is pretty much the guiding principle we've stuck to ever since. We think of our pleasurable emotions (such as joy, satisfaction, pride or confidence) as being "positive" or good, and our painful ones (such as anger, fear, envy or shame) as being "negative" or bad. In short, we've deified pleasure, "feeling good", and demonized pain.

But this view of happiness is profoundly unhelpful to us. In fact, seeking to maximize pleasurable feelings and avoid pain is a life-strategy that has seriously damaging consequences, because it flies in the face of a far more fundamental drive of human nature: the drive for progress, for genuine improvement in our relationship with life.

Progress... in our relationship with life

Evolution has endowed us with a powerful motivation to make progress in our lives – to keep on getting better at living. After all, that's what will give us the best chance not only of surviving, but of thriving.

What do we mean by progress? It seems best summed up as ever healthier and more harmonious relationships. Such healthy partnerships are our best means of surviving and flourishing, because when we partner up we achieve far more together than we ever could alone.

For these reasons, nature has hard-wired us with a strong drive to seek out and foster such health-bringing relationships. And these vital relationships are not only with the folk around us. They can also be with the natural world of flora and fauna (see Chapter 8). And they can be between different aspects of ourselves: a healthy bond between our mind and body (see Chapter 4) and between our conscious and subconscious mind (see Chapter 2) makes us resilient and ready to rise to life's challenges.

Taken together, all these relationships add up to our "relationship with life". In short, then, progress in our life is all about an ever-deepening rapport with ourselves and the world around us. *Rapport* is a skill and a state of being that is considerate, responsive, respectful of, sensitive to, and delighting in the relationship.

Fakes promising closeness

It's because progress in our relationships is our hard-wired priority in life that the likes of booze, sex, TV and fame can be so misleading. These fakes give the impression of our relationships developing, without that really being the case. For instance:

▶ Getting drunk together can seem like a short cut to companionship, but once we're sober again, we find nothing has changed.

▶ Likewise, we might hope sex will bring emotional closeness, whereas healthy sex is the culmination of emotional closeness, not the cause of it.

▶ TV shows try to make us feel a part of something, but this relationship is an illusion.

▶ And note how fame is so often sought as a substitute for love, and always fails to be so.

Beauty signals healthy partnerships

So great is the evolutionary advantage conferred by healthy partnerships that nature has found a helpful means of attracting our attention. It's called beauty. No matter it be the beauty of a personality or a face, a landscape or a building, a verse of poetry or a mathematical formula, the common denominator is that *all* such beauties comprise separate ingredients that have come together in a special partnership to create an overall effect far more powerful than the sum of the individual elements. Beauty signals healthy partnerships. We need only think of how an entrancing and inspiring voice, dance, melody or meal achieves its effect by the complementary bringing together and rightful balance of its component parts. The more daringly and unexpectedly the healthy balance is achieved, the more beautiful we deem it.

We can think of beauty as a form of energy that radiates from a fine example of just about anything. This highly attractive energy is in effect a form of information for our senses; it is nature's barcode telling us how healthy something is, because health-bringing things increase the likelihood that we and our genes will survive and thrive.

Harvard psychologist Professor Nancy Etcoff observes that with this vital equation very much in mind (something beautiful = something healthy), our brain behaves like a highly sensitive radar constantly hunting for the beauty signal. This explains why, if we're shown a photograph of a face, it takes us less than a fifth of a second to make an accurate judgement of its attractiveness.

Much of the language of this "beautiful energy" is hard-wired and universal, which explains why three-month-old babies, who are a long way from being influenced by glossy magazines and media images, will far prefer gazing at conventionally attractive faces. Likewise, adults from diverse ethnic groups and cultures can all strongly agree on how good-looking someone is, no matter that someone be from another race or ethnic group. The active ingredients creating beauty seem to include symmetry, proportion and a sense of balance. In other words, beauty signals the healthy relationship between the parts that make up the whole.

In the psychologically healthy individual, this in-born calling to make progress in our life is overwhelmingly strong. From wherever we are now in life, no matter how beautiful, rich, clever or accomplished, we still want to feel ourselves moving forward in some way. When we come to the end of one journey, we very quickly hunger for another. As the Enlightenment philosopher John Locke put it, "No sooner is one action dispatch'd ... but another uneasiness is ready to set us on work". We're pre-programmed by our evolutionary heritage to get back on the trail. This drive to make progress in our relationships is so important to us that we put ourselves through hell for it. In our hearts, we seem to know full well that pleasure isn't our ultimate goal, because we deliberately engage in emotionally and physically painful enterprises so as to live more deeply. For instance, we exercise to improve our bodies; we compromise our own wants so as to live in peace with our partner; we work hard so as to make progress in our career; and we hike in the mountains till we're hot and sore in order to feel closer to nature, and at the end of it all we'll say "That felt great!" And we'll mean it, too.

What's the purpose of pleasure and pain?

The very reason, then, that we have such trouble hanging on to those pleasurable feelings that we've equated with "happiness" is that Mother Nature hasn't intended that we should: the kind of permanent cheerfulness we've been aiming for would spell disaster for our progress in life, because we'd just grind to a grinning halt, like a drunk or dope addict. Rather, pleasure's role is to enable this progress in our lives by driving, coaxing, guiding us forward. It can be one or all of three things:

▶ **A fuel:** pleasurable feelings can help motivate us; for example, if we feel confident we can channel this energy to take on a challenge.
▶ **A reward:** pleasure can be a reward for improvement; for example, we will feel the pleasure of satisfaction at having learned something valuable.
▶ **A flashing beacon:** pleasure can be a flashing beacon, saying "over here if you want to make progress!"; for example, walking in the countryside feels profoundly good, so we're particularly keen to do it.

The crucial distinction is that our pleasurable thoughts and feelings are not in themselves the improvement. What we actually do – the activity, the challenge, the learning – that's the progress. Our brains are only interested in pleasure as a way to get us to make progress in our essential relationships with ourselves and

> **"I have never looked upon ease and happiness as ends in themselves ... The ideals which have guided my way, and time after time have given me the energy to face life, have been Kindness, Beauty and Truth."**
> Albert Einstein

Happiness for sale

Advertisers are determined to convince us that happiness is something that can be bought, ready-made off the shelf. They encourage us to go straight to pleasurable feelings as directly as possible, perhaps via boozing, over-eating, watching TV, or escaping into fantasy. But this passive consumption of pleasure leads only to stagnation and deterioration in our lives (see pp.192–196 and pp.258–260 for more on this). Rather than consuming pleasures, we need to generate them through our own best efforts to progress our relationships. In this, there can be no short cuts nor substitutes.

the world around us. And "feeling good" is just *one* means by which to achieve this far greater goal.

Just as nature hasn't intended us to be permanently cheerful, neither has she meant for our lives to be free of pain. For pain isn't our enemy, no more than pleasure should be our ultimate goal. If it is overwhelming or not channelled constructively, pain can cause us to stop trying, turn back, or become embittered. But, if we learn to ride them well, our painful emotions can be an equally powerful source of energy and guidance as our pleasurable emotions. Painful feelings can serve a very similar role to pleasurable ones. They can be:

▶ **A fuel:** painful emotions can be a fuel for self-motivation; for example anger that everyone around us assumes we'll fail at a task might spur us on to succeed at it.

▶ **A punishment:** pain can be a punishment for not making sufficient improvement; for example we will feel the pain of frustration at not having learned anything valuable.

▶ **A flashing beacon:** just as with pleasure, pain can be a signal to us saying "over here if you want to make progress!" Pain should certainly not be regarded as a red "stop" light or a skull and crossbones warning us to turn back. Indeed, the experiences that hurt and scare us most can often be the richest sources of learning and progress if only we can confront them and find ways to channel all that emotional energy.

It's as if we're steam engines fuelled by a furnace that burns both coal (pain) and wood (pleasure) so as to create the energy of self-motivation. There are no intrinsically "positive" or "negative" emotions. Both pleasure and pain can be the fuel to great progress. Equally, both can hold us back and cause

Singin' in the rain: Gene Kelly's dancing for joy despite getting soaked to the skin reminds us that it's not what happens to us that affects us, it's what we decide to do about it.

us problems if we let them. Only our skill at channelling our emotional energy determines its eventual outcome. This brings us to a theme that'll recur throughout this book: it's not what troubles or joys we run into but what we do about them that determines their net effect upon our lives.

Derailed by pleasure

Pleasure can derail us if we don't channel it helpfully. We all have our own personal anecdotes of how the sheer power of such pleasurable feelings as love, hope, curiosity, pride or satisfaction has sometimes caused our applecart to turn over because we didn't exercise sufficient skill to helpfully channel the powerful energy of those emotions. For instance:

▶ **We're so in love, we behave foolishly and upset the other person.**
▶ **We're so delighted by some success, we get drunk as a skunk.**
▶ **We're so optimistic about a project, we're blind to the pitfalls.**

It takes as much skill to prevent the energy of success from derailing us as to prevent the setbacks from doing so.

Spurred on by pain

Consider those occasions when, out of shame, fear, anger or loneliness, we have acted in very positive ways in an attempt to dramatically improve the situation... and have succeeded in doing so.

On those occasions when we've managed to turn our troubles into triumphs, we are not unlike "horse whisperer" Monty Roberts (see pp.144–145) who took his childhood experience of terrifying bullying at the hands of his brutal father, and used this pain to help develop a gentle and respectful method to train wild horses. We are not unlike eight-times winner of the Tour de France Lance Armstrong, who took his teenage anger and shame at being a fatherless boy living in a trailer park, and ploughed this energy into hours of sports practice every day. We are not unlike Eileen Collins, who took her passion for planes and flying that was frustrated by her family's poverty, and channelled it into reading every book on the subject she could lay her hands on. This intelligently channelled passion helped her become NASA's leading pilot and space shuttle commander twenty years later.

Creative anger can carry us forward

There is some compelling evidence that learning to acknowledge and positively channel our anger serves a vital role in our well-being. The Harvard Study of Adult Development (see pp.194–195) observed that those men and women who either bottled up their frustrations or were prone to explosive outbursts were at least three times more likely to have unsatisfying careers, as well as severely inhibited personal and social lives. On the other hand, those who learned to harness their anger to fuel the sort of creative action that put things right were far more likely to have well-established and satisfying careers, emotional and physical intimacy, and all-round healthy and rewarding lives. It seems we need the capacity to feel angry and not just sad when our callings are thwarted, and we need an "anger-burning furnace" if we're to drive forward our dreams in life.

NASA commander Eileen Collins grew up poor but channelled her longing to be a pilot into reading all about it and saving for her first lessons at the age of 19.

These extraordinary personalities illustrate how, when hardship comes our way, we should try asking ourselves what outcomes could possibly put the situation right. What accomplishments would enable us to look back on our dire situation (the shame, the setback, the fear) and confess that "On reflection, I am rather grateful things went pear-shaped, because without the rocket-fuel energy from all that pain, I would never have had the wherewithal to put things right and to have gone so far beyond my previous limits."

Putting our pains to good use

In *How Proust Can Change Your Life*, philosopher Alain de Botton writes: "Though philosophers have traditionally been concerned with the pursuit of happiness, far greater wisdom would seem to lie in pursuing ways to be properly and productively unhappy. The stubborn recurrence of misery means the development of a workable approach to it must surely outstrip the value of any utopian quest for happiness." To which end, de Botton studies Proust's life-guiding novel, *In Search of Lost Time*. Proust felt putting suffering to good use was "the whole art of living", and advised us to find our passions and live according to them.

Sadly, the emotional alchemy that allows us to channel our pains into something truly positive is a crucial skill in short supply. It's ironic that there's a veritable rash of books on "How to be happier", when what's really needed is knowing how to be scared, angry, lonely and ashamed – knowing what to do with those painful emotions so their energy carries us forward rather than derailing us.

How sad that so often we anaesthetize or numb our painful emotions by over-eating, boozing, retreating into fantasy, fibbing, surfing the Internet, over-spending, ill-considered sex... all the way through to the more disguised methods of avoidance, such as overwork, over-exercise, voraciously reading novels, or distracting ourselves with wall-to-wall activity. That's repressing our energy, not riding it.

Reassessing pain

Pain and pleasure are opposites but not enemies. They are the re-set switch for one another: each makes us more keenly responsive to the other. Our progress in life requires both types of stepping stone – pain and pleasure, as if hot and cold, night and day – and neither member of that partnership is more valuable than the other.

This left-right relationship has been observed long before now. The Ancient Greek philosopher Heraclitus of Ephesus wrote that "All things come into being by the conflict of opposites." This sentiment was echoed in 1790 by the poet William Blake: "Without contraries there is no progression. Attraction and Repulsion, Reason and Energy, Love and Hate, are necessary to Human existence."

What's more, pleasure and pain very often travel side by side. The nineteenth-century philosopher Friedrich Nietzsche railed against his contemporaries' obsession with the "ever easier lifestyles" that personal wealth, imperialism and the limitless horizons of technology seemed to promise: "How little you know of human happiness, you comfortable and benevolent people, for happiness and unhappiness are sisters and even twins that either grow up together or, as in your case, remain small together."

> *"Only people who are capable of loving strongly can also suffer great sorrow."*
> Leo Tolstoy

Consider the following:

▶ **How much more do we relish our food for having first felt the ache of hunger?**

▶ **How much more do we enjoy the profound satisfaction of orgasm for having first felt the longing of sexual ardour?**

▶ **How much greater is our pride in learning a skill for having first felt the embarrassment and frustration of our inabilities?**

▶ **How much greater is our love for someone when we have first experienced emptiness and loneliness without them?**

Though there is no guarantee that misery will lead to joy, it renders us ripe for it, if only we can harness the know-how. Our intense pains automatically prime us for exquisite pleasures. In Alexandre Dumas' novel *The Count of Monte Cristo*, after imprisonment in isolation for a dozen

---

Painful childhoods, extraordinary lives

A study of the biographies of seven hundred eminent individuals from all walks of life in the twentieth century was conducted by the Goertzel family (Mildred, Victor and their son Ted) *in their spare time*. Their book *Cradles of Eminence* recounts how three quarters of those individuals had suffered a childhood deeply troubled by some sort of adversity – painful poverty, a broken home, rejecting, over-possessive or dominating parents, financial hardships or physical handicaps. Yet those same children nonetheless grew into adults who rose to great heights of personal and professional achievement. Rather as a plane can most easily take off when facing into the wind, it seems that by facing and surmounting problems we can grow stronger than if our journey had been uneventful. It seems that if we can learn to harness its energy, adversity can become the wind beneath our wings.

years, the count tells two young lovers "You must have wished yourself dead, to know how good it is to live." Equally, the more ecstatically we feel love, the harder we'll cry when we lose it. If I love my friend, I will miss her dearly when she leaves me.

There are no short cuts... no health-bringing ways to bypass the pains that prime our passions, our intellect, our body and our soul for pleasure, nor those that follow when our heart-felt loves are lost or thwarted. But we do have a choice nonetheless: each of us can ask ourselves "How deeply do I wish to live?" Do we want the intense pleasures that will necessarily cause us intense pains once the pendulum swings the other way, as it surely must? Or would we rather live a more gently undulating life? There seems to be no right or wrong answer; we each of us live as deeply as our hearts and heads and bodies can manage at any particular time. This is living fully, and keeping faith with life.

It's clear, then, that pain is not our enemy. Feeling nothing at all is our enemy, because without energy, without drive, without self-motivation, there can be no sense of direction and no progress. Coming to accept pain as a necessary companion to pleasure, and to appreciate it as a powerful fuel for progress in our lives, could totally revolutionize how we live. Once we stop being scared rigid by the tears, living life becomes a whole lot easier. Once we accept our pains as no more than an occupational hazard of attempting to improve things, we'll be able to channel them more confidently, daring to venture forward despite the risk of increased setbacks or loss or rejection. By being more adventurous in what we dare to take on, we live life more openly and more deeply and this approach brings the likelihood of greater progress.

Redefining happiness

Here is this Rough Guide's proposal for a new, more helpful, definition of wholesome happiness: happiness is not permanent pleasurable feelings and an absence of pain. Rather, it is a deeply satisfying sense of all-round, well-balanced well-being and progress in our life, a sense that our life is going in the right direction, no matter the pains we might be suffering as stepping stones en route.

Happiness isn't a final goal or destination – it is and always will be a work in progress. We might find ourselves wondering what's the point of all this striving for improvement in our life. One answer might be that the journey itself is the point, the goal, the ultimate purpose of our mission. The buck stops there… en route. Mother Nature simply wants us to be in the running. It's just like granny always said: it's the taking part that counts; it's the trying. The missions we deem important, the spirit in which we travel, and the partnerships we create along the way – these taken together are the making and the measure of us.

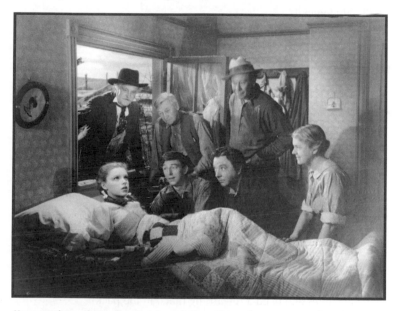

Keep on down that yellow-brick road: from Homer's great poem *The Odyssey* and Bunyan's *The Pilgrim's Progress* to the classic movie *The Wizard of Oz*, life as a journey is one of the most enduring metaphors in the arts. Note, though, how a need for a place called "home" balances the need for the voyage; how fresh nerve-tingling experiences are balanced by the friendly, old familiar. At the end of her incredible adventure, Dorothy finds herself back in Kansas and realizes "There's no place like home".

Theme 2: A wholesome life

How can we foster more wholesome happiness? One good answer seems to be to make our life as wholesome as possible. The wholesome (or "holistic") life is one which is *well-rounded* and *well-balanced*.

It's important to note here that a wholesome life doesn't mean "a full life" because a life may be full or busy with unhelpful or imbalanced activities, such as workaholic schedules or frantic socializing. However, it does imply taking ourselves as far as we can healthily go. For example, we should sleep a natural cycle till we're hungry to get up (rather than when the alarm clock screams at us), and then we should stretch our body, emotions, intellect and relationships to their fullest range and capacity.

Let's look more closely at what well-rounded, well-balanced well-being might mean in practice.

Well-rounded

We naturally want a satisfying sense of progress in each dimension of life, and improvements within one arena will do nothing to ease our hunger for progress in another. For instance, progress in our career won't satisfy our sexual longings, nor our need to climb mountains or express ourselves artistically. This is why only *all-round* progress will bring *all-round* satisfaction.

Each dimension can itself subdivide into smaller categories, so a raise in income won't make the work feel any more interesting (we're naturally inquisitive creatures), nor will extra money compensate us for a job title that doesn't afford us a sense of social status (because we're highly social creatures and need a rewarding place in the pack).

In short, if we want to lastingly improve our lives, we need to move everything forward at once, so that nothing pulls us back. This means progressing every dimension of ourselves, even the ones that may have lain dormant or under-used: our subconscious, our body, our emotions, our thoughts, our relationships. This wholesome approach is no different from when we want to lift a heavy weight: rather than pluck it up with just our arms, we should squat right down like a coiled panther so that we can use all of our body: thighs, haunches, back, shoulders and breathing. Better still if we can inspire a willing partner to share the load and make light of things.

Well-balanced

The better we can balance ourselves, the further we can reach. It seems "sustainable excellence" relies on balance, because it allows us to reach further towards our goals without desperately throwing ourselves once and for all at the problem. Chapter 7 discusses how learning to balance demanding work with restorative play can help us to do far better at work than if we single-mindedly devoted ourselves to it. Balance can apply to every component of life: we need to balance theory with practice, time alone with time with others, taking on new challenges with consolidation and recuperation. But perhaps the fundamental balance we need to maintain in our lives is between our three core faculties: emotions, thoughts and action.

Respect for the intrinsic equality of our three human dimensions is by no means commonplace. Quite the opposite: attempts to impose a hierarchy among them have been the cause of much conflict and distress across the millennia.

As far as the Ancient Greek philosophers Socrates, Plato and Aristotle were concerned, our capacity for reason was what set humans apart from other creatures. They concluded from this that reason was our guiding light, our priority purpose, and that we should take rational thinking as far as it would go. In his famous "chariot allegory", Plato characterized what he considered to be the proper relationship between reason

Both roundedness and balance benefit from healthy human partnerships, because if we team up with a loving friend, a good teacher or the right partner, we can reach further towards our passions than we ever could on our own.

and passion: our reason is like a charioteer, controlling two horses which represent our passions. For Plato some of our passions – such as courage and love of honour – carry us forward, and these are represented by a noble white steed. But other passions, such as our bodily desires and

The beautiful personality

The individual who combines thoughtfulness, passion and physical engagement, while also loving people and wider nature in equal measure, is a personality that holds a special place in our hearts. In the Renaissance, such a well-rounded personality was honoured as the ideal to which all budding courtiers should aspire: they were expected to fence and hunt in the morning, be linguists and logicians in the afternoon, and play music and write poetry in the evening. Such roundedness was embodied in the poet, playwright, wit, lover and soldier Cyrano de Bergerac, and the poet-explorer Sir Walter Raleigh.

Equally admired are those women who have broken the bonds of society's prescribed domestic roles to live a more rounded existence. Eleanor Roosevelt (1884–1962) had a difficult childhood and writes in her autobiography of how she felt herself to be an unloved "ugly duckling": "My looks fell so far below the family standards and I had no special gifts of any kind to redeem my looks." Married at twenty, she describes herself as a dutiful first lady to President Franklin Roosevelt and a mother of five, yet in her mid-thirties she very consciously transformed herself into a world-inspiring philanthropist responsible among her many other social innova-

This man, for one, wasn't afraid to break out from his assumed role in society to live a more rounded and colourful existence. Honoured for the bold and steadfast way in which he led Britain to victory in World War II, he was also a Nobel Prize-winning writer and an audacious wit. What's less well known is that he took up oil painting at the age of 41, produced 500 fine works, and was made an honorary member of the Royal Academy. He is, of course, Sir Winston Churchill.

appetites, threaten to pull us off course, and these are represented by an unruly black horse. Likewise, Aristotle viewed desire, for instance sexual desire and sexual pleasure, as a threat to order and authority because, he claimed, it undermined our rationality.

Oprah Winfrey: a woman-in-progress.

tions for the first Universal Declaration of Human Rights in 1948. More recently, Oprah Winfrey (oprah.com) fairly describes herself as "a woman-in-progress". From the days when she was reading out scriptures in church as a three-year-old child, she has overcome devastating childhood traumas and adversities to become the world's leading woman in the arenas of both media and philanthropy (she is a TV show host, author, magazine publisher and tycoon, and is founder of and contributor to many highly successful charitable and social initiatives). Somehow Oprah also made time to become an Oscar-nominated supporting actress for her role as Sofia in Steven Spielberg's acclaimed film *The Color Purple* (1985).

When one considers the beautifully colourful dimensions of the above personalities, how sad it is that our modern society encourages and reveres not well-roundedness but single-mindedness. Perhaps it is the legacy of the Industrial Revolution, but it seems to be the accepted wisdom that society's "progress" depends on ever narrower specialization on the part of its members. And so it is as if, very early on in life, society asks each of us "Are you a scientist, an artist or an athlete, because you can't be all three?" Such a limited, uni-dimensional existence would seem to go against the very grain of what it is to be human and free-spirited. Yet so long as our culture exalts the specialist, role models for a well-rounded life will be few and far between.

In assessing their views, let's not forget that these much-studied ancient philosophers were their era's equivalent of today's cloistered and cerebral university professors. Their conclusions were quite clearly *not* shared by the great majority of their fellow Athenians, for whom copious amounts of athletics and sexuality, dancing and drama, feasting and fasting, were a fundamental way of life. Nonetheless, this pitting of reason against passion, and the consequent repression of our passionate desires and physical needs, has been a recurrent theme in Western culture ever since. (See pp.151–154 for more on the Christian Church's demonizing of our sexuality and physical bodies.)

Arguably, these three ancient philosophers were quite wrong to prioritize our intellectual and logical abilities (and our modern education systems make the same mistake). But the advocates of Positive Psychology (see pp.85–101) are just as wrong to prioritize "feeling good". And we might add that sportsware firm Nike's exhortation to unconsidered action – *Just do it!* – is equally unhelpful. When it comes to our all-round well-being, our thoughts, feelings and actions

> **"It seemed to me that it would be very foolish to discard the reasons of the heart for those of the head. Indeed I did not see why I could not enjoy them both ... I could not feel that the Supreme Creator who gave us our minds as well as our souls would be offended if they did not always run smoothly together in double harness."**
>
> Winston Churchill

are all equally important to us. They shouldn't be at loggerheads; rather, in the well-balanced life, they play interrelated and complementary roles, supporting and feeding into one another:

▶ **Our emotions** (our feelings, our passions) provide not only the compass bearings that guide us, but also the fuel that drives our thoughts and actions. It is intense emotions that give us a sense that our life is worthwhile, valuable, and capable of making a vital difference. We know by the feelings in our heart and guts who and what is most important to us; and such feelings also provide us with the energy to pursue these vocations. It is particularly noteworthy that without emotion we are unmotivated, and can't make choices. Stark evidence for this comes from those unfortunate souls who

Mind, body and soul supporting one another

It seems clear that our three different dimensions are intended to work benevolently together, if only because they do so very well. For example, vigorous physical exercise is wonderfully effective at changing how we feel, and can cure a state of depression (see pp.112–113); meanwhile, the focused-thinking technique of self-hypnosis (see pp.74–76) is well able to reduce our sense of physical pain, and greatly improve a host of physical ailments.

have received an injury to the frontal lobes of the brain. Such an injury seriously weakens the emotions, with the result that though the brain might work well in every other way, the emotionally blunted personality cannot make decisions, and feels no strong motivation to pursue anything.

▶ **Our thoughts** (the products of our rational, logical mind) attempt to discern patterns in our lives and the wider world so that we can better understand their dynamics. And so, when we encounter problems on those journeys we're driven to undertake by our emotions, our reason can suggest possible solutions. Remarkably, considering his contemporaries' ardent championing of reason and rationality, it is the Scottish Enlightenment philosopher David Hume (1711–76) who best expresses the co-operative relationship that ought to exist between our thoughts and our emotions: "Reason

Complementary contrasts

Yin is not the opposite of yang; the black and white of the symbol actually fold into one other, hugging, rather than facing off and squaring up. In just the same way, man is not the opposite of woman – they naturally fold into one another, complementing each other's strengths and beauties. Opposites cancel each other out, whereas elements with complementary contrasts helpfully balance one another so as to create a compound that brings out the best of both and also generates some shared new qualities. Let's not be afraid of contrasts, then, for they give rise to complementary partnerships that foster healthy progress.

is, and ought only to be the slave of the passions, and can never pretend to any other office than to serve and obey them."

▶ **Our actions** (our behaviour) are our only means of engaging with the world, otherwise we'd be islands of isolation, and our feelings and thoughts would be imprisoned and ineffectual. Action provides our thoughts with feedback on what works best, while also stoking our emotions and sense of direction.

In support of the wholesome life

So much of modern life dismantles things into what we think are their component parts. In one sense or another, we extract the juice and leave out the pulp; refine the flour and omit the bran; bottle the milk and skim off the fat.

Consider how:

▶ **We send abbreviated emails and texts rather than conversing face to face.**
▶ **We take vitamin supplements rather than eating a balanced diet.**
▶ **In gyms, we exercise specific parts of ourselves.**
▶ **In schools, we learn subjects separately, and very often through theory rather than practice.**
▶ **Medics know too little about the mind, while psychotherapists know too little about the body.**

But is it possible that by this dismantling of so many aspects of our lives into bits and pieces, we might be losing some vital ingredients, not least of which are the synergies between the elements as they occur in their full and natural form? Throughout its pages this Rough Guide offers alternatives to this bits-and-pieces way of living – from how and what we eat and how we use our bodies to spending time with people in the flesh rather than making do with a disembodied voice over a phone line. But for now, here is one key example of how a wholesome approach very often is best:

Question: How long does it take most people learning to fly a glider or light aircraft to "go solo" for the first time? ("Going solo" means flying oneself on a circuit around the airfield, while our instructor watches proudly from the ground.)

Answer: Fifteen hours or so. Fifteen hours of being at the controls (however scared and clumsy at first) is enough to take us from being an absolute beginner to that solo circuit of the airfield.

Amazing, isn't it!

The Buddhism of His Holiness the Dalai Lama

Tenzin Gyatso, the fourteenth Dalai Lama, is the spiritual leader of the Tibetan Buddhists, though he has lived in exile since 1959 because of Chinese rule in Tibet. He received the Nobel Peace Prize in 1989, and has expressed his conception of Buddhism in a range of popular books. In some important respects, his teachings are akin to this Rough Guide's philosophy:

▶ He writes: "The most important use of knowledge and education is to help us understand the importance of engaging in more wholesome actions and bringing about discipline within our minds." He suggests practising visualizations as a practical means of achieving this (a similar technique is explored at length on pp.74–76).

▶ He believes that a compassionate, warm, kind-hearted person is healthy, and that our underlying human nature is gentleness.

▶ He believes that we do best to face up to the reality of the situation, and confront our problems rather than avoiding them. He also believes that a greater tolerance of suffering, rather than regarding it as an abnormal or unnatural state, is beneficial because the struggles of life can help make us who we are, and strong.

▶ He argues for a balanced, supple and flexible approach to life. For instance, he calls for there to be a variety of religions because the world contains a variety of people with differing needs.

However, on other important themes, this Rough Guide suggests an alternative viewpoint.

▶ The Dalai Lama does not appear to view the body as the equal of the emotions and intellect. He says "True happiness relates more to the mind and heart", and advises that our mental state, and in particular a calm mind, is "the prime factor in achieving happiness". By contrast, this Rough Guide suggests well-being is achieved through an equal balance between body, emotions and intellect, and that our deepest-felt passions are the energy and compass driving the very heart of life.

▶ The Dalai Lama says there are "negative emotions" which are harmful to us (and he deems anger to be one of these) and "positive emotions" which are helpful. By contrast, this Rough Guide argues that it is only how we use the energy of our emotions that renders them either harmful or helpful.

(The above quotations are taken from *The Art of Happiness: A Handbook for Living*, by His Holiness the Dalai Lama and Howard C. Cutler.)

But think how quickly and proficiently we learn to ride a bike or drive a car, though it seemed quite impossible for the first few hours of trying. The reason we can achieve this rapid competency is that we learn such skills *not* sitting in a classroom, *not* from a book, *not* by breaking them down into various steps, but by actually doing the whole task for real and taking full "hands-on" responsibility from the very first moment. We start slowly, awkward and uncertain, but our progress is swift because the feedback is instantaneous and the stakes are high. Given the choice of sink or swim, we invariably do the latter because our natural instincts rise to the challenge, and, coached in some fundamental principles thrown to us from the touchline, we soon get the hang of things. The point being that we learn best when we have all the elements there at the same time (and let's bear in mind that many of the key elements may be invisible to us, intangible, or so subtle as to be barely discernible). Such wholesome learning is messy and full of mistakes, but it has a magic ingredient – those synergies between the various elements of the task – that makes the whole experience so much more powerful than the sum of its parts, and that simply can't be substituted with a bits-and-pieces approach. (For much more on wholesome learning, turn to pp.200–209.)

So, however we choose to achieve it, this Rough Guide believes that living beautifully requires a well-rounded balance as its foundation.

It's surely no coincidence that the word *health* is from the Old English meaning *wholesome,* and the verb *to heal* means *to make whole again.* Much of modern life has lost this ancient wisdom.

Theme 3: Explore!

This Rough Guide endeavours to help us explore what principles, strategies, skills and experiences can create a more wholesome, beautiful life – one that is profoundly healthy, highly adventurous, good-hearted and rich in creative partnerships with the world around us. To which end, it advocates what it calls a "Universal Exploration of Well-being". This exploratory approach to enriching our rapport with life is made up of three distinct strands, each offered as an alternative to the business-as-usual in mainstream education, healthcare and the social sciences:

Exploring for ourselves

Our exploration should be universal in that every individual should take personal responsibility for exploring the possibilities of life. Rather than waiting passively for prescriptive decrees from the authorities about what they think is good for us, this Rough Guide wishes to inspire individuals, partnerships, families and communities to explore for themselves what works and when in the rough and tumble of their particular real-life situations. Understanding life going well is just too important a subject to be left in the hands of scientists, gurus or governments. All too often these so-called "experts" let us down: governments are often reluctant to make the kind of real changes that are needed to improve their citizens' well-being, and experts of all stripes make mistakes or even let their own agendas and interests skew their advice (see the box overleaf and pp.234–235 for much more on this). We all need to take far more responsibility for our own investigations of what suits best and when.

Exploring more broadly

Our exploration should be universal in that it should embrace both the theory and practice of the arts, sciences, faiths, philosophies and therapies, in an attempt to better understand how to live life more beautifully – with more breadth, depth and colour. This unifying approach defiantly rejects the artificial and enforced divisions between these disciplines, and the hierarchy of importance imposed upon them (with science and technology falsely assuming top position above all others). Both the divisions and the hierarchies are unnatural and imbalanced contrivances that do us all a profound disservice by carving up life into separate territories and setting these against each other. Similarly, schools and universities the world over are prone to academicize and rationalize the subjects they teach, with a heavy preponderance of principles and theories and only a fraction of practical know-how and

Over-scientizing how we live

If the word "scientizing" reminds you uncomfortably of the word "sanitizing", that association is quite appropriate. In his intriguing book *The Black Swan*, Nassim Taleb proposes that we've "drowned in our scientific mentality": ever since what we arrogantly call the Enlightenment, we've thought it a wonderful improvement to go from putting all our trust in the Church to putting all our trust in a tidy, linear and thus predictable world that this new tool called "science" would reveal to us. Taleb argues that science's one-dimensional, rule-bound view of the world is deeply misleading, for it ignores the intrinsically healthy randomness and messiness of real life. (See pp.101–106 for more on this.)

This shortcoming is one reason why science self-evidently has no monopoly on understanding how a life works well, or can be helped to do so. It's simply one major perspective among several others, including religion, philosophy, therapy and the arts. Even the word "science", from the Latin word meaning "to know", is a dreadful vanity, because what scientists claim they know is so often revealed to be either entirely wrong or just a small fraction of a larger truth (for example, Newtonian physics is greatly modified by Einsteinian physics, which in turn is greatly modified by quantum physics). As the philosopher of science Karl Popper wrote, "we must not look upon science as *a body of knowledge*, but rather as *a system of hypotheses*".

Problems begin when scientists forget this. Only a fraction of their evidence is convincing, and yet time and again scientists hired by governments or manufacturers have presumed to tell populations what foods to eat, what drugs to take, how to educate the young, what fuels to use... and time and again there have been monumental mistakes because of it. In the first half of the twentieth century medical doctors endorsed cigarettes (most famously in adverts for Camel – see opposite), while in the 1960s many British doctors prescribed the inadequately tested drug thalidomide, with the result that thousands of children were born with severe birth defects after their mothers had taken the drug during pregnancy.

Another reason science isn't to be unquestioningly relied upon is that while pretending to be an unbiased and open-handed pursuit of how things really are,

worldly wisdom: we read what other people have created, but create far too little ourselves. Yet neither an exclusively scientific approach nor an exclusively theoretical approach has any monopoly on how we should proceed to a clearer understanding of living life wisely. Rather, all the many disciplines through which we explore the world and what it is to be alive can equally well serve us with insights that can shape us for the better. This means inspiration can come from the creative and performing arts just as much as from the theoretical and applied sciences, and from religions just as much as philosophies, as well as from the first-hand in-the-field experience of teachers and therapists. Surprisingly, perhaps, such a broad-armed embrace doesn't render our

it's actually very much like every other human pursuit: full of passion and bias. Scientists spend much of their efforts censoring competing ideas and evidence that fall outside what's been agreed upon by those in power, who invariably have heavily vested interests ranging from personal pride to share portfolios. Though scientists claim to be building brick by brick on previous knowledge, history's most innovative scientists, such as Nicholas Copernicus, Charles Darwin, Louis Pasteur and Albert Einstein, all proposed ideas that were entirely at odds with the views and evidence popularly accepted by their peers at the time. We might well wonder whether human progress in our

understanding of the world relies not so much on "standing on the shoulders of giants" (as Isaac Newton politely suggested) as on getting out from under the shadow of some bullying self-serving Goliaths, and finding a tree to climb so we can see what's really going on.

In his fabulously sceptical book *Straw Dogs*, Professor John Gray (a philosopher at the London School of Economics) makes an apt comparison when he says that "science is just as trustworthy and stable as justice". He adds: "Ideas of justice are as 'timeless' as fashions in hats." Let's add to that the words of Richard Feynman, the 1965 Nobel Prize-winning physicist, who wrote "Science is the belief in the ignorance of experts." In other words, science should not be swayed by the reputation of the person behind the ideas – though unfortunately it often is. It's for reasons such as these that this Rough Guide champions an exploration of well-being that holds a healthy scepticism for science and its experts.

living more complicated, it actually seems to make things simpler. We begin to glimpse a bigger picture.

Exploring for real

Our exploration should be universal in the sense of our investigations being wholesome and action-oriented, whereby "life going well" is observed in its real and natural habitat, on-the-wing as it were. This sort of up-close, in-the-moment observation is what we all do naturally, and how we learn best. Such real-life exploration is what the human soul is made for: whether by kayak or on foot, by air or under sail, on horseback or bicycle saddle, we love striding forward in mind and body to feel the breeze on our face. Exploring life as we live it naturally leads to mistakes and mess, but it also brings with it a rather pleasing sense of self-efficacy, because at least we're doing something for ourselves. And that sense of making a personal difference is vital to us: youngsters learn better if they help design their own lessons; depressed individuals recover when they realize what a difference can be made by vigorous physical exercise; surgical patients heal faster when they choose their own music; old people live longer and stay healthier in care homes where they have a real say in things. So let's keep our exploration wholesome and grounded in real-life action. And finally, let's not forget to explore the very act of exploration itself, because we all have a tendency to undertake our journeys in old familiar ways. We might do well to wonder how else we might go about investigating life. Do we need to reconsider from scratch our goals, methods and long-held presumptions? Very often we don't know what we don't know, so we need to leave room for surprises.

This exploratory approach to well-being is an explicit challenge to the presiding tyranny of science and technology as the only judge and jury of what's good for us. But it's not intended to replace more traditional approaches – only to offer an alternative way of doing things. After all, by its own principles it must acknowledge that no approach will appeal to or apply to everyone; a variety of approaches is healthy, so "Vive la différence!"

To conclude: Let's not tinker!

This isn't a handbook of hints and tips on how to squeeze an extra few percent from whatever we're already doing. It believes that what we need is to team up and build better rapport in a whole host of ways, and only leaps and bounds will do. It pays to be ambitious. We fail most often not because we set our sights too high, but because we set them too low. Our journeys and goals (they are one and the same) have to be sufficiently exciting, sufficiently motivating, to overcome our inertia,

Simplicity

Leonardo da Vinci wrote "simplicity is the ultimate sophistication". In respect of which, here's a simple equation setting out this chapter's proposals:

Profound happiness = a wholesome life = well-rounded and well-balanced = yin–yang = a healthy relationship = a loving rapport = beauty

As far as this handbook is concerned, these concepts all mean one and the same thing. The founding philosophy of this Rough Guide is that well-rounded, well-balanced well-being is caused by and in turn creates a passion led, lion-hearted, nature-loving rapport with life. In pursuit of which, it proposes a Universal Exploration of Well-being, to help pull our lives together. Such exploration is, of course, a heart-felt ideal, not a fully formed enterprise – a direction rather than an achievement – and this handbook is simply a first and hopeful step.

even if once we're en route we are sustained by the intrinsic pleasure of the journey, and feel able to re-evaluate or let go of our original targets. Though we might only start with small changes, even small changes in each of our various dimensions can accumulate to make a great difference. Just think how the ancients moved great slabs of rock by rolling them on a host of small round stones. The same is true of our lives: small improvements can, if working well together all at once, enable wonderful progress.

2

Our sub-
conscious

Our sub-conscious

A source of motivations hidden even from ourselves

Learning to journey wisely through our own subconscious, learning the gentle language that this requires, offers us the most remarkable insights. By better harmonizing the workings of our conscious and subconscious mind, by improving the respectful rapport between these two states which merge together to make up our whole personality, we can greatly increase our potential for progress in every aspect of our life. This internal partnership is so important, and has been so neglected by mainstream books on happiness and well-being, that this chapter quite naturally stands at almost twice the size of its peers.

Understanding our subconscious

People have been aware of the existence of the subconscious (or unconscious – the terms can be used interchangeably) for millennia. But it was Dr Sigmund Freud, working at the beginning of the twentieth century, who first emphasized its importance. Freud famously proposed that "civilization has been built up ... by sacrifices in the gratification of primitive instincts" (see box overleaf). He regarded these instincts as

Freud and human unhappiness

For the father of psychoanalysis, Freud's opinion of its potential was remarkably modest: he thought the most a therapist could hope to achieve was to transform his patient's "hysterical misery into common unhappiness [gemeines Unglück]". For him, "common unhappiness" was the standard human condition, the best we could hope for, given our repression of our unconscious desires to behave as aggressive and sexual beasts. In his book *Civilization and its Discontents* (1930), he outlined his belief that the move towards civilization across the centuries had required that the happiness that naturally comes from the expression of our animal instincts be exchanged for the relative peace and security of urban living.

Freud had no solutions for the human condition under its yoke of polite civility that occasionally exploded into violence and war. It's indicative of his sense of impotence that he admitted using cocaine to "withdraw from the pressure of reality and find refuge in a world of one's own". But he conceded that this drug abuse was a terrible waste of energy, and was too temporary a relief to be of any good. Likewise, he felt that "the killing of the instincts as is prescribed by the worldly wisdom of the East and the practice of Yoga" was not a satisfying alternative. Nor, apparently, were the Western religions, which he viewed merely as "mass delusions" on a par with "fantasizing" and other neurotic illnesses which prevent one from engaging fruitfully with reality.

being mostly sexual, and so viewed the subconscious as a reservoir of motivational energy filled mainly with repressed sexual desires. (Freud's over-riding preoccupation with sexuality was perhaps the single most limiting factor of his life's work.)

While Freud considered the content of the subconscious to be "uncivilized" desires crudely shaped by early childhood experiences peculiar to the individual, his younger contemporary Dr Carl Jung regarded the subconscious as a reservoir of inborn ideas *common to all humanity*. This "collective unconscious", he believed, was passed down through the centuries and reflected in our culture of stories, myths and art. Jung viewed our night dreams not as wish fulfilments of our sexual and angry desires (Freud's interpretation), but as revelations of the incredible potential of the unconscious to know truth, anticipate the future, be telepathic and suggest solutions.

Dr Milton Erickson pioneered the use of modern-day hypnosis (see pp.65–73) as an effective means of communicating directly with our subconscious mind. For him, the unconscious was "everything that you are not conscious of at *this* moment … Most of your life is unconsciously determined." He didn't mean unchangeable, nor unimprovable, he simply meant that we lead our daily lives motivated by an infinitely rich mixture of helpful and unhelpful principles and memories, goals and inhibitions, the great majority of which we are not consciously aware of. In typically positive fashion, Erickson viewed our sub-conscious mind as a reservoir of experiences that were in effect "resources" that could be drawn upon to problem-solve our habitual strategies for dealing with everyday life.

> **"Your conscious mind is very intelligent, but your unconscious is a lot smarter."**
>
> Milton H. Erickson

These three men's ideas about the subconscious were, then, quite different in some ways (and we'll learn more about their ideas and their differences on pp.62–74). But they all shared a conception of the subconscious as the vital mainstay of the individual.

If our subconscious is as important as these great psychologists believed it to be, then it makes good sense to suppose that without the skill to work well with our subconscious mind, we cannot be profoundly happy. To ignore this part of ourselves would be like trying to keep our car in good running order without paying the least attention to the engine.

The theories and practice of the Freudian, Jungian and Ericksonian schools of psychotherapy are still alive and well today, each with its own international band of dedicated followers, as well as those who work more eclectically by attempting to integrate each school into a larger multi-coloured approach. Yet this whole dimension of human capability has fallen out of favour in modern-day mainstream psychology. This is very likely the result of a backlash against the oppressive dominance of Freudian and Jungian theories in therapeutic practice before World War II. But rather than restoring a balance to the field, this second half-century of antipathy has simply created warring factions which now barely acknowledge each other. The unhelpful result is that a whole generation of university-based happiness and well-being professors – along with the twenty-first century's dominant brand-name therapy, Cognitive Behavioural Therapy (see pp.82–85) – pay the workings of our subconscious mind no attention whatsoever. Their aims and achievements are the lesser for it.

How does our subconscious work?

In recent decades, therapeutic experience and experimental research have taught us a lot about our subconscious. Freud's legacy means we only have to mention the subconscious and it's all too easy to imagine we're talking about sex. Yet the best evidence suggests that thoughts and feelings about our sexuality are only a fraction of what our subconscious is interested in and responsible for. It seems our subconscious is a storehouse of all the habits and assumptions acquired from our previous experiences, kept in a place that is ordinarily out of reach of our self-awareness. But don't picture the subconscious gathering dust like some attic treasure-trove. It's far more like the engine, propeller and rudder of a boat, responsible for driving and steering our craft even though these mechanisms are well out of sight beneath the waves. We're up on deck, sure enough, but not always at the helm. This is why, when we consciously try to change ourselves, we sometimes find our behaviours returning to their original course as if they were dutifully following a route map to which we're not yet privy. On such occasions, though

In *Atonement* (2007) Robbie (James McAvoy) mistakenly sends his beloved Cecilia the wrong note – the one containing his passionate, explicitly sexual confession rather than a polite apology. We might wonder whether Robbie's subconscious had contrived to bring about this mix-up so as to lay bare his instinctive desires.

Priming ourselves for success or failure

In the mid-1990s, while researching at Harvard, Becca Levy (now a professor of psychology at Yale University) set out to investigate how our subconscious can be affected by subliminal messages and triggers (*subliminal* meaning below the level of our conscious awareness).

Some ninety Boston-area individuals, men and women, all between sixty and ninety years of age, were randomly split into two groups. Both groups were asked to respond to an on-computer test of memory, whereby they had to say whether a momentary flash of light on the computer screen was above or below a bull's-eye. Unbeknown to the participants, that flash of light appearing on the screen for around one-twentieth of a second – and thus too briefly for the eye to consciously see it (for that age group at least) – was not simply a flash but a word. For group A, the words were the likes of *senile, dependent, dying, decrepit, incompetent, diseased*; i.e. words intended to be demoralizing. For group B, the words were the likes of *wise, sage, astute, accomplished*; i.e. words intended to be encouraging.

Before and after this exercise, both groups were asked to complete a wide range of well-established memory tests. Professor Levy wanted to know whether the memory performance of these ninety senior citizens would be affected by the subliminally presented words. It turned out that on one of the memory tests, "immediate recall", the group who had been flashed demoralizing words performed on average about forty percent worse than they had the first time around, while the group who had been flashed encouraging words performed thirty percent better.

Levy's small but elegant laboratory study suggests not only that the subconscious mind can absorb information that our conscious mind does not register (those seemingly unseeable words flashed on the computer screen), but that this information can have a considerable effect upon us, predisposing us to behave in certain ways (the technical term is "priming"). When we think of how many messages we receive "unthinkingly" via radio, television or print advertisements, or how many snippets of conversation we'll happen to overhear in the course of a day, or how our homes may be full of scattered memorabilia from half a lifetime, we might wonder what effect all of this has on our subsequent thoughts and behaviour.

we might in all honesty be telling ourselves and other people that we want one thing, our subconscious may crave quite another outcome. Sometimes, to know how we truly feel about something or someone, we simply have to wait and see how we behave. That's why psychotherapy is always asking "When don't the symptoms occur? When do things improve? When have you been happy and well?" Because it's at those times that our subconscious mind is probably getting enough of what it really wants, so those occasions hold important clues to our subconscious desires.

Dr Timothy D. Wilson, a leading twenty-first-century scholar of the subconscious mind, aptly named his book *Strangers to Ourselves*, and ventured the following description: "The mind operates most efficiently by relegating a good deal of high-level, sophisticated thinking to the unconscious, just as a modern jetliner is able to fly on automatic pilot with little or no input from the human 'conscious' pilot. The adaptive unconscious does an excellent job of sizing up the world, warning people of danger, setting goals, and initiating action in a sophisticated and efficient manner."

At such tasks, our subconscious is wonderfully fast and powerful. Decisions made in an intuitive instant can be every bit as helpful as decisions made after a far more conscious, careful and com-

Trusting our instincts: in the documentary *Zidane*, the great French footballer Zinedine Zidane revealed that, before any match, he would feel his conscious mind handing over control to his subconscious. His game would only go badly if for some reason he resurfaced to what he clearly regarded as inhibiting conscious awareness. Perhaps it was Zizou's Zen-like trusting of his inner mind to read the situation and act accordingly that enabled him to out-perform even the youngest and most agile opponents.

prehensive gathering of the evidence; it's simply a matter of knowing which part of our mind to use and when. This is the observation of Malcolm Gladwell, author of *Blink* (2005). This bestselling paperback recounts some of the potential of the subconscious mind to be both a fabulous help, if we let it, and a profound hindrance if we don't. Gladwell notes that our subconscious is able to process a wealth of data at speeds far faster than our conscious mind can monitor. It's this that creates our intuitive feeling about anything from a new relationship or a business deal to a high-pressure life-or-death situation. This rapid-response processing can be highly effective. Nonetheless it can also be fallible, and what Gladwell takes pains to point out in *Blink* is that when our immediate unconscious reactions go awry and risk misleading us, they do so for quite particular and characteristic reasons. By being aware of the likely causes of error, we should be able to guard against them. For which reason, Gladwell advocates a more considered appreciation and skilled use of our subconscious abilities.

Subconscious defence strategies

In respect of the subtle, all-but-invisible power of the subconscious mind, Sigmund Freud and his psychoanalytic descendants have developed a superb inventory of the ways in which our subconscious might choose to defend its beliefs, its safe status quo and its self-image, when it feels under threat from a new situation or relationship or from disturbing memories. Many of our psychological self-defence mechanisms are so recognizable in the folks around us that the terms to describe them have passed into common usage: repression, projection, hypochondria, passive-aggression. These automatic defence strategies can be highly active and inventive, and the particular ones used will reflect the individual's level of maturity and skill in coping with life, rather than their chronological age. We probably won't be able to spot our own preferred defence mechanisms, because our subconscious will flatly deny that this is how we behave. (We'll have to ask a close and trusted friend to point out to us what we're prone to do.) On the other hand, we'll probably be all too able to spot the defences habitually used by those closest to us. The defences are divided here into three categories, representing an ascending order of psychological good health, leading from immature, to neurotic, to mature.

Immature defences

▶ **Projection:** we accuse others of having feelings or intentions which we harbour but haven't owned up to, not even to ourselves. So we might stridently claim that somebody else is "unfriendly" or "over-sexed" or "selfishly ambitious"… and not like us at all!

▶ **Fantasy:** we invent scenarios in our mind that we have little or no intention of following through with, often involving the sort of sexual, heroic, aggressive or romantic behaviours that we're hungry for but too fearful of trying out in real life. Fantasies tend to weaken our will and our ability to negotiate the legitimate demands of everyday reality, which is what makes them so insidiously self-limiting.

▶ **Hypochondria:** we use one or a host of illnesses and pains as a substitute for the direct demands or aggression we'd like to show towards others. Scared of direct conflict, we cause trouble for everyone, and ourselves, with our angry sickness.

▶ **Passive-aggression:** rather like with hypochondria, we avoid direct conflict by using subtler means to score points against the person or people we're angry at: we're late, or fall ill, or put things off, or lose things. Messing around and making a joke of everything when the topic or circumstances warrant more seriousness can also be a way of avoiding some feared competition or confrontation.

▶ **Acting out:** we impulsively and directly express some feeling no matter its destructive effects, because we are so intolerant and unable to handle the emotion. Drug abuse, violence, vandalism or self-harm might all be used to blank out the unwanted emotion of fear or love, anger or shame. We'll do anything to postpone or relieve the tension, no matter how problematic.

Acting out: *The Catcher in the Rye*

In J.D. Salinger's 1945 novel, the teenaged narrator Holden Caulfield recalls his furious and self-harming response to the death of his beloved kid brother, Allie: "I was only thirteen, and they were going to have me psychoanalysed and all, because I broke all the windows in the garage ... I broke all the goddam windows with my fist, just for the hell of it. I even tried to break all the windows on the station wagon we had that summer, but my hand was already broken and everything by that time, and I couldn't do it. It was a very stupid thing to do, I'll admit, but I hardly didn't even know I was doing it." Now sixteen and flunking out of one school after another, Holden is clearly still struggling with his grief.

Neurotic defences

▶ **Intellectualization:** we prefer to rationally contemplate inanimate things rather than face up to instinctive or socially intimate challenges. We focus obsessively on details rather than daring to look at the bigger picture; all emotion is removed from the analytical process, as is any genuine action.

▶ **Repression:** we can feel the emotions well enough, but have obliterated (temporarily) the idea that caused them. So, we cannot remember some poignant event; cannot explain why we're crying or scared; or might deny ever having held once deeply cherished passions.

▶ **Displacement:** we redirect our "unacceptable feelings" towards some less frightening target than the one that has originally aroused our emotions. We might shout at our dog, rather than our boss. Very often our phobias and psychosomatic ills have some element of displacement; for instance, we might only grow scared of flying or wide-open spaces as a self-protective substitute for being scared of some choices we need to make about the future.

▶ **Reaction formation:** we behave in ways that are the very opposite of the instinctive desires that our subconscious finds unacceptable. Perhaps we'll behave "hatefully" towards someone who deep down we instinctively love. Or we'll appear to care selflessly for someone, when what we really want is for someone to show *us* such consideration and care.

▶ **Dissociation:** our usual character and behaviour is temporarily but dramatically modified, as we attempt to avoid our feelings of distress. We might behave in a devil-may-care manner, or engage in frenetic activity, or experience an episode of manic religious joy, or simply take some drug or drink to "zone out" from an overwhelming reality. Likewise, a temporary but dramatic psychosomatic disorder (such as paralysis, deafness or inability to speak) could also serve to distract us from an unmanageable situation. Soldiers in combat will all too often have experienced these symptoms.

Mature defences

Note how these healthiest subconscious strategies cleverly integrate our personal emotional needs into good interpersonal relationships, and do all of this comfortably within the constraints of everyday real life.

▶ **Humour:** being able to laugh at adversity, to poke good-natured fun, particularly at our own prides and pains, is considered by many psychotherapists to be the most wonderful of all our psychological self-defence strategies. Time and again, those in the greatest adversity will recount that it was a sense of humour that saved their sanity.

Psychotic defence mechanisms

There is one further class of subconscious defences: psychotic defence mechanisms. These are the most seriously unhealthy and damaging of all, because the sufferer cannot distinguish between their own delusional creations and the reality shared by the rest of us. Their symptoms can be one or all of the following:

▶ **complete denial and distortion of reality**

▶ **hallucinations of people and voices**

▶ **feeling persecuted**

▶ **feeling all-powerful**

Immediate psychiatric care is vital in the face of such symptoms.

▶ **Altruism:** doing unto others as we wish had been done unto us. Perhaps we wish we'd been mentored or coached or cared for when we were growing up; so as an adult, we now take profound pleasure in providing this for youngsters in need.

▶ **Suppression:** acknowledging that something's hurting us, but not making a fuss, and bearing the strain until we find a better time in the near future to put it right. This is not the fearful avoidance of procrastination, but the wisdom of fighting battles when it suits us best.

▶ **Anticipation:** planning or rehearsing for the emotions and demands of the future in a very practical and realistic way. Focusing on what tomorrow's challenges might bring, rather than distracting ourselves.

▶ **Sublimation:** creatively channelling passionate desires in indirect ways that don't harm us or others, yet are still deeply satisfying of our instinctive urges. Aggression might be expressed through rough-and-tumble contact sport; sexual ardour might spawn a romantic correspondence in a long-distance courtship; and a volcano of artistic creativity might result from sublimated love or bereavement.

Developing the maturity of our subconscious defences

Freud's psychoanalytic approaches, as we will read below, suggest that "dream analysis" and "free association of thoughts" will reveal and spontaneously release our repressed emotions, and by doing so will heal us. However, there is little evidence that this process is sufficient. Far more promising are dynamic, practical approaches. For instance, with the help of a wise and loving friend, an inspiring role model, an encouraging mentor or a committed psychotherapist, we can all of us dare to explore in detail – in our mind's eye and then in reality – better ways of dealing with life's unceasing challenges and opportunities. By these very practical means, our subconscious mind strengthens and matures and becomes more creative and flexible as it begins to realize how new principles and possibilities can helpfully be applied to living life.

Psychosomatic illness

Psychosomatic illnesses are very real physical symptoms that are unconsciously caused by our psychological unhappiness or distress. The word psychosomatic simply means mind–body. If our mind is not happy it will express this through our body, in the same way as our body lets our mind know if it's in pain.

It's perfectly natural for our subconscious to speak to us through our bodily functions, all the more so if we've not developed other ways of communicating. (Building such a rapport is described later in this chapter.) It's quite likely that at least half of a medical doctor's patients are suffering from at least one psychosomatic disorder. The classic "conversion disorders" resulting from extreme psychological trauma would be temporary paralysis, blindness or loss of speech. But far more common among many of us is having a small cluster of less severe symptoms, albeit demoralizing, debilitating and long-term. These might include digestive troubles and sleep disturbances, skin complaints and hair loss, asthma and nausea, frequent colds and constant fatigue, or problems with our sexual and reproductive abilities. Unexplained pain, particularly if it moves around the body, can be another characteristic symptom, perhaps involving migraines, lower back pain and aching limbs. Our subconscious can either wholly create such physical woes, or exacerbate existing ones.

Sound far fetched? Think how we'll blush or perspire in response to social anxieties, or suffer shortness of breath or stomach ache when we're fearful of something. If we receive shocking news, our nose might bleed or we'll simply faint. Psychosomatic complaints are merely a longer-term, less obvious manifestation of our mind and emotions affecting the workings of our body.

Secrets kept even from ourselves

Pioneering work by Dr Ian Wickramasekera (published when he was professor of psychology at San Francisco's Saybrook Graduate School) suggests that our bodies may even be capable of reflecting inner distress of which we are not consciously aware. Dr Wickramasekera invited individuals to talk about topics or relationships they consciously rated as innocuous, only to discover that sensitive machines monitoring their skin temperature, skin conductance, heart rate, brain waves and blood pressure told a very different story, clearly indicating inner distress when a particular subject was raised. It seems that only their subconscious was aware of their disquiet and reflected this in bodily distress signals, while their conscious mind remained oblivious. Were "repressed" memories or thoughts responsible for this? Dr Wickramasekera's subsequent research has aimed to discover what might be going on beneath the surface, as well as whether by using such "biofeedback" signals to uncover hidden sources of disquiet we can alleviate troubling physical symptoms.

One explanation for psychosomatic symptoms is that our subconscious mind is trying to deter us from what it regards, mistakenly or otherwise, as one or more of three evils:

▶ **That we're going in the wrong direction in life.**
▶ **That we're travelling at a self-damaging pace.**
▶ **That we're keeping poor company.**

Another strong possibility is that our subconscious is creating these physical ills as a means of channelling a deeply felt emotion such as anger, fear, shame or despair, that we don't feel at liberty to consciously own up to, let alone express openly and directly.

Of course, in principle, it's very important to establish that there is no medical condition underlying a physical problem. But this is a tall order, not least because we, the patients, are rarely conscious of our own deeply buried psychological disquiet. Even if our medical practitioner *does* suspect the mind's initiating role in our physical symptoms, at least one third of us refuse to see a psychological-health professional because we think it's a slur on our sanity or strength of personality. But nothing could be further from the truth. Our body expressing our mind's concerns like this is in no sense malingering nor mental illness or weakness. On the contrary, it's simply our healthy brain using all the means at its disposal to signal to us, and to those who love us, that there are some un-aired feelings that need addressing. Mother Nature meant our

Are you coming or not?

Subconscious disquiet is very often at the root of our sexual problems. Though there is simply no evidence to support Freud's over-zealous assertion that repressed sexual concerns comprise the overwhelming majority of the activities of our subconscious mind (not least because so many other sorts of personal and professional relationship are either equally or far more important to us), our subconscious is nonetheless very prone to show its general angst by inhibiting us sexually. This is probably because our subconscious feels sure this strategy of "tweaking us where we're tender" will grab our attention and prompt us to remedy the root cause of what's really upsetting us.

We shouldn't be surprised that our sexual health is so sensitive to our moods. Just as our fluency of speech, our ease with making eye contact or our keenness to take on unfamiliar responsibilities may all reflect our general level of confidence, so too does our sexuality. Our ability to be comfortable with sexual arousal, comfortable with deeply intimate and exploratory sexual expression, comfortable with surrendering ourselves to orgasm in the arms of our lover, can all reflect our underlying feelings about ourselves, and the person we're with. It can also be the case that ill-considered promiscuity or harmful sexual addictions (just as much as an inhibiting sense of shame or panic at nakedness or physical affection) can reflect some form of deeply felt disquiet in our relationship with life generally. The reassuring news is this is just the sort of problem that a good general psychotherapist can swiftly help us with. See pp.291–307 for details.

body to care for our brain, and vice versa, and it's only a historical accident that has seen the healing professions of medicine and psychology artificially separated, and be far less effective for it. The mind and body may stand apart in the traditions of academic and professional training, but in our real life they walk hand in hand at all times. As we'll see, an appreciation of this relationship can help make our psychosomatic distress signals a rather less common occurrence.

Emotional trauma

Though our subconscious is always aiming to act in our best interests, its goals and strategies can sometimes be out of date or misguided, the product of our immature or emergency responses to some highly significant past experiences. Our human brain is designed to learn, but it learns unhelpful as well as helpful responses to the world around us, and if the learning process is too traumatic (perhaps an incident, an accident, or the grinding away of a long-term negative relationship), our responses can get stuck in one particular mode. From then on, we'll almost always respond in pretty much the same way to vaguely similar situations, no matter how much trouble it causes us, or how much our conscious mind tries to intervene.

In this way, emotional trauma lodged deep within our brain's circuitry can tether us to the past and make it difficult to progress with our life. Emotional trauma might express itself in the form of Post-Traumatic Stress Disorder, but it might equally reveal itself in more subtle, unexpected or paradoxical ways, such as self-sabotage, addictive behaviours, or a tendency to take on unhelpful relationship roles that simply repeat the familiar patterns from our past no matter how ill-serving.

Post-Traumatic Stress Disorder

We don't have to be a battlefront soldier to risk suffering some degree of Post-Traumatic Stress Disorder; it can affect any of us. Perhaps we've suffered a single mind-traumatizing event such as an accident or assault, some difficult surgery or a relationship shock. On the other hand, the suffering may have been recurrent and long-term, such as physical or emotional bullying that went on for years. This could have happened four weeks or forty years ago, but the outcomes can still be as strong. A child might even be traumatized simply by being told of an incident that horrifies them, or by witnessing a distraught adult.

It is by no means automatic that we should suffer PTSD after distressing events, but nor is it unusual; and it is such a potential blight on our wellbeing that it fully deserves our attention. Whatever the cause, the brain's preconscious alarm system, centred in a small organ called the amygdala, is rendered hyper-sensitive by the traumatizing experience. From then on, any elements in our environment which even remotely remind our brain's alarm system of the initiating trauma will cause us problems. No matter it be a false alarm or an imagined emergency, our amygdala hits the panic button and our panic will ensue in the form of freeze, fight or flight. It's as if the initiating trauma lodges like a piece of emotional shrapnel in our amygdala, and from that time forth we become hyper-vigilant.

In essence, our amygdala has become like a hyper-anxious trigger-happy sentry who's startled by the wind rustling the leaves.

What triggers our subsequent panic reactions may not have been the most damaging element of the trauma, it was just the feature that our brain happened to latch on to at the time: so we might be alarmed by the smell of hospitals, a bright colour, a sudden sound, an enclosed space, or an offer of intimacy.

The result might be any number of psychological symptoms manifesting in our mood, ranging from persistent anxiety to irritability, depression or emotional numbness. Perhaps we are plagued by flashbacks or obsessive thoughts or compulsive behaviours. In addition, there will very likely be physical effects: poor sleep, loss of appetite, digestive problems, proneness to perspiration, skin complaints, nervous twitches, tooth grinding, pain or panic attacks. Phobias may develop for anything from public speaking to darkness or heights. Directly or indirectly, our personal relationships may be affected. We might become evasive of commitment or emotional affection, or distrustful of even the most benign sexual feelings or advances. We might just as easily become enraged at any hint of bullying or racked with shame at some real or imagined shortfall, or filled with a sense of hopelessness. But at the root of all of these diverse phenomena will be that hyper-alert emergency stand-by state caused by the traumatizing incident or relationship. In the face of such symptoms, we might try to self-medicate through alcohol or some other distracting or self-tranquillizing behaviour, but unless the connection is identified, we'll only be dulling the symptoms, not treating the cause. What's more, our brain and body being on red-alert like this takes up a lot of computing power, and is tiring and debilitating. We can't turn our emotional energy to other things. In fact, that's how PTSD does much of its hidden damage: it distracts our resources into defending us against an unlikely or non-existent aggressor.

Removing our "emotional shrapnel"

Post-Traumatic Stress Disorder very often goes unrecognized, undiagnosed and untreated. This state of affairs is quite unnecessary, because there are at least two therapies for PTSD which, though not yet widely adopted by mainstream psychotherapy, have demonstrated themselves very promising for many individuals suffering a wide range of conditions. These techniques are known as the Rewind Technique and EMDR.

The Rewind Technique

This therapy is also known as V-K Dissociation or even the Fast Phobia Cure (though the latter is a bit misleading, because it's effective with so much more than just phobias). It can be used for fully blown PTSD, and can aid in all of the other anxiety disorders, simply by means of re-associating a vividly imagined version of the once-feared stimulus with our being in a highly relaxed state, rather than an anxious one.

The technique is not recounted in any detail here, because it is far more safe and effective if carried out with a therapist who has been thoroughly trained in its proper use. That said, the technique itself is simple, straightforward and reliable, and is founded on good psychological principles. In a nutshell, it involves us being helped to achieve a deep state of relaxation before rerunning the traumatic scene backwards and forwards in our mind's eye, several times one after the other and at varying speeds, as if we're watching it on a video screen. Throughout these self-generated re-screenings, we aim to remain very calm and deeply relaxed in mind and body. Eventually the negative emotions will fade away, and our response to the scene becomes neutral. Throughout this procedure the therapist will keep reassuring us and calming us if we become over-anxious. As with EMDR below, if we have suffered multiple traumas, it might be necessary to work with several of the worst incidents until our brain's alarm system spots the pattern – the common denominator that links the incidents – and can react calmly to *all* memories and future situations of that ilk.

At its best, the Rewind Technique will help us to find complete relief from flashbacks, and enable us to speak about the trauma or traumas without feelings of sadness or despair, alarm or anxiety. Freed from being "on our guard" against these once-painful memories, we should also acquire a more positive mood, energy and confidence for life generally.

EMDR

EMDR (Eye Movement Desensitization and Reprocessing) has elements related to the Rewind Technique, but is also substantially different. In broad terms, it works like this: while we recall the trauma, both visualizing what happened and remembering what it felt like emotionally and physically, the therapist moves a finger rapidly back and forth a foot or so in front of our face, so that it can be followed by our eyes while our head remains still. The therapist's finger or pen might make any number of these rapid left–right passes in front of our eyes. With rests in between, this process is repeated several times while the therapist encourages us to focus on the thoughts, emotions and physical feelings attached to the troublesome memory. Research so far suggests that the eye movement stimulates our brain in a way which helps us to better access and digest deeply upsetting emotions. It also seems that eye movement isn't necessary, and that any form of body movement, tapping our fingers for instance, that stimulates first the left and then the right side of the brain in quick succession is equally effective. Results have been encouraging for otherwise difficult cases, and in 2007 EMDR finally received the thumbs up from the UK's National Institute for Clinical Excellence. However, the procedure must be carried out by a clinician properly trained in its use (commonly referred to as Level 3 EMDR training, and not simply Level 1 or 2 training). They should also possess a good background of clinical training in general diagnosis and a range of therapeutic alternatives from which to choose the most appropriate for the presenting problem.

Whether the particular de-trauma technique used is the Rewind Technique or EMDR, or involves a more general use of clinical hypnosis (see pp.65–73) or energy techniques (see pp.129–134), the underlying approach is the same: associating the once traumatizing memory or event with a newly acquired physical and psychological calm on both a conscious and subconscious level. The incident or episodes that have rendered our brain's automatic alarm system over-sensitive and hyper-vigilant are in effect neutralized by our confronting the feared stimulus while we are supported by benign and therapeutic conditions. This is why it's vital that we don't fudge the experience by not fully engaging with the traumatic stimulus for fear of the consequences. It is quite likely that our ability to immerse ourselves intensely in experiences, in both our real and imagined life, has accidentally allowed us to be traumatized in the first place; and it is this very same ability for deep absorption that we must now harness to heal ourselves.

In employing such techniques, we are allowing our brain to fully process the trauma and discharge its negative energies, as if earthing a once live and dangerous electrical current. To put it another way, we are taking emotional charge of the events which once overwhelmed us in some way.

A very welcome advantage of these techniques is that for effective treatment it's quite unnecessary to disclose any of the details of the traumatizing events to our therapist. The therapist's role is simply to support us in mentally re-living our memories, while helping us maintain our physical and emotional composure until such time as we acquire a reliably neutral response to that memory or any similar situations. This procedure of calmness and privacy stands in direct opposition to any approaches that require us to re-tell our story, very probably in floods of tears: such methods may only serve to further traumatize us, depending on how much excessive emotion is attached to our re-telling.

Finally, we should note that although these techniques are not complex to learn, a well-qualified and experienced clinician is indispensable. Knowing exactly what to target and how to tailor the basic procedures sensitively and imaginatively to the individual, as well as how to cope with any difficulties that may arise, requires thorough training and experience. Besides which, finding that symptoms we've lived with for many months or years are rapidly diminishing within just a few hours, days or weeks itself brings a challenging change of horizons that will benefit from well-seasoned support. This explains why between six and a dozen or more sessions might reasonably be required to deal safely and effectively with emotional trauma.

Self-sabotage

Are we our own worst enemy, but the last one to realize it? Self-sabotage probably affects all of us, from time to time, to one degree or another. It's the phenomenon that explains why not a week goes by without a television celebrity, politician or athlete very publicly falling from grace because they seem to have pulled the plug on themselves with some self-sinking behaviour. But they're just the unlucky ones who make the headlines. For the rest of us, our own inexplicable actions may be more subtle or secret, but they're no less painful. We can find ourselves on the brink of a wonderful relationship, and yet to our own shock and dismay we start behaving badly towards the other person. We can be offered a promising business opportunity, yet we choose to pull out of the race and short-circuit our chances. Or perhaps it's our everyday lifestyle that seems tailor-made to undercut our best efforts to ride the wave of success. For instance, just when things are going swimmingly, we develop an insatiable appetite for late nights, too much alcohol, careless spending and dangerous driving. At the extreme end of the spectrum, there are the moments of madness that find us doing something horribly out of character and highly illegal, which leaves even our closest friends flabbergasted. But just as serious as these occasional incidents are the year-on-year self-punishments: the unhealthy partnerships we routinely court, the impossible goals we set ourselves, the heart-felt passions we never pursue.

We can probably all recognize at least some of these traits in ourselves or someone close to us. Such self-sabotage is the symptom of serious disharmony between our conscious and subconscious mind. The good news is it's well worth grabbing hold of those locked horns.

Our seemingly inexplicable self-harming/self-inhibiting/self-punishing behaviour is more likely than not caused by our subconscious mind labouring under some deeply unhelpful beliefs based on our childhood or teenage perceptions of how the world works. They often go something like this:

▶ **I don't deserve this love.** (So and so never loved me for all those years, so I really must be quite unlovable.)

▶ **I don't deserve this success.** (Dad always said I never worked hard enough or well enough.)

▶ **They'll only find out that I'm not nearly as good as they think I am.** (They'll call me a fraud – and they'd be right, too – just like that horrid teacher who made an example of me when I got help with my homework.)

▶ **If I shine with success, people close to me won't love me any more.** (My best schoolfriend was always jealous of me getting so much attention.)

It's internal scripts like these that are being broadcast over the loudspeakers in the control tower of our subconscious mind. Such inner voices might be quite unsuspected by our conscious mind, and even our lifelong confidantes might not realize what secret worries are driving us. One way we can become more aware of such subliminal dynamics is simply by looking for unhelpful patterns in our personal and professional lives across the years. Their effect at the mild end of the spectrum might

Are we paralysed by pleasure?

It's not only pain that can traumatize us; so can pleasure. It may help to ask ourselves what might be accidentally rewarding our unwanted behaviours, and thereby preventing us from progressing in our relationships, work or health.

Here's an illustration: a teenager who is badly bullied by a gang one day when coming home from school might show persistent symptoms of fear. These might be treated with a brief course of talk-therapy, but to everyone's consternation the teenager still doesn't progress well. What's happening, perhaps, is that the traumatic incident also brought the youngster some hidden but powerful pleasures that were felt at a subconscious level. For instance, the rush of self-righteous anger that accompanied the initial bullying event may have felt empowering to the victim, particularly to a shy or nervous boy. And, soon after, the heaps of kindly attention from friends and adults would also have been very welcome. The result is that some part of that teenager's subconscious mind might long to re-experience those rare but pleasurable emotions, and will do anything to recreate likely scenarios, even if that means "playing the victim" time and again, or perhaps having temper tantrums.

We adults are much the same. Is it possible that our persistent smoking or bingeing or TV-watching reminds us of someone we loved? Could it be that our rages or dangerous antics hark back to the rewarding sense of release we too rarely experienced while being raised by over-controlling parents?

To break ourselves free of such unhelpful patterns of behaviour, we need to identify what pleasurable emotions (and, surprisingly enough, anger can be one of these, since it can feel so empowering) may have been present but hidden in what seemed to be a purely painful scenario. This can most readily be done with the help of a therapist. Once we've discovered what's maintaining our behaviour, we can begin to release ourselves from this pleasure-driven pattern.

(The acclaimed contemporary Irish therapist Jo Griffin is largely responsible for identifying and publicizing the above phenomenon.)

F. Scott Fitzgerald, whose own life was blighted by alcoholism, ended his famous novel *The Great Gatsby* with the following lines:

Gatsby believed in the green light, the orgiastic future that year by year recedes before us. It eluded us then, but that's no matter – tomorrow we will run faster, stretch out our arms farther… and one fine morning…

So we beat on, boats against the current, borne back ceaselessly into the past.

Gatsby was traumatized – trapped in the past – but we don't have to be.

be to give us an upset tummy, a cold sore or a sleepless night just when our conscious mind so wanted us to be at our best. At the other end of the spectrum, it can be near enough a suicidal death wish: the acting out of something akin to a sobbing and powerless teenager screaming "I wouldn't care if I died now, because then all those who've hurt me would be really, really sorry!"

Addictive behaviours and relationship roles

If all this "trapped in the patterns of the past" stuff sounds rather hard to believe, consider Harvard psychology professor Steven Pinker's five-word summary of how the brain works: "brain cells fire in patterns". It's patterns that dictate and motivate our life. We search for patterns in the world around us and try to understand and have an effect upon those patterns. We are strongly prone to repeat the patterns from our past, until we realize that some of what we're doing isn't helping, and then perhaps we make very particular efforts to change our behaviour.

While negotiating life, we can all of us become accustomed to certain relationship roles, even downright horrid ones, which we learned by rote at home, at school or in early adulthood. Perhaps the negative role meant being bullied or unloved or never feeling good enough; perhaps it applied across the board or was played out only in one particular dimension such as our family, friendships, romantic relationships or work. In any event, our ingrained patterns of behaviour, generated by emotional shrapnel buried deep within our subconscious mind, can act like magnets pulling our healthier instincts badly off course. At the same time, we seem to send out faulty signals tending to attract an unhelpful or even toxic sort of person or scenario. Despite the harm this does us, what can camouflage our self-damaging sense of identity is that our enslavement can show itself in any one of three responses:

▶ **We freeze:** we get stuck submissively repeating past patterns – I'm a failure, unlovable, doomed to be alone – and live out the role by actively if subconsciously hunting down situations that are all too likely to make these harmful beliefs a self-fulfilling prophecy. In short, we repeatedly find the jobs, friends, partners and even hobbies that bring out the worst in us.

▶ **We escape:** we try to anaesthetize the emotional pain of those feelings and beliefs born of past relationships by distracting ourselves with over-work, over-study, or addictions to booze, food, TV, travel, exercise, shopping or some other bury-our-head-in-the-sand activity.

▶ **We fight:** we aggressively over-compensate for our once-painful roles. The bullied child becomes a highly aggressive adult, or the unloved youngster grows up chasing attention through fame or clinginess or promiscuity.

Bearing in mind these three responses, see if the following negative roles ring any bells of recognition:

▶ **I'm unloved and unlovable.** This role results either in our trying to partner with cold and unloving souls, or in our behaving coldly ourselves as a sort of pre-emptive strike. Either way, we foster precious little personal depth or intimacy.

▶ **I'm vulnerable...** to accident, disease, crime, bullying, going broke and even rotten luck. Living is dangerous stuff! This role results in a life dominated by fear and over-caution, in which we trust neither life nor people.

▶ **I'll be abandoned.** People will either walk out on me, or die. This role results in our being too clingy, or not daring to allow closeness.

▶ **I can't manage things alone; I have to depend on others.** This role results in our always playing second fiddle, and shrinking from responsibility.

▶ **I'm an outsider and strangely different.** This role results in our isolating ourselves and not being an active member in friendship groups or clubs.

▶ **I'm not good enough.** This role results in our isolating ourselves from others and giving up; or being hyper-critical of ourselves and others; or painfully over-striving.

▶ **I'm only fit to serve others; my needs and wishes are unimportant.** This role results in a life lived in servitude to children, parents or a controlling partner, or in destructive self-sacrifice for worthy causes.

▶ **I'm owed far more by life! Rules are for the little people, not me.** This role results in our behaving selfishly and driving people away with our lack of self-discipline.

You can probably think of a couple more unhelpful roles. (*Reinventing Your Life*, by Drs Jeffrey E. Young and Janet S. Klosko, superbly summarizes a similar range of such self-inhibiting relationship roles, and is a powerful and sobering read.) It's noteworthy that while acting out the above scripts from our subconscious automatic pilot, we tend to swing from feeling self-pitying to feeling furious, as if we know deep down something's very wrong with how we're behaving. Worse still, when we're fortunate enough to be offered a genuinely positive and helpful relationship, we might find that the honest gestures of consideration and respect will feel so alien to us that we'll reject the other person. We're addicted to what's hurting us.

Through trauma, our thoughts and behaviours can become trapped in the past, sentenced to repeat themselves no matter how unhelpful or debilitating.

If we dare to look back at our own life, or the lives of those we know best, we can begin to spot such harmful patterns. We humans are not only highly social creatures, but strongly habit-forming, and our vulnerability to repeated roles reflects both these hard-wired traits. Our salvation is to realize how we've been typecast, and then, with good companions or therapeutic coaching, our relationship with life can metamorphose very rewardingly.

Freeing ourselves from unhelpful patterns

If we've suffered emotional trauma, the paradox is that even situations which are toxic for us can quite entrance us with feelings of intense attraction and a powerful sense of "click". After all, such ingredients are what we grew up with, and we're doomed to repeat these toxic relationships unless we can break the spell.

The bottom line is, if we suspect we might be suffering from self-sabotage or addictive behaviours or relationship roles, then a specialist professional approach is needed, to help us remove or "neutralize" the underlying trauma, so our mind – and our life – can move on (see "Working Well with a Therapist" on pp.291–308). With that strong caveat, here is a brief overview of some of the therapeutic steps we might expect to encounter.

First, we require a thorough inventory of major choices in our life to spot our self-damaging passions: perhaps for cold, bullying or dependent partners; for self-punishing careers; or for self-isolating pastimes. We can only know whether our professed love or sense of mission is a healthy vocation or an addictive poison by how the role we play impacts upon our life. Do we thrive or do we wither? That's the acid test. It's hard to realize for ourselves that we're trapped in a negative cycle, but it's likely that those who've known us long enough will be all too aware of it.

Once we have an idea of what needs changing, as with all learning it's vital to visualize in rich detail how we'd prefer to behave and with what sort of person, imitating the best examples from the partnerships we see around us. We'll need to support our imaginative rehearsals with deeply relaxed muscles and the slowest, most gentle breathing. Combining these key ingredients helps us acquire skills at the level of our subconscious autopilot which is exactly where our old behaviours are deeply rooted. And if we suffer demoralizing images from the past, we should reshape these just like a film director re-shoots a scene, thereby showing our subconscious exactly what we're aiming for.

Be warned: our subconscious tends to work on the default principle of "better the devil you know", so it'll probably try some sabotage of our renovation plans. The irony is that what's profoundly healthy for us will probably feel damned awkward for a while, and we'll kick against it. Our progress will rely on our willingness to tough it out when feeling deeply uncomfortable with such unfamiliar ways of relating to the world.

Therapeutic legacies

When it comes to fostering a far healthier working harmony between our conscious and subconscious goals, thankfully there have been some outstanding pioneers. This brings us back to Freud, Jung and Erickson, whom we met at the beginning of this chapter.

Sigmund Freud and psychoanalysis

Arguably the most famous figure in the history of psychotherapy, Sigmund Freud (1856–1939) was an Austrian Jew, the eldest son of eight children born into a hard-working family of limited financial means. He graduated from the University of Vienna as a doctor of medicine in 1881, and by the late 1880s had a private practice treating so-called "nervous disorders" (such as general anxiety or panic attacks).

Freud's own health was always precarious and variable: he was prone to depression, fatigue, migraines and general anxiety, and in keeping with his generation he used cocaine to alleviate these symptoms. He eventually concluded that the best way to cope with life – and with all those unconscious sexual and violent desires that he felt sure were waiting to explode like a volcano – was what he termed "sublimation". By this he meant involving oneself in creative and productive work, particularly intellectual challenges, as an outlet for our more primitive instinctual passions. It's sad that Freud's insights into the subconscious and his suggested methods for easing the human condition could not stop him smoking some twenty cigars per day, and in 1923 he was diagnosed with cancer of the jaw. He fled Nazism in 1938 and settled in London, where he died a year later aged 83, some while after horrifically severe surgery to remove his cancerous lower jaw.

By way of therapy, Freudian psychoanalysis (which is still much-practised today) aims to have the client reveal their most intimate subconscious thoughts. To aid this disclosure, the therapist sits out of sight of the client, who reclines outstretched on a couch. This allows for "free association", whereby the client discloses aloud and totally unedited whatever comes into their mind as a stream of thought. The aim is to unearth unconscious material, and this "catharsis" – this free-ing of buried impulses – is thought to be enough to alleviate all the symptoms that are being driven by the repressed thoughts. The client is also encouraged to talk about their dreams. For Freud, dreams were the "royal road to … the unconscious": they are regarded as wish fulfilments of repressed desires, even though they, too, are somewhat repressed by being metaphorical. (Hence, the appearance of tree trunks and umbrellas in a dream might be regarded by Freudians as representing engorged penises.)

The most that the therapist will do is interpret these thoughts and dreams; they will be careful not to judge, instruct or guide. Insight and self-revelation is thought sufficient to bring about healing. Nonetheless, the therapist's skill is required because the client will, subconsciously, resist giving up their secrets. "Transference" is a key term in psychoanalysis, to describe how the client may subconsciously "transfer" or "project" all of their intense feelings for past important people in their lives (usually their parents) onto the therapist. The client is essentially expressing towards their therapist all those feelings they dared not express towards the person who originally invoked them. This transference tends to conjure deep affection for the therapist at first, but these emotions later turn to hostility and resistance. It requires a skilled therapist to channel these emotions in therapeutically helpful ways.

Carl Jung and analytical psychotherapy

Carl Jung (1875–1961) is surely the second most recognized name in psychotherapy. He and Freud met in 1906, were intensely close for six years and then, after a bitter disagreement in 1913, never met again.

Jung was the only son and eldest sibling by nine years of a well-to-do Swiss family. He graduated from Basel Medical School in 1896, and went very successfully into psychiatry, marrying into a lavishly wealthy Swiss family. Nonetheless, after his rift with Freud, Jung suffered five years of profound uncertainty that he felt took him to the edge of insanity.

In contrast to the silent, unseen Freudian therapist, the Jungian therapist is face-to-face and much more involved: there is far more of an exchange of personalities and of stories of adversities overcome. "Only the wounded physician heals", wrote Jung. Differences aside, Freud and Jung had some fundamental features in common. Like Freud, Jung believed that healing came from having consciously assimilated our subconscious impulses and ideas that were previously repressed. As Jung poetically proposes, "The secret of wholeness is hidden in the dark. One does not become enlightened by imagining figures of light, but by making the darkness conscious." It is not uncommon for both sorts of therapy to be ongoing, a weekly routine over several years; and in both therapies the aim is for the client to develop a centre of gravity within themselves, rather than being reliant on the things or people around them.

Hypnosis

Compared to the therapeutic techniques of Freud and Jung, hypnosis has a somewhat longer pedigree. Something recognizable as hypnotic techniques emerged in eighteenth-century Europe (once such activities no longer risked getting you excommunicated or burnt at the stake as a witch), and captured the attention of pioneering thinkers. Hypnosis began in earnest with the German–Swiss lawyer turned medic Franz Anton Mesmer (1734–1815) who toured Europe awing the gentry with his feats, and from whom we derive the term "mesmerized". From him the brightest torch passed to the Parisian Jean-Martin Charcot (1825–93), one of the most acclaimed doctors of his day. He demonstrated to the medical world how suggestions made to the subconscious in states of hypnosis could cure the so-called "hysteria" symptoms of mind and body brought about by over-wrought fears. However, a thorough understanding of hypnosis was still absent, and it was thought by many scientists at the time that flamboyant hand movements before the patient's eyes were required, and that "magnetism" was involved in some way. It was also widely believed that it could be dangerous and put to ill use, with "vulnerable young ladies" for instance.

The young Sigmund Freud attended Charcot's lectures in Paris, and in the 1880s he was an avid champion of hypnosis, giving lectures on the subject, translating books on it and using it in his clinical practice. Freud reflected in his memoirs in 1935 that it was through his exposure to hypnosis that he became aware that "there could be powerful mental processes which nevertheless remained hidden from the consciousness of man". However, by the mid-1890s Freud had given up on hypnosis in favour of two approaches of his own devising: free association and dream analysis (described above). Likewise, Jung quickly dismissed hypnosis and concentrated on his own original approach to dream analysis. Both Freud and Jung were zealous personalities who wanted to bring their own inventions to the newly emerging field of psychology, whereas hypnosis was already well established and belonged to other champions. Since both men were of paramount influence in twentieth-century psychotherapy, it is arguable that they effectively buried hypnosis so as to pave the way for their "own-brand" techniques. After all, these were domineering personalities, who wanted to assert their own theories, not extend someone else's. Indeed, it was arguments over their own competing theories that caused them to fall out with each other so decisively in 1913.

Nonetheless, hypnosis has been used safely and effectively for well over a hundred years in the more avant-garde circles of Western medicine, and thanks to the overwhelming clinical evidence of American psychiatrist Dr Milton H. Erickson's lifetime of hypnotic work, the American Psychological Association conceded in 1958 that "general practitioners, medical specialists, and dentists might find hypnosis valuable". However, in the UK more than fifty years on, hypnosis is rarely a sanctioned procedure for psychotherapy units, let alone for other medical applications such as pain relief. This reluctance to embrace a well-proven technique reflects a long history of professional rivalries

Hypnosis at war

In the first quarter of the twentieth century hypnosis was used with enthusiasm by a number of pioneering medics. The acclaimed medical doctor and anthropologist Dr William Rivers used hypnosis to successfully treat World War I servicemen suffering "shell shock" (what we'd now call PTSD). He helped the patient to revisit and neutralize or release the repressed emotion associated with the terrifying memories that tortured their sleep and waking hours. Among Rivers' patients at the gothic mansion turned asylum Craiglockhart, on the outskirts of Edinburgh, was the war poet Siegfried Sassoon, who had recently won the Military Cross. Sassoon's friend and fellow poet Wilfred Owen was very skilfully treated with hypnosis by a colleague of Rivers', Dr William Brown. Like Sassoon, Lt Owen returned successfully to the trenches and he won the Military Cross shortly before his death in the closing days of the war, aged just 25. Pat Barker's novel *Regeneration* sensitively captures this milestone in therapeutic history.

Many pioneering German psychologist-physicians also used hypnosis, such as Hamburg's Max Nonne, who had trained with Charcot before the war. Dr Nonne treated around 1600 patients using what he learned.

In hospitals on both sides of the war, the popular alternative to hypnosis was to give traumatized soldiers two minutes or more of intensely painful electric shocks. Tragically, dozens of soldiers died of the heart attacks that such brutal shocks could induce, or simply committed suicide rather than be tortured by this method into surrendering their subconsciously generated symptoms of horror and protest at what war in the trenches had demanded of them. It is equally tragic that by World War II, a range of drugs for anaesthetizing the brain (albeit with unforeseen physical and psychological side-effects) had become the accepted practice for treating emotional trauma; and hypnosis once again was all but outlawed by the authorities.

(medicine versus psychology) far more than any scientific reservations. It is noteworthy that the world-class psychology department of one of the UK's leading universities, University College London, has taught a professional practitioner's diploma course since the early 1990s, for use largely by psychologists, medical doctors, surgeons, anaesthetists, nurses and dentists. Moreover, coaches to Olympic athletes (such as the five-time gold-medal-winning rower Steve Redgrave) routinely use hypnosis to reinforce the effect of their psychological and physical training strategies.

So just what *is* hypnosis?

The word "hypnosis" is derived from the Greek word for sleep, but in fact, when we're in a hypnotic trance state, we're far from asleep. Our attention is simply extremely focused, and whatever we're imagining feels vividly real. We will not do or say anything we don't want to, and we'll not get trapped in that state. Far from being passive automatons, we're very able to explore new possibilities and conjure scenes.

As part of our daily lives, we go in and out of such focused trances of concentration all the time, for example when we're very intently focused on some internal thought or activity, disconnected from background realities, having tuned out all distractions. Reading a good book will entrance us, as will daydreaming to music: anything in which the surroundings fade away and we're focused. Our focus of attention can be on positive events that might conjure optimism, relaxation or some productive activity, or it can be on negative events that might muster feelings of anger, regret or shame. The depressed or anxious person is already in their own hypnotic trance: focused on one unhelpful thought. In which case, the therapist needs to help them release their unhelpfully narrowed attention and take a more positive perspective.

What hypnosis does is harness our natural ability to enter a versatile and imaginative mental state, and then guide us with helpful suggestions designed to facilitate positive change. "And change will lead to insight, far more often than insight will lead to change", said the American psychiatrist Dr Milton H. Erickson, considered one of the twentieth century's most inspiring exponents of hypnosis. This is why the self-generated, deeply absorbing, virtual-reality experience can be so helpful: by imaginatively experiencing how things could be if they got better, we allow our psychological horizons and expectations to improve to such

Some myths about hypnosis

Thanks in part to the showmanship of a long line of stage hypnotists, there are plenty of misunderstandings circulating about what hypnosis is and how it works. So let's set the record straight. We don't need a particular type of personality to be in a hypnotic state: at least eighty percent of us are likely to experience the naturally occurring state many times each day, when we become "entranced" by a good book, a conversation, a task, or the memory of some long-ago event. Nor do we have to be relaxed. Hypnosis can't help us remember the past any more accurately, nor do we genuinely regress to past lives: when in a hypnotic state, we are vividly imagining things rather than remembering them.

an extent that we think, behave and perceive things differently, and even our automatic bodily functions may respond accordingly.

Hypnosis is not a therapy in itself; it's a particular technique that can be used to enhance various different approaches. Because it's a tool rather than a broader diagnostic approach, hypnosis can only be useful once an experienced psychotherapist has diagnosed the particular problem or set of problems, and suggested how to tackle them. Hypnosis can then help to deliver those helpful strategies, but it can't replace them.

Milton H. Erickson

Dr Milton H. Erickson (1901–80) was brought up on a Wisconsin farm with seven sisters and a brother. He had not begun to talk even by the age of four, and was later discovered to be dyslexic and colour-blind. In his late teens, he was completely paralysed for several months by polio and recounts in his memoirs how he overheard three doctors in the room next door predicting he'd be dead by the morning: "Being a normal kid, I resented that!" Erickson lived another sixty years in spite of those doctors, but polio had rendered him too weak to become a farmer and so he trained first as a medical doctor, and then as a psychiatrist and psychotherapist. From there he developed his very own brand of therapy, known as Ericksonian Hypnosis and Brief Therapy.

Accessing and motivating the subconscious mind

Erickson's approach was always flexible, but the many trademark techniques he developed across his working life are the familiar tools of practitioners of hypnosis today. The aim in the first instance is to bypass the conscious mind with its analytical scrutiny and self-conscious reserve, so as to induce a hypnotic state by deeply focusing an individual's attention.

His "utilization" technique involved taking whatever the individual brought to the situation – perhaps anger, shame or fear – and using that as a first point of rapport. So, to a particularly belligerent and resistant client determined not to enter a hypnotic state, he might say "I want you to stay awake, wide awake and alert, and under no circumstances should you *permit yourself to relax and rest easy*."

This opening gambit might be followed by "confusional techniques" in which Erickson would offer small talk or even jibberish, so priming the listener to be hungry to hear something that made sense to them. At this point of hunger, he would introduce a key thought or note of guidance clearly relevant to the listener's situation. The key suggestion might be "embedded" in an otherwise innocuous line: "I don't want you to… *become adventurous*", where the words in italics are said after a slight pause, and in a quite different tone and volume, so that they stand apart from the rest of the sentence. This playing with intonation prompts the subconscious to prick up its ears and take note. Typically, the therapeutic suggestions are gentle and open: "You might find… I wonder whether… only you can know if…" The voice is slow, gentle, rhythmic, repetitive.

Dr Milton H. Erickson, the father of modern-day hypnosis for therapy and personal development, working closely with one of his students.

Entrancing tales

Erickson used "teaching tales" with his clients because he rightly saw stories as a golden road to our subconscious, enabling us to gain new insights about ourselves and our relationship with the world. But what gives storytelling – whether in Erickson's tales or in artistic media such as films and novels – its power over us? The evidence suggests two very active ingredients.

The first is that storytelling has a hypnotic effect all of its own. Take watching a film at the cinema, for instance: we block out our immediate surroundings so as to focus our attention and immerse ourselves in the unfolding story. We suspend the usual scrutiny and scepticism of our conscious mind, which gladly steps aside and allows the big-screen fantasy to engage freely with our subconscious. This process is nothing short of hypnosis, two hours' worth. This explains why we can become so physically and emotionally aroused. To all intents and purposes, we see, hear and emotionally feel the story, and this focused sensory state is enough to convince much of our brain that we are active participants. Our propensity for such visceral involvement suggests that nature clearly intends that we be able to learn from our fireside stories; and how like a fireside the flickering of the silver screen can be.

Of course, books and radio can often conjure even greater empathy within us. Music, too. We are hard-wired to move to music, and if our body doesn't, our mind will. The music will become the backing score to some movie in our imagination. The wonderful power of these seemingly less comprehensive media is that *we* are having to generate the visual images and other sensory elements all by ourselves. And as with every dimension of life, the deeper and more holistically we are involved with an activity, the more we stand to benefit.

Our subconscious appetite for stories (whether told by film, books, ballet or music) relies on a second fundamental propensity of the human brain: our drive to see metaphors in the world around us. We are primed to recognize that in some fundamental way one thing is rather like another, even though the surface detail might appear quite different. Our innate pattern-spotting mechanism means that we will wonder how a storyline might relate to our own lives.

Our capacities for the immersed concentration of self-hypnosis and for seeing metaphors are two perfect partners, because in a state of willing self-hypnosis our mind is particularly versatile and creative and more able to consider new connections, thus allowing a storyline to strike a chord of recognition with us. This is why a wet Sunday afternoon curled up on the couch with a book or an old movie can provide some intensely affecting experiences, and why our favourite stories, no matter in what medium we've encountered them, nor at what age, can be as memorable and dear to us as some of the richest experiences of our life. In most senses, we were all but there; it is as if we lived the moment. And we will re-live it in our imagination many times more, savouring it and etching it deeper into our mind, like welcome scars on our personal road map for how the world really is.

Once Erickson had guided his clients into a trance state, he would tell them tailor-made "teaching tales" rich with metaphor and symbol. In doing so he was part of a long tradition among humans of fireside stories that cause our imaginations to conjure pictures and possibilities that change our horizons. The stories Erickson told were life-enhancing, urging positive action to take charge of one's life by exploring bold new perspectives and behaviours. As we've seen, Erickson regarded our subconscious mind as a reservoir of experiences that could be drawn upon to problem-solve and to re-engage far more effectively with future possibilities as a means for personal growth and better rapport with the world around us. The therapist is simply a navigator guiding and inspiring the individual to some promising approaches that they might not have considered.

Refocusing our energies in more helpful directions

Erickson regarded symptoms as clues to a client's wider relationship with life: perhaps an *angry* skin condition, a *shaming* sexual complaint, a *self-punishing* ulcer, a *trapped* nerve, a *nervous* bladder. And like Freud and Jung before him, Erickson knew that the human subconscious was geared for safety and resistant to trying the unfamiliar: "Almost all patients will unconsciously do whatever is necessary to prevent real therapeutic change. Therefore, when the patient is on a useless track, it's important that the therapist derail him and direct him to a more fruitful one." Surprise and the unexpected, even shock, were key ways of achieving this. Erickson might set his client an unusual mission requiring them to behave differently, so as to dislodge their usual way of dealing with the world. For instance:

▶ **The hyper-anxious and self-conscious student** whose life is blighted by their shame about their facial acne or eczema might be sent for a two-week skiing holiday, on the one condition that they do not look in a mirror in all that time. (When the skin problem stops staring the youngster in the face fifty times per day, it ceases to serve as a means of communication for the subconscious mind, and so clears itself up.)

▶ **The defiant personality unable to orgasm** might be told to explore every possible sexual pleasure, "but whatever you do, I forbid you to orgasm!" (A week later, the unruly client is proud to report that she defied the therapist's strictest instructions.)

Erickson taught that the request to the subconscious had to be attractive, gentle and respectful, harnessing the client's passions and strengths so as to help solve the problem. Hence, he was always looking for ways to arouse the individual's self-motivation and spirit of exploration. His view was that feeling excited by and attracted to "a real goal in the near future" is the best antidote to depression or obsessive thinking. The power to change resides in the individual, but it needs to be brought to life.

Rather than going through life obeying a list of musts and shoulds and oughts inherited from parents and other authority figures, Erickson wanted the individual to develop a sense of their own autonomy and willpower, so that they could start making helpful changes in how they thought and behaved. Hence, he believed that the individual needed to take charge of their life by initiating innovative action, no matter how small at first: "Therapy is like starting a snowball rolling at the top of a mountain. As it rolls down, it grows larger and larger and becomes an avalanche."

NLP: Neuro-Linguistic Programming

NLP is a coaching and therapeutic system developed in the US in the 1970s. Its name reflects the perspectives of its creators: Richard Bandler, with his love of computer science, and Dr John Grinder, a linguistics lecturer. Both men shared a strong interest in therapy, and they joined forces to wonder how their specialist perspectives on the world could be fused with the subconscious-friendly techniques of Dr Milton H. Erickson. They concluded that our subconscious brain and the body activities it controls, as well as our conscious thoughts and emotions and behaviours, can all be re-programmed (i.e. re-trained) by what we choose to repeatedly associate with our past or present or future scenarios. Putting this into practice, we might imagine hearing a favourite piece of rousing music when we want more confidence for a forthcoming date, or let ourselves feel carefree laughter coursing through our body so as to counter feelings of shame or humiliation at the memory of some poetry-reading event that went awry when we were a child.

Grinder and Bandler's seminal book *The Structure of Magic* explains their theory and techniques in much more detail. NLP is an eclectic range of psychological tools and techniques that together hope to provide fast, effective improvements. However, as with any tool box, it's only as good as its user is experienced – and it helps if the user is able to admit that these are inadequate tools for some problems. But no matter because other approaches are readily to hand (see "Working Well with a Therapist" on pp.291–307).

Roger Bannister completes the first-ever sub-four-minute mile at the Iffley Road Track in Oxford in 1954, shattering many preconceptions of what's possible.

Ericksonian approaches are equally helpful in personal development, not merely therapeutic scenarios. We can all get into ruts, into self-limiting patterns of thinking and feeling and behaving. We need to stride beyond our inhibitions. One key is to explore different ways of viewing the challenge; to *reframe* it. For instance, the British athlete Roger Bannister stopped thinking about "the four-minute mile" that had never been beaten, and started thinking instead about the "240-seconds mile". Surely a second or two could be shaved off a fat number like 240! Reframing the problem allowed Bannister a different psychological attitude, to which he subsequently attributed his breaking the four-minute mile.

Erickson's therapeutic approaches are today continued through the Erickson Foundation (see erickson-foundation.org). Particularly recommended is the slim paperback *And My Voice Will Go With You: the Teaching Tales of Milton H. Erickson,* edited by Sidney Rosen. Rudimentary methods for self-hypnosis are outlined in the following section.

Teaming up with our subconscious

Learning to work well with our subconscious could be an enormous boon to our all-round well-being. Let's look at some simple methods for achieving that healthy rapport in our everyday life.

Imaginative practice

We can combine the skills of imagination and relaxation to "imaginatively rehearse" any activity in our mind's eye, so as to strikingly improve our real-life performance, whether it be on the sports field or in our workplace, on the dance floor or in a relationship. Such imaginative practice is a form of self-hypnosis.

> **"Imagination is more important than knowledge."**
> Albert Einstein

▶ **Step one: slow-motion gentle breathing.** First, we inhale very slowly and gently through our nose. Then we exhale even more slowly than we inhaled, as this ratio of breathing slower out than in will send a calming signal to our brain and nervous system. We should be aiming to breathe more slowly and gently than we have ever breathed before. Our gentle in-breath might last for seven seconds, and our gentle out-breath might last ten. It can help if we visualize the breath we exhale carrying out of us all the emotions or thoughts or physical feelings that we don't want (perhaps our irritability or worry or aches). Better still if we picture these "negatives" as a colour, so we see ourselves breathing out that unwanted colour, those unwanted negatives, exhaling them from our body. And when we breathe in, let's breathe in the feelings we do want (perhaps tranquillity, confidence and comfort); these positives can be any favourite colour of our choosing, any colour that seems to suit, or perhaps a favourite smell.

▶ **Step two: relaxing our muscles.** Now we take our mind through each group of muscles in turn, and let them fall as limp as possible. We work from our toes right up to the back of our neck and forehead. We let go our hunched shoulders and clenched stomach muscles, and let's not forget our jaw, tongue and face. The aim is that every muscle falls free and easy. Now let our imagination waft us away to a favourite oasis of tranquillity, perhaps somewhere out in Mother Nature. Feel the grass beneath our toes, smell the blossom, hear the sshhh of the waves or the wind in the willows, whatever works best for us.

Why relax?

Because a relaxed brain, like a relaxed body, is highly flexible and fast-moving. A runner at the beginning of the 200-metre sprint wants to be totally relaxed – so their muscles are flexible and fast-moving. Likewise, when we've some thinking to do, we want our mind to be flexible and fast-moving, allowing our imagination to stretch out to some new solution.

▶ **Step three: visualizing and feeling a successful performance.**
Now we should vividly imagine ourselves giving a highly successful and enjoyable performance, being sure to view and feel this from within our own body, rather than seeing it as if we were a detached bystander or a television camera looking down on things. We need to deploy all of our five senses in a systematic way, while aiming to maintain our deep relaxation throughout. Calling it imagination doesn't really do this technique justice; we need to immerse ourselves in the experience, so it feels as real as possible. We shouldn't rush, and we should be aiming to feel and see ourselves perform each step of the process clearly and correctly. As well as imaginatively rehearsing the specific physical skills, we could also run through how it's going to feel emotionally. Be sure to include an awareness of how the general atmosphere will probably be on the day. Acclimatizing ourselves to that "background buzz" of an audience or other distractions is all part of our imaginative preparation. And if a particular skill is tricky, we might need to slow-motion our way through it, or focus in on specific details.

By all these combined means – slow and gentle breathing, physical relaxation and a vividly imaginative exploration of doing things differently and successfully – we can begin to transcend the horizons of what we personally thought we were capable of.

For best effects, we should try at least a dozen such slow and thorough "internal repetitions" of the task we're trying to improve. Such imaginative rehearsal can provide a low-cost, safe "virtual" training environment in which to practise some key skills, such as preventing and relieving anxiety, building the confidence for public speaking and important performances, developing our self-motivation and overcoming our reluctance and inertia. Better still, it can also help in our social and personal relationships: inviting someone for a date, making an apology or asking for help could all benefit from a few imaginative trial runs to build our confidence and help us decide what to say and how to behave.

Let's never forget, though, that real-life experience is an unbeatably potent and quite irreplaceable training ground. Our imagination isn't meant to be used as a substitute for real-life action; it's meant to be an ally, an opportunity to prepare ourselves. So we should always be wondering how we can put our rehearsals to the real test. We can't learn to swim simply by watching or imagining; we need to feel ourselves in the water and explore what's possible *in reality*. The focused imagination that is hypnosis can only ever be one half of the coin; the other half is when we actually do things differently in real life. Together, imaginative rehearsal and exploring real life make for a very powerful partnership.

A conversation with our subconscious

Often, we know *something* is the matter – something's causing us to sleep badly, or booze too often, or constantly fall ill – but we don't know what it is. To find the antidote we need to know what we really want from life (and what beliefs or fears or memories might be holding us back). What long-held heart's desires haven't we owned up to, or done anything about? To answer these questions, it can help to quite literally have a conversation with our subconscious mind.

When setting out to work with our subconscious, we should remember that this part of our mind is as shy as a six-year-old child, as easily spooked as an Arabian horse, and quite capable of being as stubborn and determined as both. So it helps to prepare the ground gently for any communication, particularly in the early stages of developing a rapport. Our subconscious has our best interests very much at heart, but it can be over-zealous and wary of progress to the point of being self-inhibiting.

First, we need to reassure our conscious mind that we're safe enough and calm enough to speak directly with our on-board computer. Relaxing our body in the ways described above, perhaps with the help of a warm bath or bed, is a good way to do this. If possible, our eyes should be closed to help us focus our attention and conjure images. Now let's ask ourselves some questions, speaking slowly, gently and simply just as we would if addressing that shy six year old, or that nervous Arabian horse. We might simply ask our subconscious out loud:

> ▶ **"When I love or work or play, am I holding myself back for some reason? I'd like to understand what's scaring me."**
> ▶ **"I would be very happy to know why...** *[when a really good opportunity comes up, I immediately fall ill]."*

Good questions can reveal conflicting agendas in different parts of our mind, such as our subconscious wanting safety and things to stay the same while our conscious mind wants adventure and progress. They can also help reveal those self-limiting beliefs that lie behind our self-sabotaging behaviours and psychosomatic symptoms. Such beliefs might include:

> ▶ **"It's not safe to let this fear go."**
> ▶ **"I don't deserve to be rid of this albatross."**
> ▶ **"I won't feel like *me* if I lose my trademark illness."**
> ▶ **"Letting this problem go will be letting 'them' off too easily."**
> ("Them" being those people who've hurt me... and who are now themselves being hurt by my illness.)

As we gently question ourselves, we might become aware of certain involuntary muscles in our face or body palpitating slightly, as if some rarely used electrical circuit has just been switched on and is coming to life. We should take this as a good sign. It's as if we've made contact, perhaps even touched a sensitive nerve. These involuntary physical flutters will evaporate once the conversation with ourselves is over.

While in conversation with our subconscious, we should be sure to offer some self-supporting statements, such as "I really care for myself and support myself". And if something inside us winces uncomfortably at the thought of "giving ourselves a hug" like this, if it all feels too cheesy by half, then we probably need this conversation far more than we realize. Because if we can't rely on ourselves to be our own totally trustworthy supporter through thick and thin, then we're handicapping ourselves right from the start. As with many relationships, our subconscious is prone to feel unsupported and unloved, or perhaps uncertain of what we really want of it. So these conversations are an opportunity to encourage our spirits at a profound level, and make our missions clearer.

▶ "Even though Mum and Dad didn't know how to love and care for me, I am learning every day how to put my love into wonderful action with myself and those around me."

▶ "Even though in the past I felt scared by this, I choose now to do things bravely."

Note that we use the present tense – "I am, I love to, it feels beautiful" – so there is no implication that what we want of ourselves will have to wait for some time in the future, or maybe never. And there are no negative constructions. We're aiming to make things clear by setting up the goalposts with simple present-tense, positive sentences describing the behaviour we want of ourselves as if it's already happening: "I love how good it feels to sleep deeply, and I so deeply deserve to."

To help our subconscious frame its reply to our conscious inquiries, it can help if we suggest ways in which it could reveal its clues:

▶ "Perhaps I could dream this at night and then remember and understand the dream."

▶ "Perhaps I could wake up tomorrow and just realize what I want to know."

As with any relationship, we need to invest in this conscious–subconscious partnership with frequent, even regular, meeting times for a "hello, how am I?" In addition, a good therapist, particularly one well trained in hypnotic techniques (see above) or energy techniques (see pp.129–134), can teach us how to build an even better rapport with ourselves so our subconscious can more easily offer some helpful replies.

Conclusions

Our psychological good health and all-round well-being owe much to the skilful integration of the different parts of ourselves so that we feel whole, rather than fragmented. Our aim should be that every part of us, mind and body, is wanting progress in our relationship with life, and pulling together to achieve it. By harmonizing the relationship between our conscious and subconscious mind in the ways described in this chapter, we can make profound progress towards a more beautiful life.

3

Our conscious strategies

Our conscious strategies 3

Changing how we think can change how we live

Books on happiness are never more blabby than when discussing conscious strategies. They might blithely ignore the vital role of our human body, never mention the subconscious mind and care nothing for our natural environment, but they can go on for three hundred pages solid about one single psychological technique such as "flow", "prospection" or "mindfulness", as if it's the answer to just about everything. The following chapter casts a critical eye over some of the best-known conscious strategies aimed at improving our happiness and well-being. As we sort the wheat from the chaff, we'll be reminded of a central theme running through this Rough Guide: it's not our experiences that determine whether we're happy or sad or thrive or founder; it's what attitudes and action we take in response to them. And some of our responses, at least, can be consciously chosen.

A couple of big names...

The world of conscious strategies is currently dominated by a couple of big names you may well have come across: Cognitive Behavioural

Therapy and Positive Psychology. Here's what they're all about, for better or worse.

Cognitive Behavioural Therapy (CBT)

In the Western world today, Cognitive Behavioural Therapy is arguably the flagship psychological therapy for helping a troubled individual engage more effectively with life.

The word "cognitive" is psycho-talk for thinking, and the word "behavioural" (which was added later in the therapy's evolution) is there to emphasize that change is not just about how we think, but what we actually do. Doing things differently can be both a cause and a result of changing our thoughts.

Dr Judith Beck (daughter of Cognitive Therapy's founder, and long-time director of the Beck Institute in Philadelphia, US) gives in her excellent book *Cognitive Therapy: Basics and Beyond* a nutshell distillation of the premise of CBT: "distorted or dysfunctional thinking (which influences the patient's mood and behaviour) is common to all psychological disturbances".

The original tenets of CBT strongly reflect its formative era. It was developed by University of Pennsylvania psychiatrist Dr Aaron T. Beck in the 1960s and 70s as a form of fast-acting psychotherapy, i.e. taking perhaps half a dozen one-hour sessions to inspire demonstrable and substantial improvements in the client's life, rather than the weekly sessions over several years which was common practice in its alternatives. It would seem that Dr Beck created his Cognitive Therapy with at least two substantial motivations:

▶ **First, as an alternative to Freudian psychoanalysis**, which so dominated therapeutic practice with patients, and so strongly emphasized the "subconscious sex and anger" emotional motivations of all we do. CBT's antipathy for psychoanalysis is perhaps why it makes no explicit mention of the subconscious mind, and talks instead of "automatic thoughts". If psychoanalysis focused almost entirely on "uncovering" our automatic feelings, then CBT focused almost entirely on "uncovering" our automatic thinking.

▶ **Second, as an alternative to behaviourist psychology**, which had dominated university psychology departments in the decades since

World War II. Behaviourists (led by Harvard professor B.F. Skinner, infamous for electrocuting cats and other small creatures in his Skinner Box) claimed that humans and all other animals were simply computer-like machines that responded in set ways when triggered by stimuli. The behaviourists believed behaviour was all-important, and that our thoughts and feelings were all but irrelevant. CBT, in stark contrast, prioritized thoughts.

So how does it work?

In a CBT session, the therapist and client will work together to try to spot the tell-tale automatic thoughts, feelings and images that immediately occur in response to certain trigger situations. The idea is that these knee-jerk thought-responses will reveal our "core beliefs" about ourselves and how we perceive the world working.

For example, almost every time I meet someone who stirs loving feelings within me, I might feel a sinking feeling in my guts that seems to tell me to "forget it! This person will never love me." However, by asking myself when I first felt such feelings, I might realize that my unhelpful automatic reaction to new situations is probably being triggered by a long-ago traumatic episode in my teens when my mother left home, and accidentally created the "core belief" in me that "even when I love someone, they will abandon me".

Common core beliefs include such self-inhibiting notions as:

▶ **I'm unlovable.**
▶ **The world is dangerous.**
▶ **Nobody can be trusted.**
▶ **I'll never be good enough.**

Once we've diagnosed what rules of thumb (i.e. "core beliefs") we're using to deal with life, we can then arrange to test out their accuracy and helpfulness in the real world. For instance, we weigh up as objectively as we can the evidence from our lives that we are loved by some people; that we can cope well with the risks and demands we have to bear; that we can learn to be very good at certain tasks.

And so begins a process of modifying our core beliefs in helpful ways, or scrapping them altogether and replacing them with more useful ones:

▶ **I am loving and lovable.**
▶ **I make a much-valued contribution to the people around me.**

▶ **I can learn to thrive in the face of life's challenges.**

▶ **I deserve to live well because I'm a jolly good person.**

Is CBT a helpful therapy?

Having impressively challenged the uni-dimensional approaches of psychoanalysis (which exclusively prioritized feelings) and behaviourism (which exclusively prioritized behaviour), it's unfortunate that CBT instituted its very own uni-dimensional approach, by exclusively prioritizing thought. Despite referring to behaviour in its title, CBT chooses not

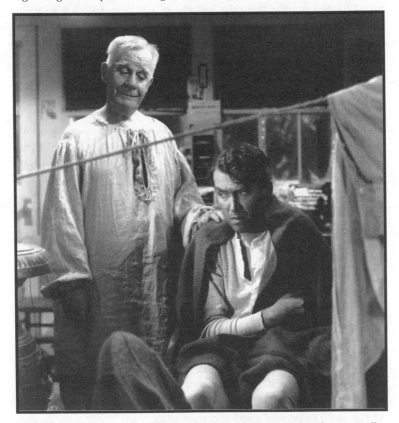

Viewing things differently: the Christmas classic *It's a Wonderful Life* (1946) tells the story of George Bailey (James Stewart), a poor soul at the very end of his tether and feeling all washed up because he's obsessing over the loss of some money. This is when old man Clarence, who's a Guardian Angel 2nd Class and eager to earn his full wings, helps George re-evaluate his life by showing him some new perspectives. And there begins a lovely tale.

to grant equality to the physical needs and drives of the Homo sapiens animal. So, in CBT training manuals, courses and books, there is little or no mention of how frequent and vigorous physical exercise, adequate sleep or good all-round nutrition are powerful complements to all psychological progress. The mind–body holistic system is simply not considered. And, of course, CBT presumes that emotions/passions are generated by thoughts, never the other way around. Control your thoughts and you control your feelings is what CBT unequivocally claims. By demoting our other essential human dimensions, CBT closely mimics the Ancient World philosophers – Socrates, Plato, Aristotle – who were equally dismissive of our passionate feelings and physical bodies, as we saw on pp.23–25.

Such an unbalanced, hierarchical approach to our thoughts-emotions-body system perhaps goes some way to explaining why CBT simply hasn't had anywhere near the beneficial effect we would want from the Western world's most commonly practised psychological therapy. Although CBT can prove partially or wholly effective for some clients, its narrow approach restricts its benefits: alas, for many clients, all the rational arguments and all the conscious reconsidering of their situation bring only minor improvements in how life feels and how they behave. CBT has thrived, nonetheless, perhaps because its emphasis on "improved thinking" appeals very strongly to the intellectually minded academic psychologists who tend to end up running university departments and heading up psychotherapy clinics. As a challenge to this, Chapters 2 and 4 of this Rough Guide explore other approaches such as Ericksonian Hypnosis and Subtle Energy therapies, which endeavour to work beyond the limitations of our conscious mind.

Positive Psychology

In the summer of 1998, this new movement in psychology was launched by University of Pennsylvania professor Martin Seligman (see box overleaf) with the help of a small band of high-flying American colleagues, among them Professors Mihály Csíkszentmihályi, Chris Peterson and George Vaillant. It is essentially a brand, a flag if you will, under which several concepts, psychological techniques and interested professors are able to sail Armada-like in roughly the same direction.

Martin Seligman

The founder and figurehead of Positive Psychology and director of the Pennsylvania Positive Psychology Center, Martin Seligman is widely regarded as one of the bravest and most innovative psychological thinkers of the second half of the twentieth century. And rightly so. In the 1970s, he and Dr Aaron Beck of the University of Pennsylvania (see p.82) devised and championed the new approaches of Cognitive Therapy that offered a highly viable alternative to the reductionist dogma of the bullying behaviourists and the dark mysticism of the psychoanalysts. During that troubled era, behaviourists ruled the roosts in university departments on both sides of the Atlantic and, with their computer-like view of human nature, attempted to sterilize in their laboratories what it meant to be alive. Against this poisonous climate and some nasty opposition, Seligman re-wrote the textbooks by documenting how laboratory dogs who received electric shocks in a high-walled pen would not try to escape once they were moved to a low-walled pen, even though escape was then quite possible. These dogs weren't acting like the stop-go machines that behaviourists claimed all animals were; they were clearly adopting a fully conscious attitude to life, albeit to give up trying. This previously unacknowledged phenomenon which Seligman called "learned helplessness" earned him an enduring place among the greats of experimental psychology, and led to his life-long advocacy of "learned optimism" (see pp.92–94) to combat such self-inhibiting helplessness among human animals. (Let it be noted, too, that on compassionate grounds he never again chose to work with laboratory animals.)

A quarter of a century after that bitter civil war in academic psychology, Seligman used his year's presidency of the American Psychological Association in

Positive Psychology is, in principle at least, a welcome and necessary extension of Cognitive Behavioural Therapy, because it aims to be not only therapeutic for our problems, but also nurturing of our existing strengths. In keeping with their CBT roots, the new techniques of Positive Psychology are united by their focus on our conscious mind (in contrast to our subconscious mind), aiming to craft and control our thoughts so as to create more pleasurable emotions and reduce the painful ones such as anger, fear, shame or regret.

Our past, present and future

Positive Psychology's most successful endeavours have been its suggestions for life-coping strategies that deal constructively with our experiences of the past, present and future:

1998 to champion a rethink of the whole focus of psychology when, as a world-renowned specialist in depression, he coined the term "Positive Psychology" to stand for "the scientific study of happiness". If it seems strange that a university psychologist should need to make a fuss about focusing on happiness, bear in mind that after World War II it was hard to get work as a psychologist if you were not studying mental illness, largely because there was so much remedial work to be done with traumatized soldiers and civilians, orphaned children and ex-prisoners. This overwhelming bias towards healing the pains of life (rather than studying the pleasures) became self-perpetuating, and lasted fifty years. Seligman describes his professional mission now as "promoting the field of Positive Psychology so as to make the world a happier place", parallel, he says, "to the way clinical psychologists have made the world a less *unhappy* place".

Seligman's *Authentic Happiness* (2002), the very first book in the field to be aimed at a general readership, was perhaps a somewhat premature attempt to sell Positive Psychology as a popular panacea, promoting as it did several strategies and conclusions which are not yet supported by rigorous studies of lives evolving over time. Though proposing bold new concepts is always to be encouraged, it is dangerously misleading to allow a reader to think such concepts are grounded safely in strong science, or to allow academic credentials to bolster our over-zealous interpretations of what is, when scrutinized, weak evidence. However, if Positive Psychology and Seligman's popular books on the subject are something of a disappointment, it is only by comparison to the achievements of his career as a whole.

▶ **Our present:** fully engaging through using our "signature strengths", finding "flow" and then "savouring".
▶ **Our future:** taking constructive action in expectation of real improvement, and being versatile in what we try.
▶ **Our past:** not ruminating about negatives from the past.

This approach, which aims to improve our relationship with our life in each of its three time dimensions, ties in closely with the foundational idea outlined in Chapter 1, that profound health is something whole and fully rounded.

Fully engaging in the present

Despite its popularity, a glass of wine in front of the TV is *not* the best way to feel better in the here and now. We're much better off being fully absorbed in some mental or physical activity that requires far greater

Focusing inflates things

Whatever we focus our attention on tends to assume a much-inflated importance to us. This phenomenon has been well documented by University of California management professor David Shachter and Princeton psychologist Daniel Kahneman, and they call it the "focusing illusion". In other words, we'll weigh up things very differently depending on what our attention is drawn to. So, ask someone how good life is, and they'll give you one answer. Ask them if they're dating someone at present, and then ask them how good life is, and you'll get a quite different response. It sounds obvious, but it's a good reminder that by altering our focus of attention we can change our emotional energy.

Such observations have often been cited as evidence that we're not very good at objectively weighing up the big picture – our focus of attention blows certain things out of proportion and so leads us astray. But Harvard psychology professor Ellen Langer emphasizes the helpful effects of such focused attention. She advocates her own brand of "mindfulness" (see p.91 for the Buddhist version), whereby one doesn't just focus on but tries to fully inhabit a moment or an activity so as to engage more deeply and gain more from it. For instance, children learning history who are asked to imagine themselves in the predicament of a key figure do far better on subsequent tests than youngsters simply asked to learn the facts in normal fashion. It seems the more actively engaged we are in an activity, the deeper goes the benefit.

involvement. This is probably because our human brain has evolved to be a rapacious problem-solver, but rapidly finding itself in a comparatively danger-free modern environment, it often has a lot of spare capacity. This means that if we don't present ourselves with a constructive but demanding task, our brain goes looking for trouble, and that's how regrets about the past and worries about the future can sometimes run away with us.

Flow

The concepts of "flow" and "signature strengths" offer two closely related strategies that can promote our complete and positive "absorption in the moment".

American psychology professor Mihály Csíkszentmihályi (pronounced cheeks-sent-me-high) first coined the term "flow" in the 1990s to describe that intensely positive state achieved when our skill and energy levels well match the task we're engaged in, so that we skate close to the edge of our ability and have to concentrate absolutely. The goals must be clear and immediate, and so must the feedback on our performance. This is why playing a musical instrument or a sport are such common sources of flow, because we can see, feel or hear from moment to moment how well we're doing. Then again, if we're cream-crackered at the end of the day, reading a good book might be an appropriate match for our energy and concentration levels. If the elements are right, we will experience a complete lack of self-consciousness, and time will pass unmeasured in a warm and lasting glow of satisfaction.

What's most likely to promote this productive "flow" state of pleasing engagement with the here and now is reducing our *passive* pursuits such as watching TV, so as to replace them with activities that dynamically deploy one or more of our "signature strengths". Positive Psychology has quite specific ideas about what these strengths might be, but we needn't be so schematic: our signature strengths are any skills (physical, emotional or intellectual) that we find so pleasurable to exercise that we feel invigorated rather than drained by doing so. Be it gardening, cooking, kissing, pitching for business or playing the fool, that small handful

As he performs on the concert platform, violinist Joshua Bell is so clearly in a state of flow, totally focused on the music he is making and the relationship between himself, his instrument and the orchestra.

Is "flow" simply a positive hypnotic state?

When we compare it to hypnosis (see pp.65–68), we will notice that the seemingly novel concept of "flow" could quite readily be regarded as fine old wine decanted into a nicely re-labelled bottle. Spot the following similarities with the above definition of flow. Our naturally occurring hypnotic states are characterized by highly focused attention: we might be entranced by some imagined scenario set in our past or future, or enthralled by the compelling activity or mesmerizing person we're engaged with. Indeed, a hypnotic state is best induced by a surprising or intriguing trigger that captures and retains our intensely focused attention and keen interest. And as with flow, a hypnotic state is characterized by time-distortion, whereby what feels like a minute or two may in reality be the passing of an hour or more. By these criteria, flow and hypnosis would seem to be all but identical. What the elegant and naturalistic term "flow" has going for it is that it deftly leaves behind all the black magic and stage conjuror baggage that has dogged the word "hypnosis" since early Victorian times.

of activities that make use of our signature strengths will be the ones we excel at and relish above all others. Engaging such strengths promotes the likelihood of entering flow.

Savour the moment

Taking five minutes to note and savour what's going well in our life is a daily routine that can make a tangible difference to our all-round well-being, particularly in times of trouble. American psychology professors Robert Emmons and Michael McCullough are pioneering the experimental work in this field with some promising results. For instance, they asked one group of research participants to keep a journal of things for which they were thankful, while other groups wrote about neutral subjects or their life's daily hassles. Ten weeks later, the "blessing counters" tended to exercise more, report fewer physical ills, be more optimistic about the upcoming week and feel better about their lives in general. In addition, they were more likely to offer emotional support or practical help to someone with a problem, while also mustering greater enthusiasm, determination and energy for their own important goals.

This savouring is thought to be particularly helpful if, before sleeptime or to turn a bad mood around, we try to focus upon three things we're really glad of in our immediate life. None of its benefits should really surprise us because savouring one's blessings is the polar opposite

Can relaxation bolster our immune system?

Psychoneuroimmunology is the neatly named branch of twenty-first-century science that looks at how our state of mind (for example, whether we're stressed or relaxed) might influence our body's immunity to illness or disease. In 2003 Professor Richard J. Davidson of the University of Wisconsin-Madison led a team of ten psychiatrists and psychologists to produce a research paper titled "Alterations in Brain and Immune Function Produced by Mindfulness Meditation".

Mindfulness is a form of meditation with its origins in Buddhism, whereby you focus your conscious attention on the here and now rather than being on automatic pilot or multi-tasking. Davidson's experimental group consisted of 25 women and men with an average age of 36. One of the major aims of the study was to discover whether after learning mindfulness for relaxation purposes these individuals would demonstrate better resistance to infection than those in a control group. The specific brand of mindfulness used, "Mindfulness-Based Stress Reduction", was taught by the technique's founder Dr Jon Kabat-Zinn. The training took place over eight weeks and consisted of a weekly three-hour class, along with a seven-hour retreat held during week six of the course. In addition, the participants were asked to perform meditative techniques at home for one hour a day, six days a week, with the aid of audiotapes. All told, that's well over sixty hours of mindfulness training.

The "control group" consisted of sixteen individuals comparable in age and background to the meditation group. They were asked simply to remain quiet and read rather than do any mindfulness training.

Was there some special ingredient in the mindfulness training that would prove beneficial to its practitioners? To find out, the researchers did something rather exciting: they injected both groups with the influenza virus (or, to be precise, the influenza vaccine) to see which group would react with the most healthy and vigorous defences in terms of the antibody-count in their blood.

The researchers reported that the mindfulness group showed "a significantly greater rise in antibody titres" in response to the vaccine than did the control group, and this result has been widely cited as demonstrating that our state of mind can influence the workings of our immune system. However, the difference in antibody increase between the two groups was barely five percent. In mathematical terms this is statistically significant, but it's far from impressive, and is arguably a poor return on the extensive mindfulness training.

The results of this study may be disappointing on closer inspection. But we shouldn't conclude that our mind cannot help our body. It seems likely, though, that it might take something more than simply relaxing our mind and focusing our conscious thoughts on the present. Chapters 2 and 4 explore alternative routes to mind body interaction which may prove considerably more effective.

of rumination – which means turning over and over in one's mind some negative thought or incident – and rumination is one of the surest ways to depression.

Feeling good about the future

Optimism means taking positive action

Irrepressible optimism is widely regarded by many psychologists as one of the most beneficial personality traits, and it's one we can readily learn like any other skill.

Let's be quite clear, though: optimism is taking the attitude that if we put some effort in we give things the best chance of improving. And that's the magic ingredient in optimism: taking positive action – not just sitting back and presuming or hoping that things will work out in our favour. Optimism is not simply wishful thinking.

With this definition firmly in mind, hundreds of studies demonstrate that compared to pessimists, optimists are higher achievers both at work and on the playing field, as well as enjoying better physical health, recovering faster from illness and suffering much less anxiety and depression.

The health benefits of optimism seem to accrue for a host of reasons. First, optimists have more friends and social supports, not least because they're such cheerful souls to be around and tend to initiate social interaction. They also do more self-care activities such as exercise because they believe it all helps; and meantime their generally buoyant mood boosts their immune system. On top of which, optimists involve themselves more actively with everyday life because they believe their endeavours will eventually reap rewards. Indeed, their worldly success is largely because they persevere in the face of life's routine setbacks and major blows, and this "dynamic resilience" often becomes a self-fulfilling prophecy.

A team led by the long-time director of clinical psychology at the University of Michigan, Professor Chris Peterson, studied the records of 1000 individuals across 50 years. The pessimists had an increased likelihood of early death, but rather than the cancer and heart attacks usually associated with the trait, "accidental death" was the most frequent culprit. Peterson's team concluded that the character trait of pessimism led to a fatalistic, careless lifestyle which led the individuals to put themselves in harm's way (for example, why bother to buckle up or stay sober when driving?). Optimists, on the other hand, habitually put themselves in situations with a high risk of *good* things happening (I wonder who I'll

The Secret

Australian media veteran Rhonda Byrne's *The Secret* is a cleverly marketed book and DVD set with an arresting proposition: that our thoughts radiate out from us and actively create what subsequently happens to us. In other words, our own thoughts and expectations become a self-fulfilling prophecy, for better or for worse. This natural phenomenon, we are told, is known as the "Law of Attraction": *ask, believe, receive*.

Rhonda Byrne has nothing whatsoever to do with Positive Psychology or any related movement, and claims none. Instead, she fields a line-up of 24 acclaimed professional "teachers", including such household-name self-help therapists as Dr John Gray (*Men Are from Mars, Women Are from Venus*) and Dr Jack Canfield (*Chicken Soup for the Soul*), as well as high-powered business consultants, scientists and religious innovators. These self-styled gurus pack *The Secret* with their motivational quotes. Notably, *The Secret* is packaged so as to bear more than a little resemblance to the bestselling *The Da Vinci Code* (which preceded *The Secret* by a couple of years), in that it aims to conjure something of an ancient manuscript, along with the suggestion that elite figures throughout history knew about the proposed Law of Attraction, and pretty much kept it to themselves.

As for its message, most psychotherapists would certainly support the idea that people tend to treat us only as well (or badly) as we treat ourselves. In effect, we lead by example. But where *The Secret* lets itself down is by portraying the universe as a vast shopping mall or mail-order catalogue in which we can send out for whatever we want (and "massive wealth" is one of its most frequent suggestions) simply by thinking hard and clearly and very positively about it. *The Secret* bears some resemblance to the optimism described in this chapter, but without any emphasis on constructive action.

Moreover, this "wish hard enough and your dream will come true" theory raises an obvious question: is *The Secret* really saying that earnest masturbatory fantasies will eventually bring us the "sexual partners" we so desire? I know of no research into this possibility, but it would surely make an intriguing PhD topic.

By far the most difficult problem with *The Secret* (and one which it fails to address adequately) is that the Law of Attraction would seem to imply that infants or adults to whom bad things happen (for example an air crash or serious illness) brought those disasters upon themselves by their negative thinking, or at the very least by their lack of positive thought. This is a pernicious and repugnant idea, and has no evidence to support it, just a carefully selected set of well-polished personal anecdotes about getting rich.

befriend at the evening class?). It's a fascinating thought that our attitude to life alters the settings in which we actively put ourselves, not just how we behave once we get there.

We can probably all learn to be more optimistic. The University of Pennsylvania's Penn Resiliency Project, directed by psychologists Karen

Reivich, Jane Gillham and Martin Seligman, runs training courses teaching optimism to teenagers. This series of twelve two-hour sessions *halves* the incidence and severity of depression, and long-term follow-ups over several years show that the gains to the individual youngsters increase rather than fade – i.e. once they get the hang of optimism, they start applying it more and more often. Of course, these impressive results have only been achieved and carefully monitored among particularly under-privileged youngsters, and we know far less about their effect on less troubled youths, let alone a general range of adults. But the results are encouraging nonetheless.

Versatility always beats single strategies

Optimism is an impressive strategy, but no single approach beats being flexible or versatile in our relationship with possible futures. To this end, we need to practise what we might call "versatile optimistic action". In circumstances where the cost of wrongly forecasting the likely outcome could be disastrously high (for instance, if we're considering drink-driving, unsafe sex or a major investment of our time or money), then it's vital that we envisage some worst-case scenarios so as to prompt ourselves to take smart precautions. By contrast, if we're simply churning out creative ideas, taking a shot at goal or asking someone for a date, that's when strategically deploying a can-do, gung-ho attitude will actively help achieve our goals, because we'll press on in good spirits.

The key distinction to be made here is that "versatile optimistic action" is always better than doing nothing at all, with the proviso that such positive action might require us to behave cautiously: to take out insurance, to put our seat belt on, to call a cab rather than drink-drive, or to seek a fourth and fifth opinion about a career choice or relationship problem. "Just do it!" might be a catchy phrase for the glossy world of Nike advertisements, but our 3-D real-life world benefits from a far more rounded approach.

Squaring ourselves with a painful past

One of the biggest enemies of happiness is rumination about the past – obsessively churning over time and time again our negative memories and partly digested thoughts, rather than putting things to rest. So how can we combat the self-torturing rumination and emotional dramatics that can so poison our mood? Martin Seligman is regarded as one of the world's leading researchers on coping with depression, and he says that insufficient appreciation of the good events in our past and overemphasis of the bad ones are the two culprits that undermine our peace of mind. Here is some of what we could do about it.

Firstly, we shouldn't replay images of our negative past. This is not denial; this is simply removing the oxygen of attention that will reheat the emotional embers. The only condition under which we should revisit a grim episode is to learn some lessons that we can directly translate into what we might call "solution-focused action" – because such action is the very antithesis of rumination.

Secondly, we should allocate a particular time of the week for this lesson-learning, action-oriented backward glance, rather than allowing negative memories to intrude whenever it suits them, and so sour other parts of our life. One hour once per week would be quite enough. And five minutes each day would also help.

Finally, when painful memories do ambush us, we must repel them immediately by conjuring positive thoughts incompatible with the negative ones. For this, we need a handful of ready-made, heart-warming memories and mantras on emergency stand-by to evoke, for instance, a sense of confidence: "Even though I had problems with examinations in the past, I practise examination technique very effectively now."

Why isn't Positive Psychology helping much?

Its *raison d'être* is an attractive one: a better understanding of how to help a life feel happier, not least because it's horribly clear that the present-day mainstreams of psychology, therapy, medicine and education are lacking something essential. Creating healthy bodies, minds and communities in harmony with our natural environments requires that we learn what helps people to thrive rather than simply survive, to flourish rather than simply stay afloat. But barely a decade since the phrase was coined in 1998, it appears Positive Psychology is running out of steam.

Positive Psychology largely made it off the ground in the US because an American billionaire, Sir John Templeton, championed this new movement with several million dollars. In the UK and continental Europe, where there has been no such financial investment angel, the movement has struggled to gain barely a foothold in even a couple of universities. Let's take a closer look at what's probably holding back this once-so-promising movement.

▶ **Positive Psychology deifies happiness.** Rather than offering big-picture explanations of how everything fits together to form a life beautifully lived, Positive Psychology has focused very largely on its priority-goal of "greater happiness!", so keeping firmly in step with the pleasure-addicted fashion of our age. On the cover of Seligman's *Authentic Happiness*, Dr Daniel Goleman (author of the bestselling *Emotional Intelligence*) cheers: "At last psychology gets serious about glee, fun and happiness." Leading Positive Psychologists have always argued that there are "positive emotions" and "negative emotions", a stance that has only served to fuel the modern-day deification of our happy/pleasurable feelings (such as optimism, love, confidence and self-esteem) as being entirely positive, and the demonization of our painful/sad feelings (such as fear, anger, shame, loneliness or regret) as being entirely negative. Professor Seligman even goes so far as to write in the preface to *Authentic Happiness* (using italics for emphasis) that *"there is not a shred of evidence that strength and virtue are derived from negative emotion"*. There is absolutely no suggestion in Positive Psychology that we should try to channel or ride the energy of our painful emotions so that they carry us forward – a transformative approach which is advocated in Chapter 1 of this Rough Guide. Alas, the new psychology has not yet realized that sadness is not the enemy of happiness but, as Nietzsche wrote, "its sister". Such a lop-sided, unwholesome attitude is challenged in some detail in this Rough Guide's Chapter 1, so suffice it to say here that in putting happiness on a pedestal, Positive Psychology is in effect legislating against the interwoven richness and rainbow colours that make up a whole life. It's outlawing everything but "electric sunshine yellow".

▶ **Positive Psychology prioritizes thinking.** Bearing in mind that Positive Psychology was the brainchild of the world-renowned specialist in depression Professor Martin Seligman, who had helped pioneer the new "thinking therapy" CBT in the 1960s (see pp.82–85), it was only to be expected that this new movement set out to use psychological "thinking techniques" to "maximize happiness". (Happiness being regarded as the polar opposite of depression.) In Seligman's Positive Psychology, the role of the body is barely mentioned (there's nothing at all on exercise, nutrition, dance, sport or song), and emotional passions are treated as something to be controlled by reason, just as Plato and his peers advocated. But as is so often the case with proclamations by academics and so-called experts (ancient and modern), the evidence of our everyday lives flies in the face of what the researchers and theorists try to tell us. Like the unruly child shouting "The Emperor's wearing no clothes!", we know from our own experience that no matter what the professors say, our feelings, thoughts and actions work together, and no one part of us is more valuable than the other.

▶ **Rushed and poor-quality research.** University departments all over the world tend to reward professors according to the number of research papers they produce, and this policy leads to plummeting quality as researchers try to find the fastest ways to throw together something to publish. The result is research that's very often based upon the questionnairing of psychology undergraduates (i.e. undergraduates ticking boxes in return for a few dollars), a fact that the resulting newspaper stories too often try to hide from their readership, because the journalists are just as desperate as the professors to fill column inches. For instance, a 2002 paper by Professors Ed Diener and Martin Seligman was misleadingly called "Very Happy People", when it could more honestly have been called "Very Happy Undergraduates"... because it questionnaired 222 undergraduates, and then allowed the impression that the results could be generalized to all other adults. (The poverty of research that has dogged Positive Psychology and the wider social sciences is further examined in the box overleaf and on pp.226–230.) Good studies of life-in-action are frighteningly demanding in terms of time, money and painstaking observation, but there's no credible alternative if we're to glimpse a clearer picture of how things really work.

Surely being happy helps our life go better?

At the very centre of Positive Psychology is the claim that happiness isn't just a symptom of life going well, it's also a cause. It's this that lies behind the movement's deification of happiness as something to be nurtured at every opportunity. So fundamental is this belief that the first ever $100,000 Templeton Positive Psychology Prize was given to Professor Barbara Fredrickson of the University of North Carolina for a range of laboratory experiments supposedly confirming this causal link. Fredrickson concluded, for example, that many people made happier by watching a DVD would then perform better on a range of intellectual tests, and be more creative and open-minded. The results were eagerly received by Positive Psychologists keen for proof of their ideas. But what happens in the real world beyond the artifice of the lab? Does our real-life experience suggest that only happy feelings can be the spur to creativity and high performance? Or can you think of testing times in your own life when the painful yet powerful emotions of shame, loneliness, fear or anger have enabled you to reach well beyond your usual comfort zones so as to achieve something clearly positive and creative?

Positive Psychology's theory that happiness helps our life go well is shored up by a couple more much-cited studies. Each is intriguing at first glance, but up close it's far more doubtful how much they can really tell us.

The first of these studies is *Positive Emotions in Early Life and Longevity: Findings from the Nun Study*, published in 2001 by Professor Deborah D. Danner and her team at the University of Kentucky (see nunstudy.org). In 1930, 180 American Roman Catholic nuns had been required to write a few pages of autobiography, at about the time they took their holy vows. The nuns were aged between 18 and 32, with an average age of 22. Almost seventy years on, these autobiographies were analysed to see if their language and their take on life were in some way related to how long the sisters lived. Was the amount of "positive, negative or neutral emotional content" predictive of the nuns' longevity?

The two language-raters were not privy to how long the nuns lived, so they could not be influenced by those results. The positive references they looked out for included happiness, interest, love, hope and gratitude. Negative references included sadness, fear, anxiety, shame and anger. Only one emotion was deemed neutral: the emotion of "surprise".

In some ways, this group of nuns was ideal for study because of the strong similarities in the lifestyles all these ladies had enjoyed in terms of nutrition, access to medical care and social environment. They were not parents, and were not married.

What Professor Danner's study found was that nine out of ten of the most cheerful quarter of the autobiographies were written by nuns who were still alive at age 85, versus only three out of ten of the authors of the least cheerful quarter of autobiographies. Ten years later, the figures were five in ten versus one in ten.

Clear proof, right, that being happy increases your lifespan (apparently by about nine years once all the sums are done)? That's what many leading Positive Psychologists would have you think. But the value placed upon this small study is out of all proportion to its significance: it can never be more than an intriguing snapshot, based as it is on a group of people with a very specific lifestyle. Any results found among these cloistered nuns might not hold true in the wider population.

An even more fundamental problem is that we know nothing else about how these nuns lived their lives. This makes it impossible for us to be sure we've identified cause and effect correctly. Even if the language-rating did accurately identify genuinely happy nuns (and that in itself is something we'll never know for sure), perhaps happiness isn't the royal road to longevity after all, but some mystery third factor is the source of both. If so, seeking happiness as a means to a long life would be something of a red herring.

The same year as the Nun Study was published, LeeAnne Harker and Dacher Keltner of the University of California at Berkeley published a research paper entitled "Expressions of Positive Emotions in Women's College Yearbook Pictures and Their Relationship to Personality and Life Outcomes Across Adulthood".

In this study, the researchers rated the yearbook photographs of 141 Californian women as to whether their smiles were genuine or not. (It has been argued that a fake smile can be distinguished from a genuine, or "Duchenne", smile because of the automatic creasing around the eyes which is only present in the latter.) The smile-rater was not yet privy to the life outcomes of the individuals, so could not have been biased. The women were aged 21 when the photographs were taken, in about 1960. An intriguing early finding was that when researchers contacted the women at age 27 they found the "genuine" yearbook smilers were more likely than their less-cheery peers to be married. The women were also contacted at ages 43 and 52, when a weak but noticeable relationship was found between genuine smiles at age 21 and self-reported good life-outcomes in middle age.

However, the information about marriage, health, work, sexual and social relations and the like on which these results were based was gathered almost entirely through the mail via self-report questionnaires. Granted, it's hard to imagine a significant number of people lying about their marital status, but beyond that we should be wary of placing too much faith in these women's self-reported levels of happiness. To really be sure these self-reports were accurate, they'd need to be corroborated by information from their medical doctors, as well as psychologists who had actually visited the individuals in their homes and their day-to-day lives so as to gauge more independently what they had made of life.

In short, the yearbook study produced some intriguing results. But rather than proving anything (such as that happiness causes a satisfying life), it raises a whole string of questions. Can a Duchenne smile be faked? And would someone good at smiling on demand be more likely to give unduly cheerful answers to questions about their life outcomes? Even if those smiles were genuinely genuine, those photos capture a single moment in time, in a single situation: were the genuine smilers happier than their peers with their life in general, or just more comfortable in front of the camera? As with the Nun Study, we simply don't have enough information to know for sure. And so, though it's all very interesting, it's far too flimsy a foundation for a claim that happiness is the be-all and end-all of a good life.

Humbug about happiness

Why is happiness hard to find and hard to hang on to? In his bestselling book *Stumbling on Happiness* (2006), the celebrated Harvard psychology professor Daniel Gilbert blames our ineptness with "bagging happiness for ourselves" squarely on the idea that we're very poor at predicting, even a little way ahead, what will make our life feel good. He calls this skill, the one we're bad at, "prospection". Self-help authors always have to coin a word, it seems, even a silly one.

Nonetheless, Gilbert's observation is undeniable: it's clear that we Homo sapiens are laughably poor at predicting what will make us happy or sad even two weeks down the line. Whether it's breaking up with our partner or losing our job, we wildly under-estimate our ability to recover our spirits and bounce back. Likewise, we ludicrously over-estimate how good a new relationship or new home will make the rest of our life feel.

Gilbert's dead right, and his account is very often refreshingly funny. But the spell is broken on the final page when he proclaims "Without a formula for predicting utility we tend to do what only our species does: imagine." Gilbert's putting imagination on a pedestal in this way is perhaps not entirely unexpected, since he is a lifelong academic. But so mesmerized is he by our brain's ability for that form of thinking we call imagination (and how exactly can anyone possibly know that we're the only animal that imagines?), he's neglected one of mankind's other massive abilities: action. If in doubt about what will make us happy, we can explore things in reality… we can experiment… we can do stuff.

Is it possible that one of the great attractions of living and doing is our not being sure, not even having the faintest idea, what's around the next bend? Is it possible that Mother Nature (i.e. our hard-wiring laid down by six million years of evolution) actually wants us to explore the future's possibilities, creating as we go?

However, there is something even more disappointing than Gilbert taking nearly three hundred pages to make one good observation on human inaccuracy that nonetheless seems to miss the likely purpose of life being so intrinsically unpredictable. For it is a deeply troubling fact that no less an august and conservative institution than the Royal Society of London awarded its 2007 prize for General Science Book of the Year to Gilbert's bestseller. The judges presumably applaud the viewpoint of the author who asks rhetorically "What could be more important than feelings?" and then in his afterword concludes "Wise choices are those that maximize our pleasure". Yet again, we have a study of happiness that puts feeling good on a pedestal – for there is precious little mention in Gilbert's paperback of the importance of doing good, or at least trying to. For Gilbert, the individual's feel-good factor is accorded absolute supremacy, and this time even the Royal Society is publicly supporting this poorly rounded and ill-balanced approach to human life.

The good news is that none of these problems is insoluble, and Positive Psychology will have much to offer if it can greatly enrich its collaborations with other ways of investigating life, while also being far more transparent and honest about its research methods and the results thereof. Meanwhile, the conscious strategies of Positive Psychology described above may not offer us a silver bullet for happiness but, used in conjunction with subconscious and physical methods, they can be a valuable part of a more wholesome approach to our well-being.

Sheer luck

No consideration of life would be complete without daring to consider the role of luck.

It's intriguing to note that the word for happiness, whether in Ancient Greek or modern European languages, so often includes at its root some clear salute to Lady Luck. In English, for instance, the root "happ" means chance (from whence comes the old-fashioned term "happenstance", meaning "a chance occurrence", and also the word "haphazard"). The enduring and universal thought seems to be that being happy requires being lucky; which poses something of a problem, because being lucky is not something we can bring about with our conscious efforts... *is it?*

In his bestselling book *The Black Swan,* multi-millionaire stockmarket trader and risk-analyst Nassim Nicholas Taleb argues that we each of us massively underestimate the role that "complete randomness" plays in carving the course of our everyday life and of the world generally. Rather than following some steady, linear, gently undulating and reasonably predictable course, Taleb proposes that our lives are far more likely to be the result of the cumulative effects of a handful of very major and totally unexpected events, some of which are helpful and some of which are handicapping. Taleb refers to these very rare, extreme-impact and totally unpredicted and unimaginable events as "Black Swans". Such events might include a chance meeting, an accident or a casual speculative venture.

Just consider for a moment your own life-course. How did the turning points come about? Were the biggest snakes and ladders caused by your good and bad planning, or by good and bad luck? This blisteringly honest self-appraisal could equally apply to your most important friendships and love relationships, to the high points and low points of your

All swans were presumed to be white until black ones were discovered in Australia. Through this metaphor, Taleb reminds us that we humans are prone to make grossly inaccurate presumptions about the future.

school experience and personal health, or to your career "lucky breaks" and "complete disasters". Ask yourself if they were the fruits of precise planning or, if truth be told, the result very largely of good and bad luck. For instance, perhaps...

▶ **At school, you only made the A-team because the other kid fell ill.**
▶ **The wonderful person you dated had just been dumped by someone and was ripe for befriending.**
▶ **The company that appointed you to that surprisingly good position were, quite frankly, desperately short of alternatives.**

Taleb argues that we might tell ourselves we planned it all that way (this is the human tendency for wanting to feel that there is order and control), but if we'd kept a diary en route, it would tell a very different story about how circumstances haphazardly emerged.

In short, says Taleb, the most important events in our life will be the least predictable ones; and they will have the greatest impact very largely because they are so unexpected and accidental.

Taleb's proposition takes some getting used to because, as he says, we're brought up to be extremely resistant to such ideas. But it is not an isolated viewpoint. Two-time Oscar winner William Goldman is one of the most successful screenwriters of the twentieth century, writer of *Butch Cassidy and the Sundance Kid* and *All the President's Men*, among many other great films. Goldman is famous for saying of his beloved industry "Nobody knows anything!", and his classic insider's story *Adventures in the Screen Trade* provides a host of examples of how top directors, actors and studios almost routinely make a disastrous flop or two (in both artistic and box-office terms) immediately after making a fabulous success. The reason for these unexpected turkeys, suggests Goldman, is that these folks simply didn't know what they were doing right or wrong, or what would strike a chord with the spirit of the time. There were simply too many variables, too many uncontrollable ingredients, for *anyone* to know which were the important ones or how to recreate them.

Taleb argues that our tendency to massively under-estimate the role of luck, in our own lives and in the world as a whole, creates a host of problems. Faced with a reality that's deeply messy and resoundingly random, we build neat and tidy models of how things *should* work. Like small children clutching a comfort blanket or a teddy bear, we crave more order, security and control than our universe can offer. So, like a small child, we make it up. And we try to convince our friends of our make-believe. We also tend to gravitate towards flowing stories, preferring them to real life, which jerks along every-which-way very disconcertingly. We like a good narrative: we like to simplify, to summarize and to explain. (Our education system encourages this kind of think-

Luck in Far Eastern cultures

While we in the West may be uncomfortable with the concept of luck, wishing to believe that we're each in control of our own destiny, in Far Eastern cultures such as Japan, China and South Korea people tend to be much more accepting of the role of luck in their lives. These cultures have a more fatalistic attitude towards happiness than we do, believing it is very much a blessing from heavenly sources. One of the consequences of such an attitude is that you don't have to feel inferior or guilty about not being very happy, since your happiness is not a reflection of your abilities. You simply need to pay your respects to luck, to the unknown and uncontrollable factors affecting any event. In Chinese culture, the number 8 is associated with good luck because it sounds like the word for prosperity. And so, in a salute to luck, the Beijing Olympics opening ceremony began on the 8th second of the 8th minute past the 8th hour on the 8th day of the 8th month of 2008.

ing, handing out A-grades for retrospectively explaining events: "What were the four main causes of World War I?") This desperate hunger for some certainty in life means that we're terrible suckers for so-called experts, i.e. the professors and consultants that "give us a good story".

▶ **"Hic habitat felicitas"** – here dwells happiness – are the words accompanying this unmistakable image on a baker's wall in first-century Pompeii. In many ancient civilizations, the "fascinum" – the phallus and scrotum (what a great name for a pub!) – was a well-recognized symbol not just of fertility but of prosperity, power and good fortune, and would commonly be carved at the entrance to a building. It seems to have served much the same purpose as a thumbs-up sign, a lucky horseshoe and a smiley face, all rolled into one. Intriguingly, the word *fascinum* is ultimately the origin of the English verb "to fascinate". That may be so, but women readers may not be entirely surprised to hear that even two thousand years ago men were making extraordinary claims about their penises.

How should we live in a luck-driven world?

Recognizing the role of luck in our lives doesn't have to result in a nihilistic attitude, because it's what we do with our "lucky breaks" and "complete disasters" – how we react to the winds of fortune – that is the making of us.

▶ **Be prepared**, Taleb tells us. OK, by their very nature, we can't predict Black Swans, but we can keep light on our feet so that their occurrence doesn't sink us, and may even bring us great fortune in one form or another. It's noteworthy that Taleb made his first financial fortune as a trader in his twenties, because he had realized that something as calamitous as the global stock market crash of 1987 was quite possible, and his own investment portfolio was well prepared to take great advantage of such an eventuality. Invest in preparedness, not in prediction. Be wary of our inborn and educated tendencies to over-concentrate on what we know, when it's probably what we don't know that will hurt us – or help us – the most. By all means enjoy the self-indulgence of taking opinions and making predictions, but just don't lose your shirt doing so, or risk anybody else's. Better to rank your beliefs not according to how likely you are to be right about them, but according to how much harm being wrong would cause. Taleb suggests that we should aim perhaps to make 75 percent of our resources as super-conservatively safe as possible, while we play wildly and ambitiously with the remaining 25 percent. Such a strategy could be applied to every aspect of our life, whether it be business matters, romantic relationships or garden design.

We thrive on feeling in control

We are hard-wired with a need to feel in control of ourselves and our future. During World War II, the factor of "feeling in control" explains why solo fighter pilots displayed less mental trauma than other air crew. Faced with danger, solo flyers always felt they could take direct and effective action by deploying their combat-flying skills. By contrast, the crew in the back of a large bomber just had to sit tight through the anti-aircraft flack and the threat of enemy patrols. Such a sense of helplessness can quickly lead to hopelessness, at which point we're prone to give up and suffer serious anxiety and depression, as we saw on p.86. This explains why bomber crews had rates of psychological illness four times higher than the solo pilots, despite their having the same 50/50 odds of survival.

Subsequent good-quality observational research has served to reinforce the truth of this World War II phenomenon. During the mid-1970s, Professors Ellen Langer and Judith Rodin found that the more control a group of nursing-home patients had over daily tasks such as choosing their plants, watering them and deciding which movie they wished to watch, the more cheerful and active they became (as rated by their nurses, not just the residents themselves). Better still, the floor on which the enhanced-sense-of-control residents lived had only *half* as many deaths in the following eighteen months as a comparison floor of residents that continued with business as usual.

These examples are a reminder that Taleb's exhortation that we face up to the role of luck in our lives is a challenge to our deep-seated need for security. As with so many things in life, we need to balance yin and yang: a brave recognition of the randomness and unpredictability of the future needs to be balanced by an understanding of our need for control and an effort to find and make such security where we can in life.

▶ **Don't look for proof confirming something, dare to look for proof against it.** Professor Karl Popper is perhaps the scientist most famous for advocating that the only way for our knowledge to progress is to take a stance on something and then look for evidence that would disprove it. Popper made "scepticism" a method that could be helpful and constructive because it helped us see how the world really works.

▶ **Detox ourselves of all the convenient stories and common fallacies**, by turning off the TV and not falling for the fairy tales sold to us by newspapers, glossy magazines or documentary series, which are just selling us tidy lies. This low-bullshit diet will help us live life more richly, closer to the truly animal nature of things with all its messy unpredictability.

▶ **Be an "avid collector of opportunities".** Taleb argues that our readiness to throw ourselves into the fray – to go where the action is and grab-a-hold of chance occurrences – is what distinguishes the accomplished individuals from the static under-achievers. (This dynamic strategy chimes with the "versatile optimistic action" that we considered above.) We should make room for positive accidents by mixing in unusual social circles, and moving outside our normal routes and routines. The more ground and variety we can cover, the more rolls of the dice we're giving ourselves, which means the more lucky breaks (and, as part and parcel of moving forward, the more painful rebuffs) we're likely to run into. Remember we very often learn most from people we disagree with, so be wary of moving only in like-minded circles.

Conclusions

Taleb's *The Black Swan* is a humbling and cautionary note on which to end a chapter that has explored how our conscious thoughts can improve how good life feels and how well it works. In short, Taleb points out that our thinking, our logic, our intellect, call it what we will, has severe limits to its range and accuracy, a fact that we should own up to and make arrangements for. In other words, the limited horizons of our thinking are very often inadequate to cope with what real life is capable of (for instance, we so often don't know what we don't know about the dynamics affecting a situation). These limitations are too easily exacerbated by our innate drives for feeling as if we're in control and for spotting comforting patterns, often illusory. In respect of which, this Rough Guide advocates we experiment with keeping *two* balls in play: actively engaging with life via our versatile optimistic endeavours to exert control, while at the same time acknowledging with good humour the intrinsically unexpected nature of things.

4

Our bodies

Our bodies

How respecting your body's nature can restore your good spirits

The respectful and thorough care of our bodies in the interests of our all-round well-being should be a lifelong mission for all of us. Yet it is a subject almost entirely neglected by mainstream religions, philosophies and psychologies. Even the best-known books on Positive Psychology and "how to be happier" fail to address the essential dynamics of our mind–body system. They go on at considerable length in praise of Ancient Greek philosophers and modern brain-science, but of words such as *dancing, singing, sport, sleep, sunlight, vitamins* or *nutrition* there is often not so much as a mention. That's like writing about romantic love without ever discussing physical attraction or sexual behaviour.

So why these glaring gaps and this disregard for bodily matters?

The omissions probably reflect the antagonistic divisions between university departments, divisions which are closely mirrored by the turf wars of their associated professions. The result is that professors and practitioners of psychology, medicine, theology and philosophy too rarely come together to learn from each other's disciplines. The integration of these naturally related subjects is, to all intents and purposes, strongly disapproved of.

Such a "mind versus body" feud can be traced back at least as far as those Ancient Greek philosophers (Socrates, Plato and Aristotle) who, in their zealous haste to champion logic and reason, relegated all our physical needs to a level of secondary importance and even shame (see pp.23–25). This demonizing of our flesh and blood was all too eagerly adopted and intensified by the early Christian Church, as we'll see below.

Flying proudly in the face of this long and unhelpful tradition, this chapter endeavours to remind us that living happily has a whole lot to do with cherishing the natural dynamics of our human body.

Nourishing our bodies

Nourishing our body feeds our spirits. Good nutrition *in all its forms* – from food and sleep to exercise and daylight – will help our mind–body system thrive profoundly. So whenever we're feeling blue, before we go blaming it on our lack of purpose in life, or our difficult past, let's test out some less psychological explanations first.

Vigorous exercise lifts our mood

When it comes to our understanding of physical activity, Loughborough University's School of Sport and Exercise Sciences is arguably one of the best centres in the world, and its long-time head, psychology professor Stuart Biddle, has been a pioneer among the thousand or so studies to date which have all agreed the following: to beat the blues, vigorous physical activity (the sort that breaks a sweat) can be part of the prevention and part of the cure. Several excellent studies have shown that vigorously exercising for forty-five minutes three times a week for sixteen weeks is as effective as the leading anti-depressant medication in treating depression, and yet the exercise achieves this with few if any side-effects, and also leaves us only one quarter as vulnerable to recurrent episodes. We should not be surprised: all of our moods, whether joyous or painful, operate largely through the chemical and electrical mechanisms which run our mind and body. Sweat-breaking exercise helps change this chemistry and so changes how we feel.

It would be well worth exploring for ourselves how many fewer psychosomatic and stress disorders (see pp.49–51) we suffer from if we exercise our whole body for five minutes (through dance or aerobics) for every hour we spend at our desk. Worth noting, too, the improvement in our productivity and the sheer liveliness and creativity of our mind.

In 2004 the UK's Chief Medical Officer himself emphasized the effectiveness of physical activity in treating depression. Physical activity might be just what the doctor ordered, but in the industrialized West our lives are more sedentary than ever. On average, adults expend five hundred fewer calories per day than fifty years ago, which means that in calorie terms our grandparents ran one marathon more than you or I, every week.

Is it any wonder that one in three British children and adults is now obese? Or that depression is reaching epidemic proportions, with the World Health Organization estimating that by 2020 it'll be the second-largest cause of ill-health, second only to heart disease? Our children are not immune, either: one in five will experience depression when they're growing up. Yet we can be pretty sure that physically vigorous social activities would help them enormously in the fight against the blues, as both a prevention and a cure.

So what could we do? Rather than faffing around with gyms, we could arrange with friends to walk briskly or jog to and from school or work each day. We could lobby for safe off-road bike paths separated by high pavements from the traffic, so we can cycle safely around town. We could rediscover the joy of riding a bicycle "hands free", or dare to perform for the first time a backward dive from the side of the swimming pool. Such adventures await us.

Commuters ride their bikes along a dedicated cycle path in Amsterdam.

Sufficient sleep supports everything

Getting enough good sleep provides a vital foundation for how we deal with life, so it's worth becoming an expert on this oft-forgotten bedfellow of much healthier moods.

Almost all individuals need eight hours or more each day, but many of us allow ourselves far less. Albert Einstein regularly slept for ten hours, and took eleven if he had some really serious thinking to do the following day. It is only an unhelpful myth that high achievers Winston Churchill and Margaret Thatcher barely slept; both were simply skilled catnappers and achieved their full quota that way. Here's Churchill in his autobiography justifying his practice of taking a siesta to break the day into two: "We were not made by Nature to work, or even to play, from eight o'clock in the morning 'till midnight. We throw a strain upon our system which is unfair and improvident. For every purpose of business or pleasure, mental or physical, we ought to break our days and marches into two."

Nowadays, we probably sleep two hours less per night than our grandparents' generation, which leaves Western society profoundly sleep-deprived. And what a price we pay...

Stanford University psychiatrist William Dement has spent nearly forty years investigating how sleep-deficiency impacts upon our quality of life by negatively affecting our physical health, energy, mood, social relationships, memory and problem-solving performance. These deficits come about not least because our immunity-boosting, disease-fighting cells drop by over a quarter after just one night's lost sleep, while the stress-inducing hormone cortisol increases by a half. It's also a startling fact that knocking two hours per night from someone's usual sleep pattern for just one week renders them as inefficient as someone well over the drink-drive limit. Exactly as if they were drunk, the sleep-deprived person over-estimates their competency and takes ill-considered risks. This is why specialists believe that more accidents both on and off the road are caused by lack of sleep than by alcohol. One in five adults admits to having fallen asleep at the wheel of a car. And official disaster inquiries have very often identified "routine sleep-deprivation" as either the key or a major contributor to human-error catastrophes, including those that befell the Chernobyl nuclear power plant, the *Exxon Valdez* oil tanker and the *Challenger* space shuttle.

There are, however, less dramatic but more insidious consequences of cheating on our sleep. It is one of the biggest triggers for migraine and digestive tract problems. Our proneness to addictive and out-of-control behaviours (such as road rage or spending or drinking too much) is also likely to be triggered by months or years of too little sleep. No surprise, then, that since sleep-deficiency increases our appetite, there has also been speculation that it in part explains the current epidemic of obesity. It would seem to be for good reason that our brain is often more active when we're asleep than when we're awake. Our sleeping brain is busy with recuperation, repair work and processing emotions. It really is no coincidence that sleep deprivation is used as a torture, the results of which can mimic the effects of severe mental illness. It takes around ten days for an otherwise healthy human to die from lack of sleep, while we can survive several times longer without food, which gives us yet another indication of sleep's primary importance.

The take-away message is that we should all sleep eight or more hours in every twenty-four, even if that requires catnapping to make up the difference. Dr Sara Mednick of the Salk Institute in California is the leading young researcher on power naps and she advises thirty minutes to a full hour midway through our waking day, usually between two and three o'clock. She says half an hour in our lunch break would be a fine compromise. This timely nap would not only lead to improved mood, alertness and productivity, but would also consolidate our learning of physical skills and mental facts. It's ironic that we sometimes think we're getting more done when we plod on through fatigue. Yet studies at the world's leading universities show us time and again that because sleepiness makes us less adept at problem-solving, creativity and modifying our plans, we are in fact far less productive. We are also irritable, sloppy and reluctant to take on challenges. The damage of too little sleep is often covert, masquerading as depression,

Does our gender or age affect our happiness?

There is no convincing evidence that one stage of life is inherently any happier than another, despite everything our parents may have told us about our school and college days being the happiest of our lives. If anything, life is likely to feel better as we grow older, as long as we are determined to get better at living it. And just as age cannot dictate our happiness and well-being, there's little if any difference between the average male and female self-ratings for happiness, though some women may be a tad more prone to intense swings.

existential angst or physical ills when all that we're desperately thirsty for is a few days with sufficient sleep, supplemented by restorative naps.

In respect of the above evidence, we could run a little experiment by adding one hour's sleep to our nightly routine, and taking a nap at lunchtime or when we get in from work, and then monitoring the difference it makes. Of course, we might need to develop a better rapport with our subconscious to help us sleep better, and Chapter 2 can suggest how we might enhance that vital relationship with ourselves.

Broad daylight prevents the blues

You don't need a clinical diagnosis of Seasonal Affective Disorder (a form of mood depression, the sole cause of which is the brain receiving

Got happy genes?

It's that old chestnut: how much is nature and how much is nurture? How much is our general level of happiness in-born, and how much is developed?

Some researchers have suggested that although our feelings of happiness change from day to day, there is a stable midpoint to these variations, to which we tend to return once temporary feelings of joy or misery have faded. If this be the case, we might wonder how much of this "default" level of happiness is determined by our genes. To investigate this question, in 1996 David Lykken and Auke Tellegen at Minnesota State University used a rate-your-own-happiness questionnaire to compare an astonishing 722 pairs of identical twins, 647 of whom had been raised together and 75 of whom had been raised apart. Whether raised together or apart, these identical twin pairs showed around a fifty percent correlation in their levels of happiness, whereas the correlation between non-identical twins was close to zero. This in itself suggests that happiness is strongly genetically determined. However, these results would of course include any temporary deviations from an individual's norm. To isolate each twin's underlying level of happiness, the researchers looked at changes over time. Comparing Twin A's happiness at one date with Twin B's ten years later, they found a significant correlation, and concluded that the stable midpoint of happiness could be as much as eighty percent genetically determined.

There are two points bearing on the above conclusion. Firstly, the reliability of the life-happiness data gathered in this study is open to question, because we have no objective evidence about how the twins actually lived their day-to-day lives to corroborate their self-rating questionnaire responses. All we know for sure is that identical twins answer happiness questions in a far more similar way than do non-identical twins. (See pp.224–230 for a detailed critique of questionnaire evidence.) Secondly, just because something can be or is highly inheritable doesn't mean that it's unchangeable. It just means we might have to make more

insufficient daylight) to benefit from ensuring your eyes receive at least an hour's broad daylight in the gloomier months of the calendar. We shouldn't be too surprised at our hunger for daylight. Our evolutionary ancestors grew up in equatorial Africa, very probably on the coast, with oodles of sunshine every day for many hundreds of thousands of years. The grey skies of northern Europe and other parts are a relatively recent human experience, which largely explains why the suicide rate leaps up during winter in the northern Scandinavian lands where several months of the year will be gloomy even in the daytime.

By way of a remedy for our daylight shortages, there are lamps and light bulbs that can produce 10,000 lux (lux is a measure of light intensity), but we could save these for plan B, because even a rather overcast winter's day produces 10,000 lux, and bright sunshine offers several times that. Why not simply whip off the Raybans to let in the natural

of an effort, perhaps by putting ourselves in environments that will bring out the best in us. Even if our default level of happiness is largely determined by our genes, learning to live regularly above that base level is where our developing psychological skill and know-how can pay dividends. How well we play the hand we're dealt could dramatically influence how we feel about life.

Further evidence of the paramount importance of how we forge our day-to-day life comes from the science of epigenetics, which literally means "beyond genetics", and refers to the second genetic code that accompanies our DNA. Every cell in our body – skin cells, hair cells, bone cells – contains exactly the same DNA; it is the epigenetic code which determines how each cell develops, by telling the DNA which genes are to be activated or "expressed" and which are to remain dormant. Whereas DNA can only be practically altered in the lab, it is currently believed that our epigenetic code can be significantly influenced by outside factors throughout our lifetime, such as our emotional relationships, and how well we eat, exercise and think. Epigenetics explains why one identical twin might develop diabetes, while her sister does not. The diabetic sister may, for instance, have had a particularly difficult emotional relationship at some stage in her life which triggered her epigenetic system to switch on certain genes that rendered her vulnerable to developing diabetes. Epigenetic changes could also trigger cancer or depression. Whereas our DNA does not change over our lifetime, it can be clearly seen through laboratory investigations that the epigenetic code of identical twins is almost identical when they're six days old, but really very different by the time they're sixty. Nurture, it seems, quite literally changes our nature. And how well we lead our everyday life – our experiences, our activities, our relationships – could well prove just as important as the basic DNA blueprint with which we were born and about which we hear so much.

goodness, remembering that mornings are the best time for an hour's light-bath? *(Let's remember, though, that we should never under any circumstances look directly at the Sun because this will very seriously damage our eyes.)* Unfortunately, we can't store the benefits of light for the brain, so our light-bath is best done every day. Our mood can lift within 48 hours, once given adequate illumination, but it can descend again just as quickly if we're starved of this health-bringing brain nutrient.

Keep yourself well watered

Our body's water level is a good example of how seemingly little things can have a major impact on our daily life. Being dehydrated can markedly reduce psychological and physical performance. Even minor alterations can have significant effects: at one percent dehydration, we might feel a tad thirsty if we bothered to think about it, but at two percent we've probably lost a fifth of our physical capacity and co-ordination, and our judgement is impaired. At just five percent below our usual water levels, we'll probably suffer aggressive, irrational behaviour, as well as nausea. This startling fact is why professional athletes are never far from their water bottles. Yet many of us are prone to run below our optimal mind and body performance simply because we're not keeping a glass of pure water to hand. Between two and three litres of non-diuretic fluid (such as water – not alcohol or coffee) per day would be an average adult requirement under ordinary mild conditions. So, when you or a loved one feel tired or irritable, consider how something as simple as dehydration may be partly to blame.

Good eating

Good eating is a habit that can be learned early. Yet no less than a quarter of British children are obese (i.e. they weigh 25 percent or more above their ideal weight), as are a similar proportion of American children. This compares to only ten percent of French youngsters. The specialists suspect that the cause of Anglo-American childhood obesity is a highly sedentary lifestyle and over-protective parenting which restricts a child's daily opportunities for exercise such as walking or cycling to school, or playing outdoors. But it's a key factor, too, that the French simply eat fewer calories, not least because they tend to eat slowly, which better allows their body to realize when it's been sufficiently fed. It can take around twenty minutes for the message that we have eaten sufficiently to reach our brain. On this vital point, nutritionists are at pains to emphasize that we should take adequate time to chew our food, because the enzymes in our saliva break it down and make it far more valuable to our body, as well as making each mouthful far more satisfying, which all helps less food to go a lot further. Nutritionists also advise that we eat in company whenever possible because it helps balance our approach to food. The company of caring people is as much an essential sustenance as is a good meal, and will stop us trying to fill the emotional gaps with food or drink. Sadly, our time-pressured, multi-tasking lifestyles mean many of us regularly turn our midday meal into a "business lunch" or simply grab a sandwich to gulp on the go. Such habits are a sure way to stomach trouble; but is it just our digestive system complaining, *or our soul*?

Guarding against nutrient deficiencies

Good nutrition can increase our positive moods and mental performance, whereas even mild deficiencies of the vitamin B range, for instance, can bring varying degrees of irritability, anxiety, insomnia, lethargy, depression, loss of appetite and poor memory. Swansea University psychologist Professor David Benton has been a prolific researcher in this field, and in one study of young British adults found that around a third of his sample were deficient in one or more of the B vitamins. He also found that fifty percent of women and ten percent of men had borderline anaemia

Being vegetarian

If we eat a vegetarian diet, it's good to know that this needn't compromise building the very finest body we have the genetic blueprints for, as evidenced by the number of vegetarians who abound in the world of professional sport. Former tennis champions Billie Jean King and Martina Navratilova both swept to victory on a vegetarian diet, as did Dave Scott (triathlon and six times Iron Man champion) and Edwin Moses (an Olympic gold medallist in the 400m hurdles). We should be aware, though, that a vegetarian diet can put us at increased risk of anaemia, so it may be wise to pay special attention to iron-rich foods and their complements that make that iron absorbable.

Astonishing evidence that food affects behaviour

When it comes to demonstrating nutrition's potential effects on our everyday moods and behaviour, Bernard Gesch, a pioneering senior researcher at Oxford University, has conducted one of the world's most respected studies to date.

In 1996–97, for a nine-month period, his team administered seemingly identical daily supplements to 231 inmates at Aylesbury high-security young offenders' prison (all of whom were young men aged 18 to 21). For those who took the capsules for at least two weeks, the prisoners who'd taken a modest but daily dose of 28 genuine vitamins and minerals as well as those all-important omega oils 3 and 6 demonstrated a 37 percent reduction in aggressive behaviour – that is, they engaged in 37 percent fewer of the sort of serious or violent offences that are very accurately logged by the prison authorities. By comparison, the behaviour of the group of young men on seemingly identical but fake pills was quite unchanged. This was an extremely well-designed study, and neither the prison officers nor the young prisoners themselves knew which half of the boys had received the truly active pills. In addition, the boys had been randomly allocated to either the genuine or fake group, so the chances of the results being biased in that way are rather slim. Yet more compelling evidence came about when the experiment was over and the inmates' nutrition returned to normal for all concerned: the behaviour of the lads who'd received proper supplements now quickly deteriorated back to its original level.

So impressed were they by Gesch's findings, the Dutch government acted swiftly to commission their own version of the above study, and their researchers have provisionally reported that those prisoners taking the dietary supplements (i.e. the full range of the EU's recommended daily allowance of vitamins, miner-

(iron deficiency), a state which can easily mimic the early symptoms of depression. However, such shortfalls usually come in groups, and iron, zinc, selenium and vitamins A, B and C are commonly low in adults. This isn't so surprising, either, since air pollution, caffeine, alcohol, sugar, headache tablets, the contraceptive pill and many other standard medications can all serve to unbalance our uptake or excretion of vital micro-nutrients. Sadly, too, modern food production methods have dramatically reduced the nutritional content of most foods. Weight-loss dieting is another way in which adequate nutrition can be compromised. In addition, a good number of us have a digestive system that's not very tolerant of cows' milk. and may find yoghurts and goats' milk (available in most supermarkets) a far more digestible source of calcium.

With all of the above risk factors so prevalent in our everyday lives, it is for good reason that psychiatric hospitals routinely conduct blood tests to screen new clients for vitamin and mineral deficiencies. What a tragedy it would be to blame life events or relationships for our

als and omega oils) committed on average 47 percent fewer offences than the prisoners taking the fake pills. Inspired by such astonishing results, the Wellcome Trust in the UK is now funding a 1000-participant study among even younger prisoners, aged from 16 to 21 years, for whom it is anticipated the percentage benefits in behaviour may be even greater because of the increased nutritional needs of young brains and bodies at that sensitive stage in their development. Gesch also plans to initiate a major project that provides supplements to persistent young offenders still in the community who are being closely monitored but have not yet received custodial sentences. The aim is to discover whether this nutritional approach is equally helpful in everyday life beyond the prison environment.

When we consider that psychological illness has now overtaken heart disease as the biggest health cost in Europe, not to mention the terrible personal and economic costs of crime, improved nutrition increasingly appears an affordable and effective way forward. Gesch writes poignantly "We need to rethink our present-day attitude to food and to understand how what we eat can positively impact upon the human condition. It may be a recipe that goes beyond individual well-being; it may literally be a recipe for peace."

It's a great boon to such aspirations that, in the UK at least, super-chef Jamie Oliver's lobbying is helping to make schools and government ministers take immediate action to begin to improve nutritional standards for those most in need. But there's a long, long way to go. Meanwhile, Bernard Gesch himself strongly advises that meals rich in fruit, vegetables and wholegrains, as well as some fish and meat, are most likely to provide the nutritional foundations for our physical and psychological well-being.

dwindling happiness if in fact we're simply deficient in some essential nutrients?

If you're pregnant or on prescription medicine, then consult your medical practitioner before taking any supplements because they could be seriously hazardous. Otherwise, consider investing in a reputable all-in-one vitamin and mineral capsule. Supplements are "team players", so the total effect of these all-in-one pills will be far more helpful than the sum of their parts. What's more, premium products are far preferable to some economy own-brand from a high-street chemist that has thrown together a limited range of cheaper synthetic ingredients.

In addition, we would be wise to eat a good variety of fresh, oily fish such as sardines, salmon, mackerel or tuna three or four times a week. If that's not possible, we should take an omega-3 essential fats supplement, readily available in a 1000mg fish oil capsule. (Note that fish oil should not be confused with *fish-liver oil*, which is rich in vitamins A

No shortage of omega-3 for this fella!

and D which can be toxic in high doses.) The omega-3 oil vegetarian alternatives would be cold-pressed versions of flax oil (also known as linseed), pumpkin seed oil or hemp oil. Even better would be to take a supplement that combined omega-3 oil with omega-6 oil (perhaps in the form of cold-pressed evening primrose oil or starflower oil, also known as borage oil). The newly emerging evidence on the effectiveness of omega oils in preventing and lifting depression might be particularly relevant to a mum with a newborn baby. She should talk to her medical practitioner about the benefits of such oils in making up for the demands that pregnancy will have made on her body's resources and in combating post-natal depression. (Vegetarian sources are probably best so as to avoid any danger of fish oils being polluted by heavy metals in the seas from which the fish came.) It may well be because our ancestors were coastal African apes, and probably eating all manner of fish, that our human brain has evolved with a reliance for its good health on the omega oils so abundant in seafoods.

Fascinating though the above possibilities might be, it's *not* a question of "the more the better". Accidentally overdosing ourselves with a daily high-potency supplement is likely to be just as bad for us as nutritional deficiencies. We wouldn't dream of eating ten times the recommended portion of even our favourite fruit or vegetable at one sitting, so let's not risk poisoning ourselves with a careless use of vitamin pills. We should *always* follow the manufacturer's guidelines when it comes to supplements because it would be far too easy to consume too much vitamin A or D, for instance, which would be particularly dangerous for a pregnant woman or a child under twelve. And let's not think that supplements are an excuse to eat carelessly. On the contrary, they should be seen as a safety net if our temporary circumstances don't allow for sufficiently healthy meals. Let's be sure to remember, too, that our best efforts towards improved nutrition should go hand in hand with increased physical activity, because the more that our nutrient-enriched blood is flowing around our body and brain, the more likely we are to be providing our vital organs with adequate supplies.

Physical dynamism beats dieting

For many folks, dieting is a more or less permanent way of life. Yet dieting only pits us against our biological defences, which are striving to keep our weight between our genetically and epigenetically (see p.117) determined upper and lower limits. When we diet, our metabolism adjusts itself to keep our body within these bounds, and eagerly takes on body fat to compensate for the famine-like conditions imitated by a low-calorie diet. This is why more than 95 percent of dieters will inevitably put the weight back on, but meantime the brain suffers nutrient shortages which impair mental performance and leave us irritable, lethargic and depressed. In addition to which, we're designed to become preoccupied with nutrition if supplies are inadequate, and these accumulated stresses might well explain how dieting can bamboozle the brain into bulimia, anorexia or obesity.

The cruellest twist of this weight-loss wild goose chase is that we blame ourselves for not being strong-willed enough, and we feel helpless and out of control. Worse still, these negative feelings can easily leak into other arenas of our life such as our studies, work or relationships. It's a good job, then, that nature has given us a far more reliable, enduring and profoundly satisfying way to improve our bodies. It's called *vigorous physical activity*: any daily routine that will perk up our metabolism, build the friendly muscles that burn body fat, and buoy up our good moods and thinking capacity for many hours afterwards.

Maybe it's dancing around the kitchen, shadow boxing in the bedroom or striding that last mile to and from work. Variety is good, it's best if we break a sweat, and all the better if we can find some pleasant company for it. No matter where we start from, fitness-wise, we can guarantee ourselves a sense of progress, satisfaction and well-earned pride, all of which beats the red-herring diets. Once we've worked up an honest appetite, we can thumb our nose at the "thinning industry" with its artificial sweeteners and counted calories. Nutritious, health-bringing wholefoods are not our enemy, so let's relish eating them… slowly, in good spirits, and in good company.

(Dancing is a great alternative to faddy diets, and the profound psychological benefits of partner dancing such as salsa, waltz and tango are explored on p.167.)

Physical nourishment alone is not enough

The vital part played in our happiness and well-being by adequate amounts of sleep, daylight, physical activity and good nutrition would be hard to exaggerate. But powerful though they are, such nourishing measures are never enough on their own. If we're eating (or drinking) unhelpful things in unhelpful quantities, we are probably doing so because we're missing some *emotional* nourishment in our life, or being over-stretched. Chapter 2, "Our Subconscious", attempts to shed helpful light on what might be at the root of our self-inhibiting, self-hurting behaviours.

Respecting our human nature

Let's not forget the profound benefit – the fundamental necessity – of respecting our animal callings and inner dynamics born of our six-million-year evolutionary history since our ancestors split away from the other forest-dwelling apes and set off to make a living in the coastal regions of equatorial Africa. We ignore our "natural history" at our peril.

The bare necessities...

The Ancient Greeks and Romans were very comfortable with nakedness. The word "gymnasium" literally means "naked place" in Ancient Greek, reflecting the fact that in these training complexes athletes would exercise unencumbered by clothes. Naturally, the Olympic Games were undertaken naked by the all-male Olympians, and it wasn't until AD 393 that powerful Christian zealots banned the games on account of exactly this. So it was that the Roman state and Christian Church of that era presided over a legacy of shame about our bodies that continues to the present day. The human frame and flesh, particularly that of women, became taboo, and this left the door open to an unhelpful relationship not only with our bodies but also with our sexuality. Nakedness and

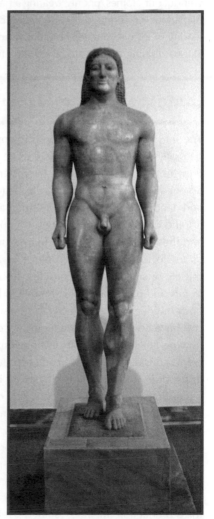

▶ Beauty in the beast: Ancient Greek and Roman statues are hung like summer orchards with dicks and boobs and bare-bottomed beauty. These were civilizations that applauded physical prowess: beauty in the human beast. Kouroi were early Greek statues of fine-bodied, athletic young men, with plaited hair and strong, regular features. Often (as in the example shown opposite) they are depicted with a cheerful turn of the mouth that is unmistakeably a rather pleased smile. These sculpted bodies cry out to be caressed. They do not hide in shame of their animal nature. They express a people comfortable with themselves and their relation to nature.

sexuality have become thought of as synonymous, and this confusion is hurting us. (For more on being comfortable with our sexuality, see pp.150–154.) We humans in the West tend to grossly under-use our bodies, but our clothes conceal our neglect. We might well wonder whether the Western world would be quite so obese, physically inactive and thus prone to serious degenerative illness if everyone could clearly see how we each took care of our physiques. It's worth considering, too, how comfortable we are without our clothes, or only wearing a bathing costume. In the glacial lakes that adorn the countryside surrounding Berlin, men and women of all ages readily swim naked together in the warm, emerald-green summer waters. Skinny-dipping is, after all, one of life's time-honoured joys.

...Mother Nature's recipes

The intrinsic goodness of a holistic approach to life, of keeping things *naturally wholesome*, is nowhere more evident than when we're considering how to treat our bodies. For instance, if we're exercising, the more all-encompassing the activity, the better. Walking, running, swimming and dancing use *all* of the body simultaneously, whereas there has been a trend of late to focus first on one quite specific part of our anatomy, and then on another, such as bums, tums or thighs. Multi-gyms require us to do this because each piece of apparatus pinpoints a particular muscle or small group of muscles. Trouble is, the body that is exercised in bits and pieces is prone to move in bits and pieces. Just think how a body builder who uses exactly this muscle-by-muscle exercise technique will have none of the harmonious grace or practical strength, speed and flowing flexibility of a dancer or swimmer or martial artist. It might be worth considering how we can keep our activities as whole and natural as possible, and this philosophy might include doing things out of doors rather than inside, and with company rather than alone.

On this very same theme, when we're choosing what to eat, it is commonplace for producers to claim they have distilled the goodness of a food by extracting the juice and oils, or cutting out the fats. But it is very likely that for the purposes of our all-round well-being, foods are best eaten as nature intended, which means whole and, very often, uncooked. This is how we ate for millions of years, until the Industrial Revolution's mass-production methods started "refining" or "deconstructing" our foods. The pulp of fruits and vegetables, and the fats that go with animal produce, all make their unique contributions to our nutrition; and let's not kid ourselves that vitamin supplements can ever be a substitute for natural-state, unrefined foods.

This "naturally wholesome" approach goes hand in hand with the school of thought that says consuming pasteurized or sterilized dairy produce denies our bodies the micro-organisms we so need for a healthy and happy digestion. Such a school might also advise that rather than using suntan creams that claim to filter out the burning wavelengths but allow through the browning ones, it might be a far healthier strategy to expose as much of our skin as possible to the full spectrum of the sunlight's unadulterated rays, if only for a very limited period of time, and then cover up altogether with clothes or shade rather than chemical creams.

Sitting around on the job

History has taught us the hard way that new inventions are not always for the best. So, in a spirit of rediscovering our healthy roots, let's consider how squatting right down on our haunches to defecate, rather than going at it half-cocked by sitting on a loo seat, could make all the difference to the healthy workings of our digestive system. Reason being, the deep squatting position naturally aligns and stimulates our colon and alimentary canals so our system can more completely and easily empty itself of what the body doesn't want. Sitting on a toilet seat, by comparison, can introduce a restrictive kink in the system and fails to stimulate action in quite the same way.

Until the know-it-all Victorians brought in chair-like toilets for the gentry in the second half of the nineteenth century, all previous generations of lads'n'lasses alike had squatted over chamber pots on the floor, or open pits outside. This wasn't unnatural, because Homo sapiens, like all apes (gorillas, chimpanzees, orangutans, bonobos and their kin), have internal organs and an outer skeleton well designed to squat for just this purpose. It's notable that very young children will automatically squat to relieve themselves. Unfortunately, just as sitting at desks for many hours every day has played havoc with the human spine, back muscles and posture, it seems increasingly likely that the past 150 years of the sitting-toilet may be largely responsible for all manner of digestive complications because our body's natural position for expulsion has been restricted. A lifetime's use of the sitting-toilet may be responsible for the bleeding from haemorrhoids (which are over-strained blood vessels) that affects half the adult population of Western nations by the age of fifty. Even more serious than that, disorders of the lower digestive tract have been associated with this Victorian contrivance called a "toilet seat", as have problems with the bladder and prostate and other organs of the pelvic bowl.

This riding roughshod over our innate needs by carelessly restricting the healthy operation of our insides is a good metaphor for much of what might be hurting us in modern life, and causing our epidemic of physical and emotional ills. We might remember from p.40 Sigmund Freud's opinion that we have only become city-dwellers by repressing our sexual and aggressive animal instincts – an uneasy pact that he felt had cost us too dearly.

Are we sitting on our assets?

Not unrelated to the above, consider for a moment how sitting in chairs, which we so take for granted, is a rather new-fangled notion. In the Ancient World, the well-to-do might have reclined on a couch

A group of people squat down to converse in the public square outside the main railway station in Beijing.

on special occasions, and only emperors and pharoahs would have to suffer sitting in a chair. Right up until the sixteenth century, chairs with back and arm rests were the reserve of royalty, clergy, lords and ladies. Everybody else perched on benches, trunks or stools; and in Far Eastern cultures, sitting cross-legged in the lotus position on floor mats was, and still is, completely *de rigueur*. In many other parts of the world today, such as India, Africa and the Middle East, people still learn to squat down flat-footed, bottom off the floor, and can be comfortable for hours in this position. Faced with these alternatives, our chairs begin to seem like our toilet seats: an unnecessary contrivance. Looking back at human history, it's debatable whether our bottoms were ever designed to be sat on. Other primates squat on their haunches, but don't actually sit on their bums as humans have of late. Might this explain why sitting on anything you're not actively riding (such as a horse or bike) looks so ungainly, and can so easily lead to all sorts of physical problems?

We might also ask: is there any human culture where the buttocks are not regarded by both males and females as potentially very attractive? And is it possible that Mother Nature intended our bottom primarily as a thing of beauty?

Body and mind united

Conventional Western medicine and psychology do not have a monopoly on healing the body and mind, or helping them to develop from strength to strength. Even within science-led cultures, accepted practices can be quite varied. For example, in Japan small magnets are sewn into mattresses to heal chronic pain while you sleep; in Germany mainstream physicians are licensed to prescribe herbal remedies for depression, not just pharmaceuticals; and in the Netherlands doctors can suggest to hyperanxious patients that they do a week or two of physical outdoors work on "therapeutic farms" (see p.241). As the French say, *Vive la différence!* In all arenas of life, a spirit of exploration will serve us best when trying to overcome an impasse in our own well-being. We should not expect our doctor or physiotherapist or nutritionist to have all the answers, nor to volunteer other possible avenues in the form of well-qualified practitioners in complementary and alternative practices. We need to educate ourselves. Particularly promising are approaches that respect the mind–body system as one whole entity, rather than treating them separately.

Our body's subtle energies

Numerous cultures have words to describe what we could call the "subtle energy" systems of the body. Subtle energy is known as...

▶ **Qi or chi in China, and ki in Japan**
▶ **Prana in the yoga tradition of India and Tibet**
▶ **Yesod in the Jewish kabbalistic tradition.**

This subtle energy is generally conceived as flowing around the body in channels or "meridians", and being concentrated in particular areas, or "chakras".

▶ **Meridians:** Just as the human body has a system of veins and arteries, and other channels for lymph or nerve signal transmission, so the meridians are conceived of as a set of interlinked pathways that carry energy into, through and out of our body, servicing all of our muscles and organs. The so-called acupressure or acupuncture points are where these channels occasionally meet the skin, and so form a particularly sensitive and accessible point for stimulation by needles, massage, tapping or simply touching therapeutically. The system of meridians, originating in traditional Chinese medicine, roughly corresponds with the nadis of the Indian yogic tradition.

▶ **Chakras:** The yogic word chakra means disk or wheel, referring to the swirling circle of energy that this tradition believes to be positioned at each of seven points in our body. These are our energy reservoirs, and the concept corresponds to what the kabbalah calls "Tree of Life" centres, or what the Chinese Taoist tradition terms "dantian". Each chakra is responsible for a distinctive type of energy (see diagram opposite), though they all spiral upwards into each other. Some cultures believe that the hands and eyes can themselves act as chakras, and can be used to initiate new chakras anywhere they are needed to heal or energize.

These subtle energy systems have as yet received little recognition from Western medical or scientific cultures. But all establishments are slow to

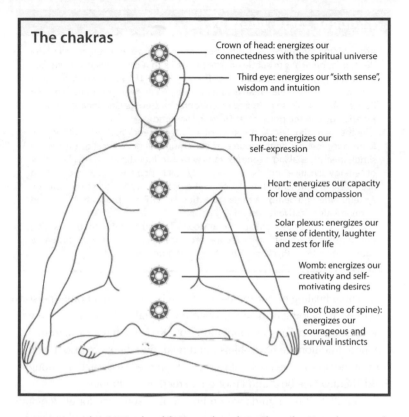

The chakras

Crown of head: energizes our connectedness with the spiritual universe

Third eye: energizes our "sixth sense", wisdom and intuition

Throat: energizes our self-expression

Heart: energizes our capacity for love and compassion

Solar plexus: energizes our sense of identity, laughter and zest for life

Womb: energizes our creativity and self-motivating desires

Root (base of spine): energizes our courageous and survival instincts

accept new ideas. We should remember that when the French research chemist Dr Louis Pasteur boldly suggested in the 1870s that infection and even deadly diseases were spread by invisible micro-organisms that he called "germs", the notion was for many years ridiculed and rebuffed by the medical establishment in France and England.

It's also interesting that the Nobel Laureate physicist Professor Brian Josephson of Cambridge University has for some twenty years now run a Mind–Matter Unification Project to explore how the energy of the human mind might affect the world around us other than through accepted mechanisms. Josephson has written that "conventional science is inadequate for situations where the mind is involved", and suggests that there probably exist unrecognized forms of energy quite comparable to electricity or radiation.

There are several well-recognized therapies that attempt to gauge, encourage, calm or otherwise influence these subtle energies in order

Thought Field Therapy

Arguably the forerunner and initial inspiration for most and perhaps all of the Western approaches to subtle energy therapies that deal holistically with the mind–body system is Thought Field Therapy (TFT). TFT has been in constant development since 1980 thanks to its creator, Californian psychotherapist Dr Roger Callagan (himself inspired by chiropractor George Goodheart's Applied Kinesiology and the psychiatrist Dr John Diamond).

In the very simplest application of this "energetic" healing method, we focus our thoughts on the source of our emotional or physical distress while simultaneously making a series of taps with our fingertips on a small number of "energy-sensitive" points on our body. Each point is stimulated in turn according to a prescribed sequence, as if tapping in a passcode to our energy system. When guided by a skilled practitioner, TFT can prove itself fast and permanently effective for very many people.

Visit tftrx.com or thoughtfieldtherapy.co.uk for further information. Leading British psychotherapist Dr Phil Mollon provides a lucid overview of this entire subject in his book *Psychoanalytic Energy Psychotherapy*.

to promote healing of our mind–body system, or that of another person whom we're helping or healing. From traditional Chinese medicine we have qigong, tai chi and acupuncture, from India we have yoga, from the Japanese tradition we have shiatsu and reiki, and there are also a whole host of therapies developed more recently in the West, such as Thought Field Therapy (see box) and Emotional Freedom Technique.

See pp.293–296 for guidance on how to find someone for advice and training in our energy systems. Or visit energypsych.org to find out more about energy therapies. Below are three approaches to promoting well-being in the mind–body system that you may find particularly helpful.

Emotional Freedom Technique (EFT or "Tapping")

Tapping with our fingertips on particular acupressure points on our body, while at the same time focusing our mind's attention on whatever's troubling us, is a mind–body combination that can substantially and dramatically help change the way we think, feel and behave, as well as relieving a host of physical ills at their root cause.

If this all sounds outlandish at first encounter, it's worth noting that acupuncture (which involves stimulating these same acu-points by puncturing the skin with sterilized needles) has been recognized by the World Health Organization as being effective for a wide range of physical and emotional ills, ranging from pain to depression.

The theory behind EFT is that it works by tapping into the body's meridian energy system. A less extraordinary explanation of what's going on is that it disrupts the pattern between what we think and how it feels. So when we confront our problem by focusing our attention on the upsetting thought, our usual pattern of upsetting responses is not only disrupted but overwritten by all the new and rather calming sensory information generated by our tapping on our particularly sensitive body points, and by all the other rituals that are often part of EFT, such as humming, counting and eye movements. This second explanation is particularly convincing, since it's already a well-established psychological phenomenon that we can benefit from intercepting and overwriting the messages sent between our brain and body. For instance, long-term pain is often the result of an unhelpful signal that's served its initial purpose but has thereafter been unable to turn itself off.

Visit emofree.com for more information about EFT.

Tai chi

Tai chi has its roots in the Chinese philosophical tradition of Taoism merged with the martial arts culture. It consists of a sequence of between 24 and 108 quite intricate but smooth, slow-motion movements (the number depends on the exact style practised), intended to create harmony within mind and body by boosting and balancing the flow of qi.

Practising tai chi at dawn on a misty lakeside in Hangzhou, China.

It is not a muscle-building or sweat-breaking form of exercise, but in a technological world so keen to rush, the serenity and beauty of its dance-like forms are a more than welcome tonic. Tai chi philosophy advocates that the soft and versatile energy will defeat the hard and rigid force not by opposing it, but by redirecting it advantageously.

Ashtanga yoga

Originating in India, yoga, like tai chi, embraces the philosophy of developing the mind and body simultaneously, and respecting our internal, unseen dynamics as much as our outer appearance. Yoga postures and breathing are said to improve the flow of prana around the body. There are a number of different styles of yoga, some very ancient, some developed more recently. By contrast with other yoga styles that hold poses for long periods, Ashtanga places its emphasis on dynamic movement between a sequence of 55 fundamental postures. The result is a fluid and heat-generating experience, full of perspiration. Breathing only through the nose and in synchrony with the movements is also an intricate part of this school of practice.

Conclusions

Our body thrives when allowed a full range of expression for our thoughts and emotions. A holistic, wholesome approach to everything we do, achieved with the aid of versatility and variety, will help give our mind–body system the very best chance of healthy development. This yin–yang rapport in which the whole is formed healthily by the coming together of complementary opposites – mind and body – well reflects the need for balance in every aspect of our life: time alone should be balanced by time with others; intellectual contemplation balanced by passionate expression; rest and recuperation balanced by vigorous action. Exploring, experimenting and pushing the boundaries of how we can better use our body to reach out to the world around us will not only allow our thoughts and emotions to deepen, it's through this rhythmic ebb and flow from tranquil consolidation to furthest stretch that we'll create our greatest satisfactions.

5

Our loves and passions

Our loves and passions

5

Who or what makes our life worth living?

Our loves, our passions, our callings, our sense of mission and *raison d'être*... all these words describe one and the same thing: the very heart and essence of who we are. It is the things we prize above all else, the things we feel driven to act upon, that define our true identity. They ignite us with a fiery energy and fabulous determination, an irrepressible *joie de vivre*.

Whether the touchstones of our passions be particular people, skills, places or pursuits, these are what make our life worth living. Time spent considering and clarifying these fundamentals is time well invested, because unless we prioritize our passions and give them air to breathe, we disrupt the very source of our will to live and what binds us to life.

As we saw on pp.23–25, for many centuries the widely accepted wisdom was that happiness is achieved by mastering our passions, subjugating them to reason. This Rough Guide believes, with David Hume (see p.27), that quite the opposite is true: the primary purpose of our intellect and our body is to serve our passions, because it is our loves and passions that determine the directions we take in life, and provide the energy for us to make headway. This is why it is vital that we acknowledge our "insides" and act to express them wisely in ways which benefit ourselves and those around us. It's this owning up to our callings, and giving them full rein, that makes our living honest and satisfying.

Doing what we love

"What is the meaning of life?" is a common enough question, but it makes no sense. It's like asking the meaning of air or water or wood. Life, just like those elements, is a limited natural resource, so a more helpful question is "What can we do with our life that would seem wonderfully worthwhile to us? How do we imbue our life with purpose?" Is it a companion, an activity, a mission, a hope? Who or what so excites us that we bother to get out of bed early, break a sweat, be brave and stay sober so we can get a good night's sleep, wake bright-eyed and bushy-tailed and try it all again tomorrow?

In 1942 Viennese psychiatrist Dr Viktor Frankl was deported to Theresienstadt, one of the Nazi concentration camps. He survived the horrors of the camps (including separation from his parents, siblings and wife, who all perished) largely, he later explained, by setting himself the mission of using the experience to improve his understanding of human resilience. From the outset, Frankl promised himself that if he survived, he would share with the world his observations upon this crucial human quality. In post-war Europe and the US, he did exactly that, developing a therapeutic approach based upon helping people find a personally motivating purpose to their lives. In his famous autobiographical book *Man's Search for Meaning*, Frankl quotes Nietzsche: "He who has a *why* to live for can bear almost any *how*." In other words, living with a sense of self-appointed purpose can give us extraordinary strength. In respect of this,

Bertrand Russell on love

Hume is not the only great Western philosopher to have honoured the importance to us of love and passion. One of the most important philosophers of the twentieth century, Bertrand Russell, writes in the prologue to his autobiography:

> I have sought love, first, because it brings ecstasy – ecstasy so great that I would often have sacrificed the rest of life for a few hours of this joy. I have sought it next because it relieves loneliness – that terrible loneliness in which one's shivering consciousness looks over the rim of the world into the cold unfathomable lifeless abyss. I have sought it, finally, because in the union of love I have seen, in a mystic miniature, the prefiguring vision of the heaven that saints and poets have imagined.

Frankl's writings urge us to seek not a *less* demanding life, but quite the contrary, a *more* challenging one that requires and deserves our deepest resources and heart-felt passions. Be it tending a garden, nurturing a relationship or building a business, it is by rising to challenges that we forget ourselves and reach well beyond the self-restricting boundaries of our own body and thoughts. Frankl believed that the journey, the doing, should be an end in itself, because the rewarding feelings will come from the route we've taken, the spirit in which we walk it, and the companionship upon the road.

> **Bring me my bow of burning gold;**
> **Bring me my arrows of desire;**
> **Bring me my spear – O, clouds unfold!**
> **Bring me my chariot of fire!**
>
> William Blake's hymn "Jerusalem" captures the thrilling
> energy generated by a heart-felt calling.

Where to look

If inspiration doesn't step up to greet us, we have to go looking for our passions, or even create them. We might find clues in...

▶ **Our childhood and teenage interests** that may have been neglected as schoolwork or other responsibilities took over, or that we may simply have been talked out of by those in charge at the time.

▶ **The subjects that never fail to grab our attention** when we stumble across them on a bookshelf or in a film.

▶ **Whatever we daydream about for the sheer joy of it**, or even the cheering thoughts we use to lull ourselves to sleep at night.

▶ **Experiencing first-hand a host of activities that we might have prematurely presumed are not for us.** (A drama class or local choir, dinghy sailing or mountain walking, landscape painting or natural science.)

Let's keep asking ourselves *for whom, for what and for where* would it feel well worth turning off the television, keeping fit and getting focused, because our heart beats faster at the mere thought of it. Whom, what and where do we hold in such value that we're inspired to set off in full sail on their behalf?

In the modern classic *American Beauty*, forty-year-old salesman Lester Burnham (played by Kevin Spacey) reminds us it's never too late to rediscover our passions: "Both my wife and daughter think I'm this gigantic loser. And they're right. I have lost something. I'm not exactly sure what it is, but I know I didn't always feel this… sedated. But you know what? It's never too late to get it back."

Is it helping or harming?

Passion is wonderful stuff, but like any valuable resource, it has its imitators. We can all hit some false notes when searching for the songs we love to sing.

Are we trying to please others?

When we're respectful of ourselves, and honouring our passions, it's as if we're hitting a ball with just the right place on the racquet. That "sweet spot" reflects the idiosyncratic mix of strengths that are born of both our joys and our adversities, and we play at our best when we're true to them.

However, if our attempts to please others by our actions lead us to neglect our true values, we can pull ourselves badly off course and thereby jeopardize our own well-being. This phenomenon was termed "the disease to please" by American psychotherapist Dr Harriet Braiker, who shrewdly discerned the self-defeating fear of confrontation that was driving some people's smiling subservience to everyone else's wishes.

Exuberance

"Exuberance is beauty" wrote William Blake. Exuberance – that appetite for life that drives us to explore and pioneer with barely containable enthusiasm – is not to be mistaken for superficial bubbliness, nor the self-possessed out-of-control state that is mania. Exuberance is pure *joie de vivre* that's being channelled constructively to carry us forward. Acclaimed American psychiatrist Professor Kay Redfield Jamison proposes that its four components are a passion to know more, a playful spirit, empathy with nature and a sense of joy.

The fruitfulness of exuberance is well illustrated by a famous episode in the life of the American physicist Richard Feynman. He recounts how his creativity seemed to dry up at age 27 shortly after the end of World War II. He so acutely felt the overbearing expectations of well-meaning folks planning his career for him that it stopped him in his tracks. Sitting forlorn in the campus cafeteria one day, his interest was caught by the distinctive but inexplicable wobble of the paper plates that some students had thrown high into the air. This plate conundrum prompted Feynman to play around with some calculations to explain the wobble, just for the sheer fun of it, and it was these diagrams scribbled down over the next few days which later earned him a Nobel Prize, not least because they had major relevance to the stability of rockets used in America's forthcoming space programme. Who knows to what heights exuberance might lift us?

Our motivation to please can equally be the fear of being ignored or rejected, so we set out to do whatever we think might make the other person love us, or at least win their nod of approval. Yet someone's approval or pride in our achievements is not a true sign of their caring, not if they disregard our essential make-up.

Is it passion or obsession?

It's a wonderful thing to feel a calling, whether it's to share our life with someone, raise a family, practise an art, a faith or a profession, or even to live in a much-loved place. But such a heart-felt desire is only worthy of being dubbed a "calling" if its passionate pursuit brings us profound well-being en route. If our going about it damages or unbalances our life in some way so that the costs outweigh the benefits, then that activity is tainted with some degree of obsession that is merely masquerading as vocation. Such unhealthy obsessions can have many disguises, ranging from excessive physical exercise or academic study right through to round-the-clock parenting or a workaholic job routine. Most often such over-wrought, narrowly focused activity is serving either as an escape from painful emotions or as an attempt to compensate for them, but in either case such an inflexible and airless fixation will be harmful rather than helpful.

To guard against this possibility, we need to balance our passions with some other activities which recuperate us (shared adventures with loving people is often the best). By doing so we allow our pursuits to provide a lifetime of nourishing enjoyment.

Are we true to ourselves?

If an alien being secretly observed our daily lives, our weekly routines and how we spent our weekends and holidays, what would they presume? That our desk, our commute or our TV were more important to us than our loved ones, our creativity, or time in the countryside? Is that alien misapprehension possible?

It's all too easy to live our daily lives out of sync with our priorities, out of kilter with how we'd rank who and what is most valuable to us if we listed them on paper. Sometimes, by accident, we can be distracted from what's most important to us.

Do you still play the sports or musical instruments you instinctively loved as a teenager? Do you still make time to dance or sing or read for pleasure? And what did you promise yourself with hand on heart when you were 16 or 21 or 30 or 40, when trying to cheer yourself at a particularly bleak time? Perhaps it was learning to speak a foreign language, ride a horse or glide a plane? Perhaps it was winter on the equator, spring savouring a special city, summer hiking in the mountains, or autumn swimming in tropical seas? You probably planned to set aside a whole year to exercise your passions – the grand tour, the four seasons, fully rounded. You might even have promised yourself a profession you could thoroughly enjoy, or a love affair, or to live life in a far-off foreign land better suited to your sensibilities.

Of course it's not just the big stuff that can be neglected; the everyday things that once mattered to us can fall by the wayside too. We all-too-quickly forget how we told ourselves things would be: the hat we would wear, the weekends with friends, the bike ride to work, the view from the window we'd look out from.

Now dare to ask yourself how and when you're planning to realize such long-held, heart-felt daydreams?

Because, truth to tell, though our most personal treasures probably need dusting off and bringing up to date with what we've learned about

Sublimation

Of course, sometimes our passions can cause us problems: our passionate love may be unrequited, and our deepest desires might be damaging to ourselves, or quite unacceptable to those around us. Freud coined the term sublimation to describe what he regarded as one of our most successful human traits: our ability to channel our passionate instinctive energy away from its original target, and towards something seemingly quite different, which nonetheless satisfies our original longings. Just as a hydro-electric dam harnesses the energy of water to produce usable electricity, it is through the channelling of sublimated energies that desires which might otherwise prove highly problematic for us and those around us can metamorphose into something creative and most welcome. Artistic pursuits, sports, beloved hobbies and professional careers can all be the fruits of highly successful sublimation.

life since then, that's quite different from turning our back on our original inspiration. It's those daydreams that should ground us, give us a sense of ourselves, a North Star. They're what we're made of. They cry out for expression, and for every year we postpone them, at the very least we are imprisoning some important part of ourselves, and more likely we'll begin to feel sour about life. We might find ourselves suffering a range of psychosomatic illnesses (see pp.49–51), because such a state of affairs saddens our soul. After all, if we can't trust ourselves to honour the best of our daydreams, what can we trust ourselves to do? The more honest we can be, and the more dynamically we act, the better things will be, because if we respect our fundamental hungers, our essential desires, we are less vulnerable to superficial cravings for the sorts of daily anaesthetics that distract us or dull the pain of what we're sorely missing: the treasure-hunt journeys that only our heart can choose for us.

Soul to soul

One of the most powerful callings we can experience is the calling to share our life with other people. Whether it be a close friend or lover, a marriage partner or a child, those most dear to us can be the very touchstone of our existence.

Loving friendship

In his great work *Nichomachean Ethics* Aristotle devotes two full books to the subject of friendship. For him, a true friend is, quite simply, "another self". Yet it's all too easy to take our closest companions for granted and to squeeze them around the pressing demands of our everyday life.

Creating rapport

Whether we are hoping to foster a loving friendship or a romantic relationship, our first step must be to establish rapport. No one knows more about this than Monty Roberts, the real-life "horse whisperer" and the inspiration for the Robert Redford film of the same name. "My greatest accomplishment was learning to be gentle", writes Monty; "without that, I would have accomplished nothing." Monty has spent a lifetime training horses, as well as fostering 47 troubled youngsters, and having three children of his own with Pat, his wife of 50 years.

His life story is all the more remarkable because by the age of 12, Monty had sustained 71 broken bones at the hands of his cold and brutal father, who used threats and acts of violence to extract fearful compliance.

Disillusioned by the world of adult humans, as a child Monty found comfort and love among horses. And then, as a teenager, he gained extraordinary insights into animal rapport by spending days out on the high desert ranges of Nevada studying wild herds through binoculars. Through his caring observation of these powerful and profoundly social creatures, he did not simply transcend the bullying he'd endured as a youngster, he created its very opposite: the active application of gentleness to achieve what he calls "Join-Up", which is a willing partnership between man and horse built upon trust and mutual benefit.

In his book *Join-Up: Horse Sense for People*, Monty explains that the very same principles can apply to our relationships with other human beings. His success as a foster parent clearly shows that with people, just as with horses, gentleness reaps far greater rewards than the harshness of an abusive or coercive atmosphere.

So, for example, when trying to nurture a romantic partnership with someone, we can in our enthusiasm push too hard, which only leaves the other person feeling bullied by our insistence and inclined to pull away. By offering our warm invitation and then gently and patiently withdrawing, we send the signal that any decision to develop the hoped-for relationship is the other person's free choice, and this in itself provides a strong foundation for partnering up. If our initial offer is met with reluctance, rather than using our determination to push harder, we would do better to look for an alternative way to bond. In all of this, it is vital that we respect the values and goals important to the other person, and the language and rules of engagement they're willing to accept. This considerate approach is further helped by keeping our own breathing and heart-rate calm so as not to radiate any sense of urgency, agitation or irritability. In short, we should channel our determination not into greater outward pressure, but into greater mastery

This laissez-faire attitude is quite unwarranted given their extraordinary role in our physical and psychological well-being. A loving friendship halves the troubles and doubles the joys and by doing so makes life's journey all the more enjoyable. That much we know already; but let's also appreciate that there are dimensions of our personality that would not blossom half so well, if at all, without the catalyst of the right relationships. For this reason, our best friends help create who we are, and

of ourselves. Likewise, rather than chasing, we should seek to make a sufficiently attractive offer, and then back off so that the other soul can feel they have full ownership of the next move.

Monty Roberts would tell us that no matter whether we're offering romance or friendship, inspiring others to learn, doing business or negotiating peace, it is by being gentle, by self-calming and by seeking to understand the language and values of the other person that we are most likely to foster a helpful rapport. It is by so gently inviting "Join-Up" that we salute the spirit's need for autonomy and self-respect just as much as for companionship and love.

Horse whisperer Monty Roberts earns trust and warmth through gentleness and respect.

our growth and progression is reflected in who among them we let go, and who we deepen our roots with. As with so many facets of life (such as our thoughts, nutrition or exercise), a rich variety is a very healthy thing, and it should be no surprise if our dearest companions are quite different from each other.

What distinguishes these rare individuals as so valuable is that they feel our pains and pleasures, our setbacks and triumphs, as if they were their own. For this reason they encourage us in our best endeavours, and haul us up if they think we're letting ourselves down. Their level of empathy is matched by their level of intimacy with how we think. After all, in the company of a true friend, we dare to think aloud without the need to edit ourselves. These privileged insights enable our confidential ally to question the very process of our thoughts and to suggest better ways of approaching things. This presents a crucial opportunity, but only a kindred spirit

> **"What is friendship? One mind in two bodies."**
>
> **Aristotle**

will take it. It is because they think we're worth it that a true confidante will dare to risk our irritable indignation, when less caring friends would shy away. But the health of our relationship is reflected not in how hotly we argue, but in how well we make up afterwards. Best friends may bruise each other, but they are loath to bear a grudge. For all of this and far more, such folk deserve an honoured place on our list of priorities.

The pain of loneliness prompts intimacy

Loneliness tells us so much about the human spirit, it should be no surprise that the sorrow of enforced isolation is a key theme in popular tales from *Robinson Crusoe* to *Cinderella*, from *The Count of Monte Cristo* to *Bridget Jones's Diary*. But loneliness isn't our enemy. Like hunger, it reminds us of nature's insistence that we make progress in our relationship with the world around us. After all, loneliness is our hunger not simply for proximity, but for closeness of spirit, for something deeply shared. What's more, this intimacy we crave requires not just knowing but also understanding and caring, and this can be for the place we call home or the skills of our vocation, just as much as for another living creature. Seen this way, rather than fearing or resenting the pain of loneliness, we might regard it as a benevolent feeling, and a reminder to us that pain is not in itself a bad thing. On the contrary, nature has helpfully endowed us with two systems for motivation: the pains which repel us, and the pleasures which attract us. So when it comes to loneliness, nature scolds us for being too detached, and rewards us for getting to know things better.

Marriage partnerships

What does the best research flag as the essential principles for a fruitful and enduring partnership between two adults? Professor John Gottman of the University of Washington in Seattle (gottman.com) is a leading figure in this field, and has observed carefully and at close quarters several hundred married couples. For instance, he films them interacting as they spend the weekend in an apartment (see box below), and keeps in touch with them for several years thereafter.

It seems that couples who've profoundly enjoyed several decades together invariably describe each other as their very best friend, and such profound friendship has certain distinguishing qualities. Above all else, it's a union of equals, and though they might not share every role, they nonetheless regard each other's activities as equivalently important to the welfare of the team. In short, their different needs and resources are a good fit and dovetail into one another very nicely, allowing the two halves to make a well-rounded, well-balanced whole that is far greater than the sum of the parts. (It's noteworthy how a "wholesome" approach to life once again suggests itself as the most helpful; a theme explored as a cornerstone to this Rough Guide.)

Gottman's evidence also suggests that we can foster such a friendship of mutual enjoyment, support and respect through sharing enjoyable activities in which we can grow and progress together, whether those activities be gardening, drama, sport, travelling or child-rearing.

Research in the Love Lab

Professor John Gottman has done much to enhance our understanding of marriage and partner relationships by taking the trouble to observe, in unprecedented detail, the habitual interactions of couples. The Gottman Institute in Seattle, founded by Gottman and his wife Dr Julie Schwartz Gottman, has a fully functioning, very comfortable apartment (the so-called "Love Lab") in which study-participant couples (and their pets if they wish) typically spend a whole weekend being observed by researchers. In this way, the researchers can see how the couple really interact with each other, verbally and non-verbally, rather than relying on how they would like to think they behave. From 9am to 9pm (there are no cameras in the bedroom or bathroom), they are automatically filmed, and perhaps watched from behind the two-way mirror in the kitchen.

Such "shared adventure" is the crucible in which are born all of our loving companionships, and under no circumstances should work commitments or other worldly demands – *not even child-rearing* – be given priority over those companionship-building activities. Children are like evolving planets that thrive best when basking in the warmth created by the loving adults whose profound partnership cre-

> **"We know it is not the joining of another body will resolve loneliness, but the uniting of another compliable mind."**
>
> John Milton

ates the sunshine at the centre of their life. If, however, the parents' lives revolve around the children, it's all too easy for mum and dad to be accidentally separated from each other. In such a situation, the children are "spoiled" by the imbalance of love and attention, while the parents grow cold from neglecting one another. Professor Gottman estimates that eighty percent of couples who split up do so because they stop thinking and behaving like a "we", and retreat into unhelpful and self-protective "me" strategies. Two such individuals who are not working sufficiently as one entity will only wind up feeling lonely inside their marriage. Falling out of love, or having an affair with a third party, may be the eventual *consequence* of this loneliness, but it's very rarely the root cause.

To prevent such drawing apart like this, partners can actively seek to deepen their sense of shared purpose. Seeking ever-increasing intimacy requires us to develop our capacity not only to love another, but to let ourselves be loved; and it's this latter skill which most often needs some practice, particularly if we were brought up by parents who accidentally or otherwise gave us (as children) the impression that we weren't loved or lovable. It's only by feeling love-worthy and love-deserving – and so actively investing in our well-being in every aspect of our lives – that we will nurture the resources with which to comfortably and keenly love those most dear to us.

Gottman's own over-riding message is this: never miss an opportunity to engage positively with our partner through affectionate gestures, cuddles, compliments, taking a genuine interest, and sharing at least one romantic date per week. Reason being that *one* special factor can override all of our shortcomings, and that factor is simply to let our partner know on a daily basis that our loving partnership together is the one thing we treasure above all else.

Parent and child

"I love you and because of this I will help you progress in whatever positive directions your passions take you." When a parent makes this clear to a child, for that child life can be a delight. These are the happiest, strongest youngsters – the ones who are urged to develop themselves and make progress in their rapport with life; the ones who are absolutely and equally supported in these endeavours, no matter if they are faced with mistakes and setbacks or achievements and plain sailing. Those who love them *do not* withdraw support as a punishment for insufficient results or for passions that are disapproved of. Such reliable back-up from parents or life-mentors leaves the young individual free from any hunger for

The legacy of childhood

The Harvard Study of Adult Development (see pp.194–195) has analysed the personalities of over eight hundred Americans as they evolved over a lifetime. Its director, Professor George Vaillant, has concluded the following about the adults who eventually emerged:

▶ Compared to unloved children, those cherished by their parents grew into adults who were five times more likely to play competitive sports. They were also five times more likely to play games with friends and to take full and enjoyable vacations.

▶ The best predictor of an adult's high income was not their parents' social class, but whether their mother had made them feel loved.

▶ The best outcomes were achieved by children whose parents did not treat their emotions – whether anger, fear, sadness or joy – as misbehaviour to be punished, but as energy to be channelled.

▶ Children are enriched by learning to take people inside themselves, i.e. by loving and being loved.

▶ The most vital turning point for a once-troubled child was "meeting a caring friend and marrying an accepting spouse".

These sobering observations aside, Vaillant makes it quite clear that such patterns are merely likelihoods, and that any particular individual might live their life quite differently despite the odds.

approval or liking, and free from any shame or despair at their own sense of falling short in the eyes of the adults they most care for. With no need for any painful introspection as to their own imagined inadequacies, it is the world around them that becomes the focus of that child's attention, and they're not afraid to take it on. They are outgoing, confident, warm. Their emotional acumen will at all ages allow them to be a deeply loved and loving person who plays special roles in the lives around them.

Deliberate abuse and cruelty aside, most psychotherapists would argue that few relationships are as inhibitive as those in which love is offered only as a reward for what the parents deem as desirable outcomes (for instance, that the child deliver beauty, A-grades or obedience), rather than the love being offered as a support to healthy behaviour (such as good humour, close friendship and a passion for life). Put another way, the most troubled children and adults are those whose parents only offered approval and a show of affection when it suited the parents, rather than when the child needed it most. Thankfully, alternative well-springs of helpful love can be found among best friends and benevolent mentors at any stage in our lives.

Sexual fusion

If we lose the compass and fuel of our passions, our subtle natural senses, our wish to thrive in harmony with all that's wild, then we lose the very essence of what it is to be alive. We become like dairy cows or caged birds: domesticated. As we saw on p.40, Sigmund Freud warned more than a century ago that we urban-dwelling humans were paying too high a price to live so many and so close together in so-called civilization. One casualty of this constructed and constricted life may have been our innate animal intimacies.

The demonizing of human sexuality

The Ancient Greek philosophers were deeply distrustful of heterosexual passion. According to his disciple Plato, Socrates described romantic love between a man and a woman as a "disease" that makes them first lustful and then obsessed with parenting: "First they are sick for intercourse with each other, then sick for nurturing their young." For Socrates and Plato, only the love between an older man and a younger man was ennobling, because such homosexual expression did not risk parenthood, and the physical partnership between the wiser man and his mentee might readily lead to instruction in such intellectual themes as virtue, philosophy and beauty.

We shouldn't forget that Plato and Socrates were in many ways out of step with their times: sexuality played a rich and welcome role in the everyday lives of the majority of Ancient Greeks. Likewise, the gods and goddesses they worshipped were frequently engaged in love affairs and lustful adventures. Yet the sexuality-embracing pantheism of Ancient Greece stands in stark contrast to much of what has followed. Ever since that time, in all the major religions and faith beliefs, the body's sexual appetites have been demonized as something to be suppressed. Put another way, it's hard to find a religion that champions the sexual expression of romantic desire.

Why might the religious authorities be so keen to outlaw romantic love? Is there something more to it than care for our spiritual progress? One explanation goes something like this: to assert greater control over the general population, the mainstream Christian Church from its earliest days sought to take ownership of nakedness and sexuality so as to monopolize the supply of sexual experience to men and women. (In support of this assertion, it's notable that Chinese Confucian philosophy openly regards sexual desire as a threat to loyalty to one's father and one's superiors.) The early and medieval Church authorities effectively outlawed all sexual experience that was out of wedlock, or for any purpose other than procreation. By edict of the Church, even

William Blake on passion

The poet, painter and thought-pioneer William Blake (1757–1827) championed the human body as an extension of the soul, the individual undivided. He protested against the orthodox Church's demonization of our physical desires, particularly sexual, regarding them as wholly natural and a wondrous source of earthly joy. In his *Vision of the Last Judgement*, he writes "Men are admitted into Heaven not because they have curbed & govern'd their Passions or have No Passions, but because they have Cultivated their Understandings". And in *The Marriage of Heaven and Hell* he declares "He who desires but acts not, breeds pestilence."

Married to his beloved wife Kate for 45 years, the visionary Blake believed in and practised equality in their relationship, more than a century before women were given the vote in the UK.

Modesty, or hypocrisy?

Notoriously, Victorian women's clothes were armour designed not only to conceal the curves and chicanes of the female form, but to protect it. Bustles and corsets were little less than mobile fortresses to keep men locked out and womanhood locked in. Likewise, men were restrained in frock coats, tight trousers and boots that you needed help to pull on and off. Yet the Victorians' strait-laced fashions were only one side of a deeply contradictory, even pathological relationship with their sexuality: not so far from the upright domesticity of the family home, child prostitution was rife in London's streets.

It wasn't only Victorian England that was suffering from its repressed animal nature. Across the waters in Europe and the US the hypocrisies were much the same, and nowhere more evident than in the reception of some of that era's most famous works of art. *Madame X* (see right) is one of the most celebrated paintings of John Singer Sargent. The aloof high-society Parisian beauty stands full-size, red-haired and resplendent, not even deigning to look at her viewer. She represents all that contemporary society deemed untouchable: the female sexuality of which gentlemen could only dream. When first displayed at the Paris Salon in 1884, her right dress strap hung suggestively off her shoulder, but critical outcry at such indignity persuaded the artist

masturbation could bring you eternal damnation. We might perceive a degree of hypocrisy in the Church fathers' repudiation of our sexuality. After all, St Francis of Assisi and St Augustine – just like Buddha – both drank deep from the cup of carnality in their youth, and only after many, many years renounced such ways, because they finally decided that such lustful practices were a hindrance to their spiritual progress.

to repaint the strap in its proper and decent place.

Now compare that presentation of "womanhood out-of-bounds" with its polar opposite, *The White Captive* (1859). This life-size white-marble teenage girl, carved from a live model by the American Erastus Dow Palmer, was immediately celebrated as one of the finest nudes produced in the US that century. This entirely vulnerable adolescent is presented to her viewer with an all-too-convenient story that she has been stripped and tethered to await whatever "uncivilized ends" her Native American captors have in store for her.

These two strikingly different images seem to illustrate the deep schisms, the pathological hypocrisies, of the age in which they were created. Sexuality and nakedness were deeply taboo, but if a pretext for depiction of the female form could be found – if the figure could be distanced from contemporary society in some way – then viewers were all too happy to satisfy their instincts to admire the female body. There was no outcry at the unveiling of *The White Captive*, for it depicted an "exotic" scene far removed from viewers' own lives. Likewise, the Salon was packed with far more revealing paintings than Sargent's, deemed acceptable because the ostensible subjects were goddesses or mythical figures, not contemporary Parisian women.

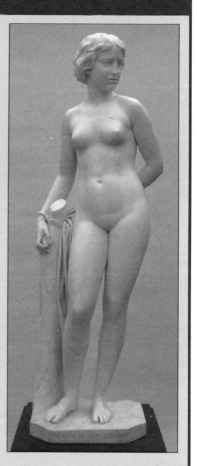

In the centuries that have followed, like any restricted activity or black-market commodity, sexual experience has taken on a grossly inflated and distorted super-prized value in most societies. It's a sad fact that pornography via magazines, DVDs or the Internet is a huge and growing industry. Seeking to quench our sexual passions for each other has been so painted as an act tantamount to depravity, to criminality, to evil, that even today otherwise healthy careers and partnerships can be jeopardized not by illegal sexual relationships, but by taboo ones. Whether it be one-night stands or extra-marital affairs, co-worker liaisons or state-licensed prostitution, though these behaviours are not illegal, they nonetheless can earn individuals a far more severe punishment from a reproving society than any number of law-breaking activities.

It's not wicked, it's wild!

Dr Alfred C. Kinsey (1894–1956), a zoologist at Indiana University, wrote *Sexual Behaviour in the Human Male* (1948) and then *Sexual Behaviour in the Human Female* (1953). The avant-garde and painstaking research upon which his findings are based (research that involved face-to-face interviews, confidential self-report questionnaires and the filming of copulating couples in Kinsey's secret attic studio) seems to confirm what had for two millennia been a much-contended point: that mutually exciting sexual exploration between two eagerly consenting mature individuals is wholly in keeping with our identity as animals who cannot choose to be other than part of the natural world. Kinsey's research seems to confirm that vaginal, oral and anal sex are all part of that animal-intimate repertoire of behaviour. Our sexual needs (widely varying in strength from one individual to another) for intimate sights, touch, taste, sound, smell and penetration all make very clear our innate drives, no matter these be masked or outlawed by the artifice of culture, state or church. The explicit illustrations of sexually active men and women on Greek clay amphoras dating from 600 BC bear ample testimony to the longevity of our intriguing desires for each other's bodies. In such light, the so-called sophistications of modern civilization seem not so much refinements as *con*finements. We are wild at heart.

Tantric sex

The Sanskrit word "tantra" means "to weave". In the tradition of Tantric sexuality, this has come to denote the weaving together of the subtle energies of two individuals when they conjoin. Tantric sexuality suggests an intriguing alternative to regarding ejaculation as the zenith of a sexual encounter. It is proposed that the man should resist ejaculation altogether, refraining from it completely during most sexual encounters, focusing instead on the myriad other sensual pleasures: the scents, touch, taste and sheer seductive sight and presence of the other. The woman, by contrast, should indulge in as many orgasms as she cares to.

Our heart's regret

Because life is so much bigger than we are, things never go quite the way we've planned, often not even close. One upshot of being unavoidably swept along on the current like this is that from time to time we find ourselves mourning painfully for "the lives we have longed for but not yet lived".

It's surely no accident that "what if" stories are beloved the world over. Perhaps this theme proves so popular because our human brain is highly adept at generating a host of alternative possibilities. It's what our imagination excels at. And "what if" thinking is rarely more powerful than when it tastes strongly of hope and regret, the latter of which is too often regarded as a self-punishing mug's game and best avoided.

It's good news, then, that psychology professor Neal Roese at Illinois University takes a refreshingly positive perspective on that bitter pain of loss in the pit of our stomach. He builds his case on the key observation that although in the shorter term we regret the things we've done, as time passes we increasingly regret the things we didn't do but could

Death inspiring life

Is it possible that far from being malevolent, death is simply a necessary counterpoint if life is to have meaning? After all, if our time for living was not finite and uncertain, we'd feel no imperative to "carpe diem". Just as happiness needs sadness to help us appreciate it, so life needs death – something to push against. They are complementary to each other, rather than opposing.

Dame Cicely Saunders was the founder of the modern hospice movement. Before her own death in 2005 she said reassuringly: "There can be something very creative about bereavement." Bereavement is one of life's most painful emotions, but grieving does not necessarily lead to depression. For a healthy recovery, it seems to help us to have the example of those who have experienced bereavement and are living happily now. It also helps to have at least one close and confiding relationship in which we can talk openly about the pain of loss. Most of all, it seems we will cope well if those we live amongst need us to. By letting go of one much-loved individual, our heart and hopes are set free to embrace another, and life renews itself.

There is much wisdom in the traditions that allow us, perhaps even require us, to grieve deeply and openly, *and then to put away our mourning and re-engage with living life.*

have. This characteristic is evident in studies as far afield as the US, Russia, China and Japan, and it probably reflects the following two phenomena. As time passes, we're not only very good at seeing the silver lining in our gaffes, but we also start to see the bigger picture of our life-course, and realize that trying something bold but risky wouldn't have been so bad after all, even if it hadn't worked out. In essence, psychology would agree with former US president Theodore Roosevelt in declaring "Far better it is to dare mighty things, even though chequered by failure, than to dwell in that perpetual twilight that knows not victory nor defeat."

So, when some promising course of action calls to our heart, we should take it. Be it the kiss ventured, the friendship offered, a career explored, or an adventure undertaken, we should remind ourselves

Love and regret: Ang Lee's *Brokeback Mountain* (2005) compassionately dramatizes the forbidden love between two young cowboys in the 1960s. A couple of times a year the two men head out into the hills to be secretly in each other's arms. But the rarity of these moments takes a great toll on both their hearts. Jack (played by Jake Gyllenhaal) reproaches Ennis (Heath Ledger), "We coulda had a good life together! ... Had us a place of our own. But you didn't want it ... You count the damn few times we have been together in nearly twenty years..." In the film's closing scene, Ennis caresses a shirt worn by the man he loved, and declares to an empty room "Jack, I swear..." We sense that, for him, the pain of loss is made greater by his regret that he did not dare more.

Angels who awake our soul

The word *angel* comes from the Ancient Greek *angelos* meaning "messenger", and many cultures ascribe common attributes to such beings and our mystical encounters with them. In traditional writings, it seems understood that when we are visited by an angel, we might be the only one able to see him or her, but for *us* at least our angel will radiate not only a light but a palpable energy that can be felt passing through us, like an X-ray revealing our innermost essence. Their very presence fills our human heart not only with awe but with fear. They can fairly be called a messenger because they inspire within us a passion to change our life for the better. Their energy is the fresh bright morning that stirs our soul from sleep. How like an angel is the being with whom we fall in love.

that if all we risk is embarrassment or a painful sense of setback, these aches will quickly fade, and by the very act of trying, our spirit is making progress.

Such a pioneering philosophy reverberates with one of the first principles of the human condition: it's not making mistakes that's a problem, it's what we do about them that determines whether they bring a net loss or a net gain. Accordingly, for our regrets to be productive rather than toxic, we should harness our pain to spur the versatile and creative actions that will put right what feels wrong. We should view regret as a natural warning bell that lets us know we're missing out on a longed-for course of action; and we could use this feeling as a compass to create a future that fully compensates for the past in some positive way.

With this in mind, we might ponder all those things we won't regret were we to be squished tomorrow by a grand piano falling from forty floors. We *won't* regret all the TV we missed these past twenty years from not having one; nor the times we stayed sober when we could have got drunk; nor the calls and texts we didn't take because the friend we were with felt far more important. We will, however, regret all those fears that we didn't dare face so they held us back for half a lifetime; regret the weekends walking in the wilds that we didn't find time for; regret the individuals we never took lovingly in our arms; and regret all the other very personal projects that never got further than the pieces of paper we wrote them on. In short: we will regret our heart-felt passions unexplored.

Conclusions

It has been argued that there can be no free will if we do not exert control, just as a rider is only truly riding if she is actively directing her horse. Likewise, in the intellectual tradition of Plato, Victorian poet Lord Tennyson wrote "The happiness of a man in this life does not consist in the *absence* but in the *mastery* of his passions."

As a counter to this position, it might be said that the very nature of our passions is that they are never mastered, never domesticated, never channelled and always wild. Perhaps passions would not be passions if they were under our control; they would be skills. Perhaps it is their distinctive value to lead us wildly where they will. Perhaps our passions would not be so precious to us if we could always have things our own way. We can't make people love us, no more than we can make love last for ever. But it's this very uncontrollability that makes our loves all the more dear to us while they last.

6

Our social nature

Our social nature

Being good with our friends and neighbours

"**I** belong therefore I am" is a far more helpful observation upon our fundamental human motivations than René Descartes' "Cogito ergo sum: I think therefore I am". For we are first and foremost social animals, and we need the physical presence and companionship of others, or the hope of it at least. Need, that is, in the sense of its being essential for our all-round well-being. It's no accident that solitary confinement is still the most feared form of psychological punishment for a prisoner. We are each born alone inside our bodies, alone with our emotions and our thoughts, and to feel truly alive it seems we must be reaching out to take a hold of the world. Hence we hunger to belong – to another person, a family, a tribe, a profession… to a social world that welcomes us.

So it is that a life can only really blossom when we manage to push aside all the isolating activities we accidentally invent for ourselves: the studying alone for exams and travelling alone in cars; the Internet surfing and TV watching; the work projects needing overlong hours; the texts, emails and mobiles that are no substitute for actually being together. We can only blossom when we see through all the glittering bling of our so-called civilization and digital technology, so as to fully appreciate our natural social needs: for respectful recognition, liberal acceptance, valued roles, self-expression and warm companionship. All deserve to be honoured at the centre of our lives, because they are the motivation, the goal, for most if not all of our other activities. The work, the play, the recuperation are only a means to our sense of belonging.

Camaraderie and esprit de corps

The breadth and depth of our personal relationships are crucial to our well-being. If we have a small handful of soul mates and confidantes, as well as neighbourly neighbours and supportive co-workers, we are, just for example, far less likely to experience depression, hyper-anxiety, low self-respect and problems with eating and sleeping. These are the conclusions of no less a social commentator than Professor Robert D. Putnam, a former head of Harvard's JFK School of Government and author of *Bowling Alone: the Collapse and Revival of American Community* (bowlingalone.com).

Putnam's research teams analysed massive amounts of already existing data, in an attempt to see what overall trends emerged. Two of the largest sets of data were:

▶ **The Roper Social and Political Trends Archives**, which contained 400,000 responses from interviews conducted in person with a cross-section of Americans between 1973 and 1994

The camaraderie created by a shared mission is finely portrayed in *Das Boot* (1981), directed by Wolfgang Petersen. One of the most acclaimed films in the history of German cinema, it tells the story of a World War II U-boat crew. Suffering the deep-compression and rivet-tearing tension of Atlantic ocean combat, these 42 conscript submariners are not fighting for the Nazis, nor harbouring malice towards the Allies; they are fighting for each other, and for the hope of returning home.

▶ **The DDB Needham Lifestyle Archives,** which added 87,000 surveys to the research pot, conducted between 1975 and 1999.

These are both questionnaire-style national surveys about how people spend their time: everything from when they last threw a dinner party to how often they attend a social club or society. The strength of Putnam's research method is that it does not rely on just one survey, but on numerous bodies of evidence, including official records of crime levels, educational attainment and illness. The surveys also tracked trends over many years, rather than taking what could be a highly misleading one-moment snapshot. (Ask people how safe they feel one week after 11 September 2001, and it should be no surprise that you'll get a very different answer from two weeks before.)

Professor Putnam's work has popularized the term "social capital", by which he means all the mutual support, trust and good-will networks we have accumulated in our "social bank account" by dint of our personal relationships and community involvement. Social capital, Putnam concludes, is vital to our well-being, and has been diminishing dangerously for several decades now. Putnam illustrates the power of this social ingredient in the following way: if you have a choice between

▶ **giving up smoking twenty cigarettes per day, or**
▶ **joining a weekly social club if you're not already a member of one**

then he advises that to considerably increase your physical, psychological and social health, you should *join that club!* No matter it is for badminton or bowling, acting or religious worship, the statistics from studying how other folks have lived their lives tell us that a social club will do far more good for you even than giving up such an unhealthy habit as smoking. The fact is that the great majority of the most healthy and satisfied individuals decorate their rooms with photographs of loved and loving people, and fill their diaries and calendars with sociable activities, notably ones that don't centre around alcohol. The message of such lifetimes is clear: no matter our age, it is vital that we cultivate a strong and richly varied social network. And no matter whether we count ourselves as outgoing or introverted, we should put our past habits aside and set out to boldly join group activities so we can eventually feel welcome and valued. (Overcoming shyness is considered later in this chapter.)

After all, *the group* is a natural denomination for humans. Whether it be a Girl Guide troop or a college choir, a military regiment or a sports team, institutions that inspire a collective pride and camaraderie in their fellowship bring a great added benefit to those who take part. That sense of belonging and shared values is a tonic for the soul. It is a tragedy that so many educational and working institutions so over-laud *an individual's* accomplishments that esprit de corps is compromised.

Professor Putnam is quite unequivocal in his assessment of the decline of social capital particularly evident in the Western world since the early 1960s. He blames too much television watching, overlong working hours and overlong commuting, all of which only serve to isolate us from each other, and to weaken the health-bringing bonds and bridges that are formed by a rich variety of frequent social contact.

Benevolent touch

No matter two people are holding each other in order to dance or to practise a martial art such as judo or jiujitsu, their "benevolent touch" is respectfully considerate of the other person's body and spirit; and such benevolent physical contact appears to provide a powerful nutrient for such social creatures as ourselves.

We shouldn't be too surprised.

At the University of Wisconsin-Madison in the 1960s, psychology professor Harry Harlow demonstrated that touch, *the very feel of things,* was even more important to newborn primates than milk. He offered eight baby rhesus monkeys a choice between two surrogate mothers, one covered in soft terrycloth, the other simply a monkey-shaped wire frame. For four of the infants, the terrycloth mother dispensed milk; for the other four, it was the wire mother. If all the babies needed from their mothers was food, then they should have become attached to whichever offered them milk, but Harlow found that all of them clung to the terrycloth mother, whether or not she provided food. A famous photograph from this experiment (see opposite) shows a young monkey clinging determinedly to his cuddly cloth mother with his back legs while stretching across to the wire mum to suckle.

It's a tragedy that Harlow's quite unnecessary experiments became increasingly cruel: keeping monkeys from birth in absolute isolation

We were all at one time umbilically attached to our mother's body. We know what it is to feel connected, and we hunger for this.

from other living creatures for months and even years. Had he bothered to leave his torture-chamber laboratories, he would have discovered that World War II had left Europe and the Far East strewn with ready-made proof of the need for comforting physical contact. A British contemporary of Harlow's, psychiatrist John Bowlby, worked in orphanages and with homeless children across Europe in the aftermath of the war and was commissioned by the World Health Organization to write a report about what he learned. He recorded how babies placed in isolation wards (because they were born premature or for fear of contagious diseases) would die without human touch, and noted that older children who received insufficient physical proof of love most often became either aloof loners or frightened clingers, depending on which strategy they adopted to try to cope with the "hug-less" circumstances that had traumatized them.

The vital nutrient for the human soul contained within the benevolent touch of other creatures, then, is not a new concept, but it's one we too frequently neglect in our increasingly "virtual" world.

Maslow's hierarchy of needs

Harry Harlow's first PhD student, back in the 1930s, was one Abraham Maslow, who would go on to become the founding father of Humanist Psychology and the head of the American Psychology Association. Perhaps it was Maslow's apprenticeship with shamefully deprived rhesus monkeys that sowed the seeds for his proposal that we humans, like all creatures, have a hierarchy of essential needs that go well beyond food and water.

Maslow envisaged these instinctive needs as forming a pyramid. The closer to the base of the pyramid, the more powerful the need. Only when the lower, more fundamental needs are met can we comfortably concentrate on higher needs, said Maslow, and if a level of needs is not met, we will obsess or over-compensate. For example, if a child doesn't feel sufficiently secure when growing up, they might become a highly nervous adult who finds it hard to trust anyone. The pyramid below is derived from Maslow's original proposal of five levels, but with two additional levels (for understanding and beauty) which were inserted later by those studying Maslow's work, in order to clarify what he seemed to believe was required for self-actualizing.

Self-actualizing – striving to be the best person we can be

Appreciating and creating beauty

Understanding and gaining knowledge

Social status, recognition and self-esteem

Love, belonging and intimate relationships

Safety, shelter, order

Physiological needs for air, water, physical contact, sleep, food, warmth, sexual fulfilment

Maslow's pyramid makes for an intriguing explanation of behaviour. But do we really prioritize safety before love or status? His proposed hierarchical ordering of needs is perhaps a less accurate and helpful observation on human nature than his simply recognizing our need for a rich range of psychological and social nutrients that go well beyond the physical if our life is to flourish.

Partner dancing

All forms of dancing are a wonderfully positive expression of our intimate self, and are very healthy for it. Dance brings more joy than just about any other leisure activity. If solo dancing is a channel for instinctive self-expression, then partner dancing is an opportunity for intimacy and the sheer joy of holding on to someone else. And folk dancing in all its forms is equally nutritious. When it comes to the ways and means of living well, we're very quick to wonder what new breakthroughs we can invent. But what have we forgotten? What classic wisdoms? For instance, have you ever been to a wedding in the Scottish Highlands? It's to be wholly recommended, for the Highlanders truly understand the joy of social dancing and the power it has to bring people together. Even the most varied bunch of wedding guests will find themselves united by the hand holding and partner spinning of a ceilidh, and soon Home-Counties ladies will be swirling arm in arm with city fellows, and even the grannies will be stomping like Cossacks.

Alongside the esprit de corps that can be conjured within minutes by a simple ceilidh we might set the experience of teachers at tough inner-city schools, who have often witnessed how even the most troubled and difficult lads find a transforming sense of identity in learning "modern partner dancing" to competition level. It seems to channel their painful emotions into a welcome form of physical expression, and every dimension of their lives grows more gentle and considerate as they learn on the dancefloor to work empathetically with their female partners.

There's time-honoured wisdom in the hand-to-hand dance.

Nelson Mandela (left) spars with professional boxer Jerry Moloi.

Adult play-fighting

If dancing together can achieve wonders, there is compelling evidence, too, for the psychological goodness of rough-and-tumble activities. Let's not forget that Nobel Peace Laureate and the first black president of South Africa Nelson Mandela was an accomplished amateur heavyweight boxer in his twenties and thirties (see above). Amateur boxing clubs have long been a way of bringing self-control and compassionate consideration to angry young men. Studies of lifetimes support this observation:

Aikido: the way of love

In the Japanese form of self-defence called Aikido, "do" means "the way of", and "Aiki" means "love". Denis Burke Sensei, 7th Dan Aikido Yuishinkai, of the Isshinkai School of Aikido, explains some of the philosophy behind this martial art:

When two or more opposing forces meet, the result can be creative, perhaps forming an idea, a team, a friendship, or love. In physical-contact sports, judgement and apathy are attitudes that are not remotely viable; they have to be left behind for players to progress, which as I see it leaves the way open for love. As people become more accustomed to physical contact they seem to become more connective and open to others ... more open and comfortable with unconditional love. What all that boils down to is how easy it is to work with them and get on with them socially, and that can only be good for their prospects in life.

Boxing clever

A psychological study of the 1997 Cambridge University Boxing Club in their centenary match against Oxford observed some of the transforming qualities of contact sports. After one hundred years, the score in terms of matches won and lost stood neck and neck, and the century's decider was fought in front of a capacity crowd of over a thousand spectators. Wearing heavily padded gloves and head-protectors, the young men (aged between 18 and 35) weaved around toe to toe while swapping punches with a complete stranger. What made it all the more remarkable was that none of these chaps had ever boxed before, and their six months of intensive preparation had entailed quite a journey, not least of which were the traditional matches against the officers of the Royal Military Academy Sandhurst, and then the ratings of the Royal Navy. Interviewed alone, every one of these boxers-in-training ranked the whole experience alongside the greatest challenges of their lives thus far. This is quite a claim when one considers that among their ranks was a former RAF fighter pilot reading philosophy, a Californian physicist studying for his PhD, a millionaire barrister, a quietly spoken first-year boy with a karate black belt, a black Texan who was a West Point-trained army lieutenant turned investment banker, and a local Cambridge lad who'd left school apathetic aged sixteen only to feel ravenous for a university education several years later. Each told of the psychological transformation wrought within them by the ritualized confrontation of boxing – how it brought self-respect and respect for the other fellow, and a calm gentleness to their behaviour outside the ring.

the Harvard Study of Adult Development (described on pp.194–195) revealed that young men who, in their teenage years and early twenties, frequently played contact sports (which in those days meant wrestling and American football for that group) were far more likely to meet with health and success in *every* aspect of their future lives than young men who did not take part in such sports. Such is the magic of hands-on.

In light of its nurturing effects, it's deeply regrettable that while educators at the coal face are increasingly aware of the benefits for young people of all ages of having their hands on each other, nonetheless educational policy-makers are still promoting screen and keyboard technologies and learning-on-your-own as the dominant methods for classroom work. Quite the opposite approach would seem to be required: we should help our young people become truly comfortable in their physical relationship with themselves and those around them. We're better at this strategy with primary-school children, but it is teenage boys and girls who most need to develop this physical-social comfortableness, at a time when touch too easily becomes tainted as a sexualized or violent act, rather than something playful, sporting and benevolently social. (Of course, *welcome* sexual contact can be one of the most exquisite forms of benevolent touch, and is considered on pp.150–154.)

We all of us put ourselves at risk of illness when we neglect our sociability by cutting ourselves off from others and moving through life as if in a vacuum-sealed bag. Far better that we learn to move together cheek to cheek, hand in hand, body against body, whether in dance, contact sports or play-fighting. There was a saying among the old Italian Mafia: "A good friend helps you move house. But *a really good friend* will help you move a body."

Full-bodied relationships

The face-to-face real-time presence of another person has a magic to it that communication technology and modern lifestyles should not be allowed to jeopardize. There are many things that no amount of emails and texts can tell us. Those technological substitutes are literally unwholesome, in that they lack the vital dimensions of a full-bodied personal exchange: the physical posture and gestures, the scent and skin complexion, the facial expression and eye movements, the rate of breathing or a breath held. Like hearing live music compared to its digital equivalent, there appears to be a reverberation and intensity in being with someone that cannot be mimicked. Besides which, simply making time to be there with the other person, time in which to converse patiently, already communicates a great deal of good will.

Seeing eye to eye

Our being able to look long and deep into someone's eyes tells us much about how we feel about them, and how we feel about ourselves. If we find eye contact difficult, if we shy away from it and catch someone's gaze only fleetingly, then this is telling us something we need to listen to and understand:

▶ **Do we lack self-confidence or self-esteem?**
▶ **Is it something about the other person that's putting us off?**
▶ **Or is it just possible that we're falling in love?**

In any event, we should do something about it. It's worth taking stock of just whose eyes we're willing and happy to meet. Being around people who are wrong for us, who don't bring out our best sides, is something we had best be aware of and put right.

A word in your ear

A voice can be as attractive as any face, body or movement, and many of us can quickly recognize the voices of film stars from a previous generation: the *shlurred* speech of Humphrey Bogart, the slight hesita-

A song in your heart

When was the last time you sang out loud at the top of your lungs? Because it seems singing really is a tonic for body and soul. Scientists at the Goethe University of Frankfurt took saliva samples of singers in an amateur choir before and after an hour's rehearsal of Mozart's Requiem. They found that the singing had dramatically stimulated the immune system that fights disease, as well as notably improving the performers' mood.

Likewise, Professor Gene Cohen of George Washington University has followed a group calling themselves the Senior Singers Chorale, whose ages range from 65 to 96. Compared with their elderly neighbours, the senior singers suffer less depression, require fewer visits to the doctor, take fewer medications and partake in more activities.

Better still, it's not just the singer who benefits. Studies suggest that hearing singing voices can contribute to premature babies being able to leave intensive care a few days earlier than they would otherwise. The remedial effect of musical sounds is also evident in a study by the International Society for Music in Medicine, which looked at 90,000 patients in post-operative phases of surgery. Nearly all the patients said listening to their own choice of music during their recovery helped them relax, a claim substantiated by their using fifty percent less than the recommended dose of sedatives.

So the message is clear. Our singing voice should not be confined to campfire circles, shower rooms and car journeys when an old favourite comes on the radio. Let's join a local choir, or a Gilbert and Sullivan light opera group. Let's team up for some a cappella, or search out some blues or soul. But whatever we do, at work or at play, let's practise using song not only to reflect but to rally our spirits. And if someone demands of us "What is there to sing about?" we might well borrow the words of the mandolin-playing Captain Corelli. When held at gunpoint by the passionate young Greek woman who asks him how he can sing when there are people dying in the world war that has come to her island, the Italian captain replies in all earnestness: "There is singing when babies are baptized; when you celebrate a marriage; men sing as they work; soldiers sing as they march into battle; and there is singing when people die. I have always found something in life worth singing about, and for that I cannot apologize."

tion of James Stewart, the deep burr of Richard Burton or Sean Connery and the musical butter-smooth intonations of Cary Grant or Katharine Hepburn. These days, film-star voices are far less distinctive, largely because the emphasis is now on action rather than character. But for you and me "resting" from our Hollywood careers, our voices are still a remarkable asset.

"Let your breath and voice be connected to your groin!", says Patsy Rosenberg, one of the UK's leading authorities on voice training, and the ways in which we might develop our voices to better reflect the richness of our personality. We are urged to use wide-open mouth movements, and to support our voice with full, deep breaths, which in themselves require, create and project confidence. All of this conveys information. It's a well-documented phenomenon that a profoundly deaf person will speak with the accent of the region they grew up in, because they will have observed so acutely how the people around them shape their mouths to produce speech. Many of us, without consciously being aware of it, routinely take short, hurried breaths that barely reach beyond our upper chest or even the back of our throat. We then tend to creep the words out apologetically through half-closed mouths. Little chance there of reverberation, depth or conveying a sense of ourselves as a vibrantly physical person. We may have observed that so often the most self-assured person in the room is the one who feels comfortable speaking slowly and gently, as if the words are being freshly minted for the listener.

In respect of the importance of communication, General Lord David Ramsbotham, a former HM Chief Inspector of Prisons for England and Wales, believes that many crimes of violence and theft are committed by young offenders frustrated by their inability to express themselves verbally. Which is why, he argues, communication therapists can work wonders on a young persons' prison wing.

When YoungLivesUK.com (see pp.174–176) asked young men and women through anonymous open-ended questionnaires what features they found most physically attractive about another person, it was eyes, smiles and *voices* that came top for both genders, very probably because these "windows to the soul" said so much about how that person felt about themselves in relation to others. It's worth considering how we could learn to use our voice better, so as to bring alive one of our least developed but most potent physical qualities.

Clothing signals

We naturally use our choice of clothes to broadcast messages about ourselves, just as other creatures might change the colour of their feathers or skin to indicate their intentions. Since we each comprise several different identities depending on who we're with and what we're doing, it doesn't seem extravagant to have an outfit for each of our personality dimensions. And it's worth remembering that the characteristic thoughts, feelings and behaviours that comprise our identity are constantly evolving, which begs the question "Does our present wardrobe reflect our progress, or are we wearing a personality from the distant past?"

Such questions deserve our consideration because our clothing automatically communicates something to those around us, and all we can choose is to what extent we actively craft the message. This is quite an opportunity because how well we get on with the world depends not only on how we view life, but on how life views us, and some part of that impression will be shaped by our appearance.

Mentorship matters

Among the many studies of wonderfully impressive lives, you will not find one single example where someone has achieved creative heights without having at least one powerful source of deeply supportive love… a supportive relationship, whether in childhood or later years, that has served as a catalyst to their flourishing.

It is equally notable that studies have repeatedly shown that youngsters surrounded by troubles are nonetheless likely to do extremely well if they have at least one close relationship with a caring and competent individual. This might be a neighbour, teacher, coach or school friend. Even a profoundly troubled child can internalize their mentor's benevolence and so begin to view themselves as worthy of care, and treat themselves accordingly.

The transforming role of a supportive person

In the 1990s Columbia University psychology professors Charles Harrington and Susan Boardman jointly interviewed for a full three hours sixty very high-achieving mid-career professionals who had thrived despite seemingly disadvantaged backgrounds. Three quarters of these individuals reported that mentors had been very important in their careers, i.e. some guiding individual outside of their immediate family or closest relationships. This ratio prevails in all the subsequent research: most people who are living life with flying colours can point to a mentor, often several, even though there are some souls who make it through simply fuelled by at least one loving person, though no mentor.

The GoodWork Project is a joint research venture between leading psychologists at Harvard, Stanford and Chicago Universities, and the fields under investigation include genetic research, journalism, business, law, medicine and education, i.e. wherever the pace of development and market pressures might urge some form of corner-cutting when it comes to quality. The project has to date interviewed more than a thousand professionals, each of whom is widely regarded as quite outstanding by their peers. The essential question posed to these exceptionally high achievers was this: how did they tackle the challenge of consistently producing work that was of excellent quality yet also considerate of the well-being of the wider community? Or, as the researchers put it, what promotes "honourable work"? One of the findings so far seems to be that a key ingredient for good work to take place is good mentorship. It's particularly noteworthy that whereas the veteran professionals who were interviewed tended to recount how their own apprenticeships had strongly benefited from mentors and role models, by stark contrast the relative newcomers in our ultra-modern era felt an unhelpful sense of loneliness and being left to get on with it.

Our lives lack mentorship

"How to achieve your goals in life" and "How to enjoy the journey" were the two questions at the heart of the YoungLivesUK.com project which, on the brink of the new millennium, set out to garner the experience and insights of some of the most accomplished individuals of their generation, ranging in age between 16 and 78. The research team visited the UK's leading schools, blue-chip companies and elite organizations: from Eton College and Gordonstoun through to management consultants McKinsey & Co, the Rambert Dance Company, the Royal Marines and the Royal College of Art. Each establishment was asked to invite a handful of their most outstanding members to take part, in addition to which the project interviewed at length several dozen well-known indi-

Missing Dad

In the 1990s, the iconic "good" Terminator played by Arnold Schwarzenegger in the film *Terminator 2* (1991) was far and away the most popular fictional character for the imprisoned teenage boys serving sentences in the massive high-security Feltham Young Offenders' Prison near London's Heathrow airport. The explanation for their adulation seemed to be that the character was not only a physically and emotionally invincible man-like robot possessing the exact same qualities these pained and frightened boys desperately wished for themselves, but, even more poignantly, he had been sent back through time *to protect and befriend a fourteen-year-old boy who had no father*. It seems that this role of surrogate dad made the robot character all the more psychologically resonant and satisfying for these young inmates, above and beyond any other tough-guy film character that existed at the time.

The Terminator (Arnold Schwarzenegger) has been reprogrammed and sent back in time to protect the teenage John Connor (Edward Furlong) from a robotic assassin.

viduals, including authors Nick Hornby, Helen Fielding and Bill Bryson, footballer Gary Lineker, journalist Kate Adie and former SAS commander General de la Billière.

The YoungLives research was attempting to harvest some hard-won life-skills wisdom from these highly successful individuals, but the responses also highlighted a worrying trend visible across British society: in short, our technology-driven, high-pressure lifestyles are leaving less and less time for mentorship and emotional support by parents, extended family, teachers and trainers. (For more on the detrimental effects of our high-tech, high-pressure lifestyles, see Chapter 9.)

Particularly telling were the results of the one-to-one and small-group interviews with some of the younger participants in the study. Two aspects of growing up had far and away brought the most pain to these young people in their teens and mid-twenties. These were:

▶ **their lack of self-confidence**, i.e. the confidence to speak their mind, ask for help, declare their most pressing hopes, fears and passions, or to step out from the crowd

▶ **the absence of a mentor** with whom to freely broach life topics felt to be of crucial importance to them, from career choices to personal relationships.

This universal hunger for mentorship is reflected in the blockbuster films of our era – everything from *Star Wars* and *Men in Black* to *The Lion King* and *Harry Potter*. But it is by no means a uniquely postmodern ailment. *All Quiet on the Western Front* was published in 1928 by Erich Maria Remarque, who as a working-class German teenager had seen action as an infantryman in the trenches of World War I. The story is narrated by a young German soldier, Paul, who sums up his generation's feelings of betrayal as they come to realize that those they have looked up to as father figures are not, after all, worthy of their respect and trust but are responsible for starting a senseless war:

> For us lads of eighteen they ought to have been mediators and guides to the world of maturity … We often made fun of them and played jokes on them, but in our hearts we trusted them. The idea of authority, which they represented, was associated in our minds with a greater insight and a more humane wisdom. But the first death we saw shattered this belief.

What makes a mentor?

At its best, mentorship is a one-to-one, non-parental relationship that allows the mentee to confide in someone who understands something of their wider life, as well as their past experiences and aspirations for the future. To mentor, we don't need to be wise, we just need to be willing to care and to teach by our own good example. This close and considerate relationship between mentor and apprentice is a recipe for progress. Nobel-Prize-winning physicist Richard Feynman underlined just this point when he wrote: "The best teaching can be done only when there is a direct individual relationship between a student and a good teacher – a situation in which the student discusses the ideas, and thinks and talks about things." In respect of the potential for goodness contained within this benevolent role, we might each of us wonder to whom we could offer mentorship, and from whom we might request it. There are a number of formal mentoring schemes out there looking for volunteers:

▶ **NCH's independent visitors** befriend and support children who are in care in the UK; see nch.org.uk/getinvolved/index.php?i=117.
▶ **MENTOR** Is a US organization that puts would-be mentors in touch with mentoring schemes across the country; see mentoring.org.
▶ **BBBSA.org** is the website of Big Brothers Big Sisters of America, the largest mentoring organization in the US, where volunteers provide support and advice to youth.

If you feel you would like the help of a mentor in your own life, you may find that your employer or university or college offers a mentoring scheme. But probably you can think of someone you already know whom you admire and respect. If you feel uncomfortable about asking them to be your mentor, remember that most likely they will be flattered to be asked. Perhaps start by asking them for advice about a particular problem, and build on the relationship from there.

From mentors to role models

In the absence of a suitable mentor, identifying a role model in our everyday life can be a guiding beacon. In the late 1990s, Cambridge University's Dr Sarah Fitzharding conducted a quite unprecedented exploration of the coping strategies of over a hundred very highly accomplished men and women in the UK and US, all of whom were lesbian, gay or bisexual, and nearly all of whom had endured considerable adversity because of their sexual orientation. (Among their distinguished number were editors-in-chief of national magazines, leading entrepreneurs and world-recognized actors.) Towards the end of each interview, many of which went on for hours, Dr Fitzharding asked "What one thing above all else would have made the greatest improvement to your experience of growing up?"

More than half the participants gave essentially the same answer: "The example close at hand of an adult who was gay and out, and thriving in their personal and professional life."

As well as looking for role models in our everyday life, we could read the autobiographies of those people we most admire. This way, we can read in helpful detail how their progress in life was not overnight or unearned, as it can so often appear from afar, but was in fact a natural development of their well-channelled passions, leading to determined and realistic practice, supported by enduring positive relationships. (Chapter 7 expands upon these themes of what it takes to excel.)

It's rather nice to know that even Albert Einstein had the portraits of Isaac Newton and Michael Faraday watching over him as he worked at his desk. It's a reminder that all of us benefit from the inspiration of other people's lives, which can help us invest our own grand plans and humble day-to-day activities with something of their winning spirit.

Volunteering help

Giving of oneself to bring joy to another is one of life's great pleasures, but such actions should nourish the giver just as much as they benefit the recipient. The Harvard Study of Adult Development found that *personally satisfying altruism* was one of the hallmarks of the most healthy, fulfilled and accomplished lives. However, such health-bringing altruism should not be confused with the urge to self-sacrifice that comes from a shortage of self-worth masquerading as generosity to others. If we wish to be a force for good, we must be good to ourselves first of all. The more we can recognize and respect our own centre and sources of well-being, the more we will respect those of the people around us.

First off, we need to find something which speaks to our heart-felt interests. This can mean passing on the good that has made a difference in our own lives. Indeed, some of the healthiest personalities are characterized by individuals taking "creative revenge" on their own painful past by engaging in the sort of highly constructive charitable work which puts things right for the next generation.

We also need to be realistic about our own emotional resources, because planting trees with an environmental group is going to make very different demands on us than working with hospice patients close to death. If we're feeling fragile, then we should start off with something manageable, perhaps a couple of hours per week assisting someone who knows the ropes. On the other hand, if we feel game for it, why not partner up with a friend to create our very own voluntary project, and then offer to run this under the umbrella of an already registered charity, so as to minimize the admin required? If we're short of ideas, there are thousands of volunteering vacancies advertised on the following websites:

▶ **do-it.org.uk (UK)**
▶ **volunteermatch.org/search (US)**

Asking for help

Our volunteering to help others should make it far easier to ask for help ourselves. And the more it scares us to ask, the more we have to gain by doing so. The fear or shame or despair we feel in confiding our troubles in another are not signals warning us not to, they are simply saying "This is important, so pay attention and do something". By stark contrast, an ignored or inadequately resolved problem may not only hold us back, it will more than likely drag every other aspect of our life out of kilter too. This phenomenon simply reflects the profoundly holistic, interwoven nature of our well-being. We can't just vacuum-seal some part of our psychology and stick it in the deep freeze. Better we face up to things, whether it be a health scare or sexual anxiety, money worries or a relationship impasse.

In our quest for wise counsel, we need to own up to the possibility that even our best friends and family could, quite unwittingly, be jamming our problem in place, perhaps by their well-meaning acceptance of it, by their turning a blind eye, or by their treating it as taboo and not to be talked about so as to spare pain or embarrassment. That's why we might require a confidante well outside of our usual circle, someone who can see the whole picture through fresh eyes, and help us to do the same. What's more, we will probably have to broach things with several people before we hit upon something that works for us.

We should remember that asking for help is not the same as acting helpless. Quite the contrary: it can demonstrate our fighting spirit. In the snakes and ladders of life, we grow strong not in spite of fighting problems but *because* of fighting problems. The struggle strengthens us. But there's no rule that says we must do it alone. And let's be honest: what passes for a spirit of independence may in fact be masking our childish need to appear perfect. We should keep in mind, too, that it's not the problem that does the damage, it's what we do about it. If we wall it away, it can go rotten on us; but if we open it up to fresh air and bright light, it can heal and we can learn from it. What's more, by asking for help, we can be a role model of inspiration for those around us, sending a message that progress in life is not about concealing our demons.

Overcoming shyness

Are you too shy to offer a kiss or a helping hand, or to ask for one?

Shyness is a brutal jailor. If we're shy, though we might crave companionship, we cannot easily or freely declare our true hopes and hungers, nor ask questions or invite mentorship. We might also be timid about expressing our heart-felt affection, or be overly wary of accepting affection from others because we fear that we'll only be a disappointment to them. Shyness can indirectly bring us even more pain if we try to bolster ourselves with alcohol, or occasionally blow our tops with ill-judged outbursts of self-expression. We might even resent those who don't seem to suffer shyness. If any of these symptoms rings a bell of recognition, it might come as some reassurance that the BBC's Kate Adie, former SAS commander General Sir Peter de la Billière and Indian spiritual and political leader Mahatma Gandhi are just three individuals among many who have led lives as inspiring pioneers, yet have written about having to overcome considerable shyness. Funnily enough, if you trouble to ask them, *everyone* has been painfully held back by shyness in one type of situation, or at one time of life or another: the accomplished public speaker who's awkward with romance; the confident actor who's uncomfortable being themselves; the business person who's great talking money, but embarrassed by their body. Shyness is part and parcel of being a social animal.

Nonetheless, shyness is a phobia; that's to say it's an overblown and unhelpful fear. At both a conscious and a subconscious level, we fear being evaluated by our audience very likely because we fear being disapproved of or even humiliated. Paradoxically, our excessive anxiety to do well and create a good impression will not only inhibit our performance, it will also put our audience on edge. And as with any other phobia, we can accidentally allow it to dictate how we lead our lives, perhaps by narrowing our educational or career horizons, or by negatively affecting how we behave in our outwardly social or our intimately personal lives. However, we shouldn't think that the opposite of shyness is showing off, since the need to be the centre of attention is simply another form of being overly anxious about the impression we're creating, and to all intents and purposes the exhibitionist is woefully subservient to other people's opinions. The true opposite of shyness is being able to forget ourselves so completely that we can enter the psychological "flow" state (see pp.88–90) characterized by focusing our attention entirely on the task in hand and thereby increasing the likelihood that we will perform at the height of our abilities. All the better if we can put our audience so at ease that they, too, forget themselves.

But how do we achieve such a useful level of skill?

When faced with bullies, the more we try to dodge and avoid them, the more restricting they become. By far our best bet is to arm ourselves with some relevant know-how and then face up to those things that bring us dread. The good news is that when it comes to tackling shyness, what's known as Cognitive Behavioural Therapy (see pp.82–85) can be an ally to us in challenging all of our self-defeating assumptions which more often than not are rooted in out-of-date thinking habits from our earlier life experiences. As soon as we resolutely challenge their accuracy, our out-of-proportion fears, perfectionism, pessimism and self-consciousness will begin to melt away. By using imaginative role-play or a state of self-hypnosis (see pp.74–76), we can experience the possibilities of success in ever more demanding situations, and so gradually desensitize ourselves to being observed or evaluated. From there, we can move on to some manageable real-life try-outs, which by then will have lost much of their sting. Throughout all of this, we'll be aiming to associate the once feared situations with new feelings of physical relaxation and emotional pleasure. Aiding us in such work is the bread and butter of any good coach or therapist.

Dealing with difficult behaviour

The most difficult behaviour we'll ever have to deal with will probably be our own. Just think of all the unhelpful aspects of ourselves that we first have to spot, then own up to, and eventually do something about. We have our fears, our jealousies, our regrets and embarrassments; and then we have our loves, our passions, our pride and hopes. And all the time, we'll be fighting with ourselves and saying one thing and doing another. If we can begin to make progress when faced with these internal challenges – and we can turn to Chapter 2 for help with this – then working better with those around us will come all the easier for it. All the same, in the course of our life we are bound to encounter some who wish us harm and it's worth thinking about the best ways of responding when faced with such behaviour.

Those who wish us ill

We are social animals, for sure, but self-evidently we are not wired solely for peace. The frequent and commonplace conflicts and full-blown wars that have characterized human relations since the beginning of time have made that horribly clear. We are aggressive, competitive, acquisitive creatures, and whether as individuals or nations, these behaviours frequently run amok, when we seem to feel the urge to bully, beat or even obliterate one another.

It's unpleasant to think about, but some people will want to harm us. Perhaps because we're too beautiful or ugly, too rich or poor, too this colour or that size, too religious or too secular. They have their reasons, they wish us ill, and they may even act upon it. We might decide to challenge their behaviour with a surprising move of our own, perhaps enlisting peer pressure to derail their spite. Or we might simply distance ourselves as best we can from such embittered personalities. But perhaps our best defence against such behaviour is, for want of a better phrase, to count our blessings: if nothing else, these self-appointed enemies make us grateful for those who just as spontaneously wish us well, and who put themselves out to help us in a host of considerate ways. We might also be prompted to start taking better care of ourselves. Ironically, it can take someone else's *Schadenfreude* to set alight our own will to thrive.

Do unto others?

Reciprocity is advocated by most – perhaps all – of the major faiths. Confucius wrote: "What you do not wish for yourself, do not do to others." Sounding a similar note, Rabbi Hillel (in the first century BC) wrote:

Lessons from the War Room

The 2004 Oscar-winning documentary *Fog of War: Eleven Lessons from the Life of Robert McNamara* focuses on one man's time as US secretary of defense during both the Vietnam and Cold Wars. This riveting and moving film demonstrates how it was the sheer nuts and bolts of individual personalities and how well they did or didn't communicate with one another in difficult situations that determined the outcome of major world events.

One of the film's eleven lessons is "know thine enemy", illustrated by Mr McNamara's suggestion that the Cuban Missile Crisis (that brought the world to within hours of nuclear war) was resolved largely because President Kennedy was able to communicate with the USSR's President Khruschev via a hotline that printed telex messages. This medium allowed the two leaders to broker a solution which accommodated the personal and public needs of both.

A strongly related lesson is the importance of understanding the drives and goals of those who we *presume* oppose us. Mr McNamara explains that no such hotline existed between the leaders waging the Vietnam War, and this mistake was compounded by the American administration's having little appreciation of the history of the Vietnamese people. After speaking many years later with his North Vietnamese counterpart, Mr McNamara believes that a proper analysis of Vietnam's vehemently independent fighting spirit would have predicted that the country would have been extremely unlikely to acquiesce to USSR-backed communist forces, any more than it acquiesced to America's capitalist ones.

Finally, Mr McNamara emphasizes the transforming potential of empathy. In the closing frames of the documentary he observes that *rationality* is not enough for successful human relationships. Logic is only half of our decision-making repertoire, and when dealing with those around us we greatly benefit from our emotional insights.

"That which is hateful to you, do not do to your fellow; this, in a few words, is the entire Torah. All the rest is but an elaboration of this one, central point."

On the other hand, Oscar Wilde disagreed with this principle, pointing out that if our golden rule is "do to others as we would have them do to us", then we are simply imposing our own limitations on the other person. For instance, this would be a licence for the perfectionist and unloving parent to bully their child to greater work and to deny them love, or for a self-loathing individual to be cruel to others. Would it not be better to treat others compassionately according to their needs at that particular time?

Conclusions

It's probably because we're anxious creatures that we've survived for six million years and rule today, albeit tyrannically, in our animal kingdom. We have *evolved* to be nervous: nervous in the company of people, and even more nervous without them. It's not an illness – it's the way we're wired – but it's a challenge. There are other seeming contradictions, too, or are they simply complementary needs? We want to be accepted, but we want to be distinctive. We want to feel cared for but we want to feel free. Yet again, yin and yang are at work within us.

But why should all this matter so much? Why bother to reach out to the other?

Perhaps by honouring our social nature, by making friends and getting on with the world around us, we are creating a fertile medium in which to develop our passions so we might one day fall in love with life.

7

Playing wisely, working well

Playing wisely, working well

The better we balance, the further we reach

We tend to think of work and play as fundamentally opposed to one another, conflicting priorities competing for our time and energy. Yet they are just another example of how complementary opposites – yin and yang – can work together to help our lives flourish. The ability to "play wisely" often distinguishes those who excel in their work, because the better we are at balancing our lifestyle, the further we can reach out in any direction without derailing ourselves. In this chapter we'll learn how any one of us can achieve a high standard in our chosen endeavour, and how we can restore our energies and expand our skills through invigorating play.

What's play and what's work?

Play is any pleasurable activity that is done for its own sake; the joy is in the journey itself. Any appointed goals are only an excuse for our participation, and though it might be naughty and rule-breaking it is always good-natured. Playfulness in adults, just as much as in children, might take the form of humour, of games and sports, of hobbies and of holidays. It can include our gardening, our fishing, our carpentry and photography. Play needn't be *all* pleasure, though. It can be challenging and exhausting, and we often get hurt accidentally as part and parcel of the horsing around.

By contrast, we know something is work when it is *seriously* goal-motivated with painfully high real-life stakes, such as earning the money or the social status that will maintain or improve our quality of life. Professional sports and Olympic competition are *not* play, not least because the experience of taking part is deemed less important than the goal of winning. There's no room for the good humour and carefree experimentation that characterize true play. Our team-mates wouldn't laugh with us because there's too much "serious stuff" riding on the final score.

We also know something is work when, if it didn't offer the rewards of social status or money, we wouldn't choose to do it. Play is something we do for the sheer intrinsic joy of it, whether that joy be physical, emotional, intellectual or social.

Playing wisely

"As people grow up, they cease to play", wrote Sigmund Freud, "and they seem to give up the yield of pleasure which they gain from playing."

We tend to think it's just for children, yet "playfulness" can be one of our most helpful capacities throughout our lives, and warrants as much serious consideration as our work.

The benefits of play

As we learned in the previous chapter, regularly taking part in hands-on "play-fighting" such as wrestling, boxing or American football can be highly beneficial for every aspect of a young man's present and future life. Such rough-and-tumble play seems to put individuals at ease with themselves and the world around them. The same is true of such playful hands-on activities as partner dancing: they help develop the all-important social aptitude and easy rapport which is one of the cornerstones of a deeply healthy life.

Some arresting evidence for the benefits of play comes from an investigation of play in adult primates (including humans), recently conducted by the pioneering young Chilean evolutionary anthropologist Isabel Behncke-Izquierdo (a researcher at Oxford University). Isabel has found that species which are prone to play more, particularly as adults, tend to be more intelligent and social than less playful species (for example elephants and dolphins compared to sheep and deer).

On an individual level, the more playful individuals in a group tend also to be the more exploratory, and an exploratory spirit is a wonderful quality that can lead to increased capacity for innovation and creativity. Many of the most fulfilled and contributive lives around us are characterized by the spirit of adventurous exploration, experimentation and

Dolphins are famously playful and extremely capable mammals.

well-intentioned rule-breaking which lies at the heart of play. (This vital theme is further explored in Chapter 10.)

Very importantly, too, adult individuals that play more spend far less time scratching or picking at themselves in self-damaging ways. Zoo-keepers have reported how even an adult turtle will begin to self-harm

Laugh away the pain

Psychotherapists have long observed that if we can dare to pair an inner chuckle with our most painful or haunting memories or fears, we can significantly neutralize their emotional poison and erode their ability to hurt us. In strong support of this assertion, the Harvard Study of Adult Development (see box on pp.194–195) concludes that "a good sense of humour" – most particularly being able to poke good-natured fun at our own excesses of pride and painful failures – is probably the strongest single predictor of a life well lived; i.e. it is the skill most likely to create individuals characterized by rewarding intimate bonds, vigorous physical health, strong social networks and career success and satisfaction.

We know, too, that when hostages recount how they survived years of brutal confinement in desperate conditions, they invariably explain that their sanity was spared not only by escaping into their imaginations (see box on p.198), but by good humour – theirs, and that of their companions.

Such phenomena tally with findings from the New England Centenarian Study, founded by Dr Tom Perls in 1994 and now based at the Boston University Medical Center. The most comprehensive study of its type anywhere in the world, it has to date analysed several hundred centenarians (i.e. individuals aged 100 years or more). Of particular interest have been those even rarer folks who not only live until they're 100 (which is about 1 in 10,000 of us) but are still firing on all twelve cylinders in mind and body (which is about 1 in 7 of centenarians). The researchers have found that what most distinguishes these extraordinary individuals is their good-natured humour.

These remarkable human Volvos don't fit a single stereotype: some are rich, some poor; some are vegetarian, others love meat; and they represent a broad range of ethnic and racial backgrounds. But there are some common denominators: none of the centenarians studied so far reports ever having been a heavy drinker, and the five percent who *have* smoked gave it up by midlife. Very few are obese; the men particularly are *nearly always* lean. Crucially, they have been physically, intellectually and socially active people; living testaments to the motto "use it or lose it!" These healthy characteristics will have contributed to their disease-free lives; but their not needing to over-eat, drink or smoke may well have been a direct result of their being able to cope with the "slings and arrows of outrageous fortune" by dint of their good-natured wit and humour. The weakness of the study is that it relies on people's own accounts of their lives, and the accounts of their children (who are often themselves in their seventies and eighties), and such memories can be rose-tinted or just plain inaccurate. But the present speaks for itself; and the ability to be actively good humoured at 100-plus is hard to fake.

if kept in a tank with too little to interest it. The implications for adult humans are not hard to draw, says Isabel: "The more social playfulness we can engage in, the less prone we'll be to neurotic self-damaging behaviour, and the greater will be our capacity for resilience in life."

What's more, she says "creatures who play together tend to stay together". If we want creative and lasting partnerships, we must frequently make time for playfulness.

Play is our "wild card"

Play's greatest virtue in our lives is its versatility. Being flexible in our thinking, feeling, behaviour and attitude towards all that befalls us is a regular life-improver, and play helps us to do just that. In an upcoming publication Isabel Behncke-Izquierdo has deftly coined the term "Adaptive Joker" to capture the wonderfully versatile nature of play. Just as in a game of cards the joker is the "wild" card that can assume any role we choose for it, so our playfulness can be adapted to serve an infinite number of roles: we can be play-acting (perhaps to amuse), play-fighting (such as wrestling) or play-sexual (when flirting or dancing). We might offer a witty comment to defuse a tense situation, or poke fun at ourselves to heal some pain. Play, then, can be whatever we need it to be so as to help us adapt to a situation, and to progress within it.

Play practises our powers of deception

Successful work and successful play can both benefit from some element of "deception", i.e. concealing the truth for the purpose of a helpful surprise. The other person mustn't know what we're about to do, our true intention, because, if they guess it, our actions will fail or have their impact greatly reduced. Hence deception, as a complementary contrast to transparency and predictability, is a very useful ingredient in many aspects of our lives. Just think how a feint move on the sports field can easily wrong-foot our opponent, or how the feigned disinterest between a wanting-to-kiss couple can heighten the exciting chase. Some of the most captivating stories and arousing sexual experiences, some of the most successful business ideas and unstoppable crimes, rely upon their defying expectations. Pretending can work a treat; and our playtime very often practises our ability to fake things.

Yet, if deception can be very "winning", then so can unexpected honesty and frank self-disclosure. For instance, sharing personal truths in an unguarded way can surprise the other person and promote dramatic progress in a relationship. As ever, yin benefits from yang, and the wisdom is in knowing not simply how but when to apply one, and when the other.

Passive consumption pretending to be play

One of the special ingredients in play is that it always involves *active engagement* – physical, psychological or social – it's *never passive*. Let's not deceive ourselves about this: watching television or getting drunk are *not* play, yet they are very often our default options when we're trying to unwind after work.

The trouble with too much television

Watching television is the commonest pastime in the modern world, and the average person will spend more time doing this than any other activity other than work or sleep. Nothing else has so rapidly and profoundly affected how most of us use our free time. In 1950, barely ten percent of American homes had television sets, but by 1959 ninety percent did, which is probably the fastest ever spread of any technological innovation. (The uptake of the Internet has rivalled TV's record, but hasn't beaten it.) Yet the evidence is mounting that TV's detrimental effects on our lives are legion:

▶ **Television doesn't help our brain.** By measuring brain activity, it has been clearly shown that it takes considerably more brain involvement to read a book than to watch television. Reason being that when reading we're creating images in our mind's eye, whereas TV watching is simply the consumption of pre-packaged images. It is for this reason that many scientists believe too much TV allows our thinking skills to weaken. And because we're so passive in the face of television – because we're not processing the information by interacting with it, discussing it or generating responses – we learn very little, no matter how many documentaries we watch.

▶ **Television doesn't help our children.** No less an institution than the American Academy of Pediatrics recommends that infants under two be exposed to absolutely no television at all. This is because even very young babies just a few weeks old will strain to locate and look at the source of all this light and noise, and could grow up expecting television to be a necessary part of their environment.

▶ **Television doesn't help our social life.** Psychologists have observed that when it comes to leisure activities, the more you do of one thing, the more you do of all the others. So if you're big on DIY or

TV values

How can we be so sure that TV is to blame for all these social ills? Luckily for us, back in the early 1970s a team of researchers from the University of British Columbia documented what happened to the social life of a small Canadian town when television signals finally made it through to their valley. This "naturally occurring experiment" clearly exposed the detrimental effects of too much TV: not only did people take part in fewer community activities, but physical and verbal aggression increased among the town's schoolchildren, and their reading skills declined. In 1999, much the same phenomenon was repeated in the isolated kingdom of Bhutan when its ruler lifted a ban on television, allowing numerous cable channels to broadcast TV programmes to this tiny nation for the first time. The kingdom has suffered the dire consequences ever since: considerable increases in family break-up, crime, drug-taking and violence in schools. Bhutan's experience has been so shocking to its people that the king has since tried to re-take some of the ground sold to the small screen by passing laws about the sort of programmes that can be broadcast.

Brothers Sangay and Gyembo Dorji, from a village in eastern Bhutan, are mesmerized by the satellite TV they got just last year.

going out to the movies, it's likely you also take part in lots of other activities such as playing sport, hosting dinner parties or helping out at a voluntary organization. This equation is very reliable; but when it comes to TV, quite the reverse is true: we do less of everything. These past fifty years, TV watching has been a major culprit in the severe decline of every form of positive social involvement, within or outside of the home. Husbands and wives now watch three hours of TV for every hour they spend talking together, and six hours for every hour they spend in community activities.

What's the problem with a couple of drinks?

Harvard Medical School professor George Vaillant is one of the world's leading authorities in this field (not least because of his leadership of the Harvard Study – see box below), and he notes that rather than keeping tabs on how much we drink in terms of units, it's more revealing to consider what effect it has on us. Does our drinking cause us problems in any arena of our life: physical, working, social or personal? For instance:

▶ **Are we fully in control of if and when and how much we drink?**

▶ **Does it affect our behaviour in ways we'd rather it didn't?**

▶ **And does our drinking stop us doing the things we really want to, perhaps as regards our relationships, hobbies and work ambitions?**

The finest study of lifetimes ever completed

The Harvard Study of Adult Development is widely and justly regarded as the finest examination of twentieth-century lifetimes ever completed. Begun in the early 1940s, it originally set out to observe how the most promising youngsters of their generation (i.e. the healthiest in mind and body) would lead their lives. It was hoped much could be learned from tracking their "healthy development". (For this alone it is remarkable, because the vast majority of studies in medicine and psychology focus on those who are sick in some way.) The core group of participants, known as the Grant Cohort, comprised 268 Harvard undergraduates (largely from middling or wealthy families), recruited between 1939 and 1944. (It's said that the young JFK was among their number.)

The research began with a thorough evaluation of every aspect of the young men's lives and their family backgrounds. This involved medicals, psychiatric evaluations, tutor reports and in-depth face-to-face interviews with the participants and then their parents. From then on…

▶ **Every two years**, questionnaires asked the participants for information on many aspects of their personal, social and working life.

▶ **Every five years**, questionnaires asked the participants about their health, and this information was cross-referenced with reports from their personal physicians.

▶ **Every fifteen years**, the participants were interviewed to assess in greater depth how they were coping with life.

Since he took over directorship of the study in 1970, Professor George Vaillant has added data from two other long-term studies of human development:

▶ **The Terman Women Sample**: 90 women from Lewis Terman's study of 672 "gifted teenagers" from middle-class families (a study begun at Stanford University in the early 1920s)

One sobering realization is that overdoing alcohol is very likely to be the root cause, rather than a symptom, of serious difficulties such as chronic stress and depression, and a downward shift in our social and economic standing. We know this because the very best studies show that no amount of analysing the hardships of people's lives can predict who will and who won't develop problems with alcohol. By stark contrast, a person's problem drinking, if unchecked, will all by itself very likely foreshadow a clear degeneration in their physical well-being, personal relationships and career. In other words, alcohol can manufacture life-problems all of its own making. Just as poignantly, Professor Vaillant's work suggests that too much alcohol stops us developing emotionally, because it would seem that the anaesthetizing effects of

▶ **The Glueck Study**: a group of 456 men who grew up in comparative poverty in inner-city Boston, recruited in their teens between 1940 and 1945.

The participants in these studies were similarly questionnaired and interviewed at regular intervals over the course of their lives. Altogether, this amounts to a vast treasure-trove of data, which Vaillant and his team have used to explore what makes for a wonderful life. They have been particularly interested in the life-coping mechanisms of each individual. When faced with adversity, did they for instance retreat from problems into fantasy, alcohol or psychosomatic illness? Or did they negotiate the problems by skilfully channelling their emotional energy through such mechanisms as humour, dynamic action and mental rehearsal?

The researchers are now adding the results of DNA testing, brain-imaging and brain autopsy to their formidable data bank. What's very impressive is the negligible drop-out rate among participants over the seventy years the study has now been running, which means the picture that emerges should be unusually complete. Everyone gets counted, warts and all. Perhaps the study's greatest strength is that it is "prospective", observing what happens en route, rather than being "retrospective", i.e. asking people to recall and explain (often very inaccurately) what happened in the past.

Of course, the study does have its limitations: so many men, almost all white folks; the use of questionnaires which can be inaccurately and misleadingly answered (though these are supported by face-to-face, in-depth interviews and, in the case of the men, physician's reports). Nonetheless, the length and size and varied approaches of this study make it one of the best windows we have on how everyday lives develop across a lifetime, for better and for worse. For this reason, its conclusions on various key topics are referred to throughout this Rough Guide.

Professor Vaillant has written two excellent books based upon this marathon study to which he has devoted so much of his career, *Adaptation to Life* (1975/1995) and *Aging Well* (2002), which both make compelling reading.

Living deeply by drinking lightly

Many of us, from our early teens upwards, have probably spent almost every social occasion "just a little bit drunk". Not lying under a table singing "Yesh-terday", but just on the second glass of something that's left a warm glow inside and made everything seem rosier. We feel bolder, smarter, funnier and far more attractive, and all those well-laid plans and good intentions suddenly begin to seem strangely dispensable. But although boozing helps us feel bet-ter for a few hours, do those feelings come at too high a price? Perhaps it's time for a stock-take of the net benefits of boozing:

▶ **Does drink help me be more myself?** Nope, quite the opposite: the more we drink, the more it flattens out any distinguishing characteristics. Alcohol literally dilutes our identity: we begin to behave just like every other drunk person.

▶ **Does drink help me relax and unwind?** Sure, but it leaves us tired and irritable the following day.

▶ **Does drink help me get on with people?** Actually, this is the thing we might most regret about getting drunk: it comes in the way of our getting close to someone. Drink pretends it's making friends for us, but that's all part of the blur and illusion. The truth is that by not boozing, it's as if we're saying "I don't need to be drunk to enjoy your company. I don't need to be drunk to relax with you, confide in you and laugh with you." Staying clear and sober shows the other person just how much we appreciate them.

It's not a case of being anti-alcohol; it's more a matter of being pro-intimacy. A glass of fine wine or cold beer tastes a treat, but the second glass runs the risk of blurring our relationship with the *real* life around us. If we want to live more deeply, we need to focus hard so we can be closely connected and fully engaged. And if what we're doing or who we're with isn't sufficiently moti-vating for us, we don't want to mask that by consuming a chemical sticking plaster. We want to keenly feel what's going wrong so we can start to put it right. If our reality is to improve (and reality is, after all, the only place we can be together with the people we love), we've got to stay with it and learn to ride the ups and downs.

the drug prevent us from learning to react helpfully to the demands of life. We get stuck with the emotions of an angry teenager, until such time as we sober up.

We're probably the only person who really knows the full impact on our life of our relationship with alcohol, but if drinking is a problem (our drinking, or that of someone we love dearly), our medical practitioner will know a well-proven therapist who can help us develop the attitude and strategies to deal with it.

How's your relationship with reality?

In other words, what proportion of your thoughts and actions are intended to bring lasting improvements to your real-life circumstances, perhaps through careful planning or problem-solving or practising a skill? We might call such actions "reality-investing". By contrast, what proportion of your thoughts and actions do you use simply as a "quick-fix" so that you feel better immediately, with little regard for the medium or longer-term consequences? These quick-fixes would include bingeing on food or alcohol, making unrealistic plans, or lying and exaggerating; they are in effect "reality-distorting". Finally, how much of your time do you spend "reality evading" – that is, indulging in pure fantasy about absolute impossibilities, or wishful daydreaming about things that you're doing little to make happen? This third category also encompasses those activities we partake in because they allow us to disengage discreetly from the world, such as watching TV or surfing the web.

Thinking about these three categories, we may find that seemingly insignificant and unrelated activities we partake in are, on closer consideration, united by their common goal as regards reality, whether that be investment, quick-fix or evasion. It's worth becoming aware of any such bias in our behaviour, because our characteristic style of dealing with real life can have substantial effects on our well-being and progress. When interviewed at length in the YoungLivesUK.com study (see pp.174–176), young adults who were clearly high-achievers in various walks of life reported having resorted to far less reality-evading or reality-distorting practices while growing up than were recounted by their peers who hadn't gone on to excel at anything. The implication was that reality-investing thoughts and behaviour paved the way for more accomplished and satisfying living. It was equally striking that although all the young adults interviewed – both the high-achievers and the under-achievers – considered "wishful daydreaming" and "pure fantasy" to be a vital safety valve for unfulfilled needs and desires, they also recognized there was a danger of dreaming so ambitiously that real life seemed quite a let down. The study's conclusion was that fantasy and fiction might well refresh our spirits, inspire us or protect us from overload, but we're always better off guiding their fruits back towards real life with all its potency, unpredictability and camaraderie.

Hostages

Retreating into fantasy instead of engaging with life's challenges may be a wasteful move when we have everything to play for, but in extreme situations where we have no control over our external situation it can be a vital self-protective measure allowing us to preserve our psychological well-being. The memoirs of kidnap victims Brian Keenan (*An Evil Cradling*), Peter Shaw (*Hole: Kidnapped in Georgia*) and John McCarthy (*Some Other Rainbow*) recount how they would very often imagine lengthy conversations, flamboyant expeditions and vast undertakings in order to remove themselves from the physical and psychological tortures of solitary confinement in filthy, lightless cells and the constant threat of beatings, mutilation or death. The post-traumatic mental health of these men is testimony to the effectiveness of their doing so.

In support of this critique of fantasizing and wishful daydreaming, the Harvard Study (see box on pp.194–195) noted that individuals who took frequent and full-length holidays, being sure to leave their work far behind them, went on to lead some of the healthiest lives in all possible terms: mind, body and relationships. By stark contrast, individuals who were prone to spend a lot of time in extravagant fantasy lives would rarely if ever take holidays. These high-fantasy/low-holiday individuals seemed to lead much-troubled lives precisely because of their unwillingness to engage with reality, and their unwillingness to disengage from work by means of active play and holidaying. Fantasies were no substitute for the health-bringing nature of real-life playfulness.

Active recuperation

If we spend sixty hours per week desk-bound in highly cerebral conversations, or staring at a computer screen, we can be sure that sitting in front of the television is a useless antidote. What we need to do instead is counter-balance our working life with an equal and opposite activity, which means maximum refreshment would come from getting outdoors for some highly physical and emotionally expressive pursuits. Perhaps gardening or hill-walking, sailing or singing, or the local amateur dramatics. If they're carefully designed to fulfil our deepest needs, these compensating worlds will make our time off-duty a real asset. It seems that the greater the difference between the various parts of our life, the more thoroughly we can play each part and yet still balance our mind, body

Albert Einstein relaxes with his fiddle while sailing on the S.S. *Belgenland* in 1931.

and soul. The better we learn to "actively balance", the further we can stretch ourselves. It seems that rather than being diluted by this approach, our calling in whatever form will, like a log fire, burn all the more brightly for us letting in some air. Albert Einstein loved to play the violin to calm his mind. The young Luciano Pavarotti played soccer and tennis every spare moment throughout his growing up; and when he became an acclaimed opera singer, he made time to be around horses to calm himself before and after performances.

As these folks illustrate, having a healthy life-balance doesn't mean settling for a sort of beige-coloured mediocrity. Rather, this ebb and flow between investing in ourselves and expending our energies allows us to feel renewed each morning, and to enjoy journeying ever more deeply into our passions. To excel at something, we need to excel at recuperating ourselves. Play contains elements of exploration, laughter, relaxation and surprise, all of which are foundational ingredients of the well-balanced well-being cake. Which is why we adults would do very well to bring a larger slice of it back into our lives.

The Lord is my shepherd;
I shall not want.
He maketh me to lie down
in green pastures.
He leadeth me
beside the still waters.
He restoreth my soul.

The familiar words of Psalm 23 remind us of the restorative effects of the natural world.

Working well

If ever you find yourself pondering wistfully those things you dearly wish you were really good at, you'll be interested to hear the following: just about any individual of average learning ability is quite capable of acquiring a professional level of competence in virtually any field of endeavour, no matter whether this be with a musical instrument or foreign language, fiction writing or fine art, science or sport.

That's a wonderful thought, perhaps rather unbelievable, so how do we know it's true?

Old dogs and new tricks

When it comes to learning new skills, it's good to know that it's not our age that's important, it's our attitude and our actions. Our brain, like so much of our body, is extremely malleable and at any age we benefit from stimulating ourselves with new learning, whether physical, emotional or intellectual.

For instance, if musicians in their seventies keep practising, they remain almost as dexterous in body and brain as much younger souls, and their depth of experience more than makes up for any shortfall. As long as we pay heed to the principle of "use it or lose it", we've little to fear. Sadly, Pablo Picasso admitted he allowed himself to stagnate in later years and even joked bitterly that he was painting fakes of himself. By contrast, Verdi's writing of time-honoured operas spanned fifty years largely because he remained so determined to develop and keep versatile by exposing himself to new and diverse ideas. Yes, it seems pure mathematicians do some of their finest work in their twenties, while athletes very often peak in their early thirties. We might also note that the Fifth Symphony, the Sistine Chapel and *Hamlet* were all works of art achieved by individuals in their late thirties. However, Winston Churchill was sixty-five when he set out to lead Britain against the Nazis in World War II, and Titian was still producing great masterpieces, such as *The Death of Actaeon* (see opposite), right up until his death at the age of approximately ninety.

In short, it seems that Mother Nature does not intend that old age be the price we pay for living. Ageing is not a disease, nor does it bring inevitable decline. It's an opportunity – extra time with which to make a positive difference and explore more deeply our relationship with life so that the "old familiar" can be seen through fresh eyes. The American poet Henry Wadsworth Longfellow wrote:

For age is opportunity no less
Than youth itself, though in another dress,
And as the evening twilight slips away
The sky is filled with stars, invisible by day.

Some of the best evidence is from the lifetime's work of Michael Howe, one-time psychology professor of Exeter University, who carefully analysed the routes to expertise of some of history's most eminent achievers, as well as modern-day athletes and musicians. After a whole career spent studying the development of exceptional abilities, Professor Howe declared he had found absolutely no evidence to support the widespread belief that we need some inborn head start by way of special gifts or talented genes. On the contrary, we can all of us *learn* to get good at things, so long as we can muster a few key ingredients (of which more below).

In support of this assertion stands the work of one of America's most celebrated professors of educational psychology: Tufts University's

Titian, the Venetian master, was around eighty when he painted *The Death of Actaeon*, but nonetheless his work conveys a deeply sensual and sweeping vitality. The goddess Diana, in revenge for Actaeon spying on her bathing, transforms him into a stag, whereupon he's devoured by his own hunting dogs.

Robert Sternberg, who is a world leader in the field of competence and expertise. He, too, argues that high levels of skill must be learned in the course of life rather than inherited at birth, and that what we commonly and unthinkingly refer to as "talents" are actually skills developed through practice.

The views of these two professors are largely based on thorough interviews with performers of different skill levels recounting their training regimes since their earliest days. Top performers (in music, sports and chess, for instance) have often had highly structured practice routines from an early age, so the number of hours and the nature of such practice can be recalled with some accuracy. These autobiographical accounts are then cross-referenced with the memories of the performer's parents and coaches to give as clear a picture as possible.

These retrospective studies (which are of course prone to over- and under-estimates and other accidental distortions of what actually took place) are backed up by other studies by psychologists tracking the development of promising individuals in real time as they progress from early studentship to maestro status. (You will recall that this studying of lives as they evolve is one of the great strengths of the Harvard Study of Adult Development, outlined on pp.194–195.)

The work of these and other researchers in the field of expertise suggests that there are at least four key ingredients which need to be in plentiful supply if we're to learn to excel in our chosen pursuits. These are:

▶ **Lots of determined and realistic practice** that always aims to improve rather than just go through the motions. This determined practice, the sheer amount of it and how realistic it is in terms of what will be required of us on the day are the most important factors determining how good we get at something.

▶ **A heart-felt, self-motivating passion** to fuel those long hours of challenging practice. Pushy parents or bullying teachers might extract results for a while, but such "outside" motivations will eventually backfire.

▶ **Warm support**, enthusiasm and encouragement from someone deeply important to us.

▶ **A rich learning environment** comprising keen-as-mustard practice buddies, mentoring coaches and inspiring role models.

Let's take a closer look at these factors.

Putting in the hours

Aristotle was a great believer in the importance of practice to strengthen our performance in every dimension of life, and observed that "we grow self-controlled by exercising our self-control, and courageous by performing acts of courage". One-time US president Thomas Jefferson seconded that notion more than two thousand years later when he wrote that "disposition of the mind, like limbs of the body, acquires strength by exercise".

We are used to thinking of artists as being naturally gifted, but even great painters have insisted that their ability is simply the result of practice. J.M.W. Turner put his accomplishments down to "dammed hard work", while Joshua Reynolds believed that the faculty to draw could only be acquired by "an infinite number of acts".

Musical ability is another quality that is commonly considered to be something you've either got or you haven't – and child prodigies such as Mozart are held up as proof that it's all in the genes. But studies have shown that 3000 hours of determined practice will reliably turn a novice musician into an impressive amateur (perhaps the best in their school). In other words, getting good at an instrument requires the equivalent of two hours per day, six days per week, for five years. Yes, Mozart was a competent violinist by the age of six, but his father was a pre-eminent music teacher who made his three-year-old son practise for several hours per day. Bearing in mind the 3000 hours that little Amadeus must have notched up by age six, we should be more surprised if he *hadn't* become a prodigy.

This 3000-hour rule of thumb seems to apply across almost any field of endeavour, whether it be salsa dancing, horse-riding or speaking a foreign language. By way of comparison, it requires on average a total of 10,000 hours to reach professional standard. Numerous studies have also confirmed that it takes at least *ten years* of full-time dedicated practice to become world-class in just about any domain.

This is not to say that personal motivation, training techniques or the quality of tutoring are not also vitally important; it's just that the number of practice hours which individuals recollect doing, or are known to have done, will all by itself accurately predict the heights to which they have soared – whether that be state, national or international standard.

TV versus expertise

On average, we watch between three and four hours of television every day. But even if we clock up "only" two hours a day, we'll still be spending a whopping one eighth of our waking life watching TV. If we live until we're eighty (which most of us will), we'll have spent the equivalent of nearly ten solid years of our waking life watching television. And, as we've seen, ten years of dedicated and realistic practice would be enough to make us an international authority in our chosen field.

So there's the trade-off right there: do we want ten years of TV, or would we prefer the pride and rewards of expertise?

We have no choice about the 25 years of our life we're going to spend in the health-bringing state of sleep, but we do have total choice about that ten years in front of the TV. On our deathbed, are we really going to whisper to our friends "My only regret is that I didn't catch more episodes of *The Simpsons*"? For sure it's a great show, but there are so many other things that deserve to be done… and done well.

For instance, by the time they're 21, music academy scholars with 10,000 hours under their belts have the skills to become professional concert performers, whereas the ones who've clocked up only 5000 hours can only become teachers.

Real-as-possible practice

We learn to do things well much faster and more effectively if we learn under the very same physical and psychological conditions in which we intend to perform them. This principle applies to all activities of mind and body, no matter it's football, self-defence, conversing in a foreign language, giving a speech or a musical performance, dancing or going out on a date. It's a shame, then, that so many training regimes are artificially subdivided into an activity's component parts, rather than being holistic.

Take sports, for example. Whether it's tennis or rugby, there is little or no gain in practising our ball skills in isolation: we need to develop them as part and parcel of our in-the-moment strategies against a wily opponent who is trying equally hard to outwit us. For sure, we might practise our serve fifty times in succession, but it should always be against a live opponent on the other side of the net, who is shifting position and trying everything in their power to distract us. This way, we practise together all the physical and psychological demands of the task.

The story is similar when it comes to learning a foreign language. Many of us will have had years of grammar lessons and classroom practice, and perhaps even a fortnight's visit overseas, but at the end of it all our speaking and listening ability probably reached, at its snow-capped peak, to about the level of a six-year-old child falteringly ordering a Big Mac, and yet not understanding the waitress's question about fries and mayonnaise. We never came anywhere close to being able to talk ourselves into a friendship, a love affair or a job. A far better way to learn a language would be to go live among the native speakers for a year, and completely leave behind our mother tongue. If we immerse ourselves in the new language – listening to the radio, reading a daily newspaper, writing it every opportunity we can create, and even trying to think with the new vocabulary – we'll be passably fluent before the year is out.

Formal education and professional training in general, whether at school or university level or beyond, seems to repeat the limitations of such approaches. Even in the applied subjects, we spend the majority of our time reading vast textbooks of supposed facts and fashionable ideas, and spend just a fraction of our time actually generating and writing up our own ideas, let alone actually doing things for ourselves in meaningful real-life situations. Which of us hasn't spent weeks reading up for examinations only to discover that we're rubbish at writing it down in sixty minutes, or answering questions "on our feet", let alone applying our hard-won knowledge when we suddenly find ourselves in the world of work?

Keeping things whole in the workplace

Work, like everything else in life, benefits from a holistic approach. Karl Marx criticized capitalism for creating the Industrial Revolution and the factory conveyor-belt system that fractured production into a series of stages, and so deprived the artisan of the satisfaction of seeing his product or service from first idea to final form. And for sure, there's something very demoralizing about only doing one part of a job. Modern car companies have discovered that it's better to allow people to create small teams and let these teams produce their very own cars from start to finish than to simply have individuals perform one small part of the production-line process. In light of this, it's worth considering how we could foster such a holistic approach in our own workplace.

Which of us hasn't tirelessly practised our ball skills against a wall, but then found ourselves awkwardly out of position on the field of play? Who hasn't rehearsed the warm embrace in one's head, but floundered when it came to the doorstep kiss? We learn far, far better when things are for real, or as near as makes no odds. It is perhaps for this reason that when General Sir Peter de la Billière took charge of the Special Air Service halfway through his career in the regiment, he insisted on his troops using live ammunition in training exercises, despite the obvious risks. The SAS fast earned its reputation as one of the most reliably effective military units in the world.

There is no substitute for undiluted reality. The real world is wonderfully interwoven and we need to learn to live it that way.

Warm encouragement

In the 1980s, the young psychologist Dr Lauren Sosniak studied 22 young Americans who were the leading concert pianists of their generation. In trying to work out how they'd done so well for themselves, she found some unexpected results. For instance, rather than coming from musical dynasties as we might have presumed, half of these pianists had parents who didn't play an instrument themselves. Nor did the young pianists show precocious early ability. Though they began with their instrument at around six years of age just like all of their contemporaries, most of them weren't shining in competitions even in their early teens. It was sheer determination to succeed that helped them to keep going. Nor were their first teachers musical virtuosos. Their later teachers were certainly top musicians, but the distinguishing qualities of those early teachers as remembered by their pupils were warmth and encouragement. The only finding that wasn't surprising is that the mums and dads were equally warm and encouraging, not only towards their children and their frequent and regular practice, but also towards the teachers themselves. For instance, a parent would frequently sit in on lessons to show their support.

Sosniak's findings have been borne out by recent research with much larger numbers of musicians, across a wide range of instruments. They're also corroborated by the rags-to-riches tale of world tennis champions Venus and Serena Williams. The sisters' parents had never even played

Ten-year-old Venus Williams basks in the loving support of her father Richard.

tennis – their father was a security guard and their mother a nurse. Nor did the girls receive expensive coaching: remarkably, Dad only stopped coaching the sisters himself, despite having no prior experience, when the girls were about fourteen years of age, at which time he handed their training over to a seasoned professional. But the sisters were encouraged by their parents to play from their earliest days and, very importantly, they had each other to play against. Their subsequent career vividly illustrates that even stark poverty need be no hindrance to developing exemplary skills, provided realistic practice is combined with warm encouragement from those we love.

Rich learning environment

There's often a presumption by parents and educators alike that strengths will automatically flourish of their own accord. But the fact is that strengths need specialist nourishment if they're to thrive.

Professor Howe of Exeter University has studied the lives of many famous high-achievers, and found that for the most part their exceptional achievements didn't come out of thin air: these people's strengths and passions had been nurtured in a rich learning environment full of opportunities and inspiration.

Let's take for example Charles Darwin. After a thoroughly privileged childhood happily engrossed in natural history and surrounded by excellent mentors, the young Darwin then had five years on H.M.S. *Beagle* with bags of cabin-time to swot up on his subject, and then the thumping good example of the Galapagos Islands. Within two years of returning home, he had formed his theory of how "natural selection" could explain evolution.

Michael Faraday, who made such great contributions to the development of electricity as a form of power, came from a far less privileged background. But nonetheless circumstances combined to supply him with a splendid scientific education. After leaving school at just thirteen in 1804 he went straight into a seven-year apprenticeship as a bookbinder, a job which exposed him to all the finest scientific books of his era. Better still, he could take full advantage of this because his devoutly religious parents had taught him to read so well. He was also deeply influenced by an inspiring self-help book called *The Improvement of the Mind* by Isaac Watts, and his kindly employer set up a mini laboratory to indulge the teenager's burgeoning interests.

The lives of Darwin and Faraday demonstrate how helpful the right circumstances can be in allowing our passions to develop: if Darwin hadn't got that place on the *Beagle* voyage (and he very nearly didn't), perhaps he'd never have put two and two together in the way he did.

But what's more, these examples raise the possibility that dedicated practice and the right environment in which to excel could be enough to take any one of us from beginner to big shot, no matter what genes we're born with. Once we see what enriching educations these great men received, perhaps it's no longer necessary to assume inborn gifts to explain the heights to which they reached.

It is through the study of such wondrous lives that we can begin to appreciate how these acorns did not necessarily fall from a different oak tree from you and I; they simply fell into extremely fertile soil. It's no accident that so many giants of history strenuously denied possessing "special thinking powers" of any kind, claiming instead that they were distinguished only by the sheer joy they took from their work.

The power of concentration

Making major improvements requires absolute concentration, and such an intense focus of attention is a strain to achieve. It's notable that Charles Darwin and Isaac Newton were both able to focus their attention not only for hours but for days at a time, as they worked through a problem. (They would then take to their beds for equivalent amounts of recuperation.) Today's fashion for multi-tasking is the nemesis of concentration, which means if we're half-heartedly practising our salsa steps or golf swing while making a mental grocery list, we're severely reducing the benefits. One classic study demonstrated that stroke patients trying to relearn physical skills while being chatted to by a cheery nurse recovered far more slowly than a comparison group of patients who were simply encouraged to attend completely to the task. It's telling, too, that many world-class novelists work only in the mornings, just until their

Relaxing our minds for rich rewards

Air Commodore Professor Christopher Andrew, a historian for Britain's Secret Intelligence Service (SIS), has studied how World War II cryptanalysts such as Alan Turing broke the enigma code used by German forces. He observes that code-breakers required an eccentric mind capable of thinking laterally and intensely at the same time. What's really noteworthy is that a couple of these chaps were notorious for doing their best work in a hot bath, for hours at a time; and indeed one man's allotted office was simply a bathhouse. (He eventually married the female soldier who valiantly served him the soap and loofa.) The highly relaxed mind can stretch far more broadly and quickly than a tense one, just like a relaxed body, so this story of the "bathhouse breakthrough" isn't so daft. Learning to relax deeply and often is a vital mind–body skill if we're to excel in our work. Play produces just such relaxation of mind and body, which is part of what makes it such an important ally of our work. We can also all benefit from some simple relaxation techniques, as described on pp.74–75.

full concentration can no longer be maintained. Then they park their quill and spend the rest of the day recuperating in readiness for their next intense immersion.

The acclaimed musician and conductor Daniel Barenboim (latterly of the Berlin Philharmonic) said he tries always to "play as if it was my first time, and will be my last".

Pushing beyond the skills plateau

To win, you have to dare to lose.

A study of first-class ice skaters by Professor Janice Deakin of Queen's University, Canada, observed how the best among them spent nearly fifty percent more time than their rivals attempting new moves and so incurring numerous mistakes, while their less accomplished peers more often repeated what they could already do well.

It's this absence of self-editing, self-inhibiting fear about doing "the wrong thing" that can unleash a performance that has the throttle wide open. It is by these means that high-flyers distinguish themselves, because while reaching for the stars, they do not allow themselves to be daunted by the number of times they fluff it. If we become afraid of the consequences of failure – these might be criticism, embarrassment or blame – then this fear will tend to inhibit or even paralyse our skills, and we simply "choke". Either that or we play for safety and take too few risks, which only leads to underachievement. Our performances, our career, our whole life could remain lacklustre because of such self-defeating anxiety.

Perfectionism is the enemy of success

Nothing is more inhibiting of a pleasurable sense of progress than its arch-enemy, perfectionism. Perfectionism is a "false ally" pretending that it's merely trying to do a decent job, while secretly it feeds the malign feeling that whatever we are, or have, or try to do just isn't good enough.

Perfectionism tends to result in painfully slow progress or full-blown paralysis – either that, or the sort of manic activity that ends in isolation, self-damage and exhaustion. No matter which, perfectionism cruelly

John Baldwin and Rena Inoue made history in 2006 when they became the first couple to land a throw triple axel in Olympic competition. The move is extremely difficult, but for that reason earns high marks from the judges.

scuppers our loves, our health and our happiness. Worse still, it can too easily infect any and all parts of our life: from how we shop (for instance, never being able to make a final decision, or overspending in an attempt to get the best) all the way through to how we regard our body, our choice of romantic partners and our professional progress.

One antidote is realizing that high performance most often comes from being productive, not perfectionist. Professor Dean Keith Simonton's analysis of accomplished lives shows this fundamental rule holds fast across all disciplines and applies at any age. He notes, for instance, how Shakespeare wrote his smash hit *Hamlet* one year, and the not nearly so successful *Troilus and Cressida* the next; and though he produced 37 major works, we only really celebrate a quarter of those. This means that this wise old writer simply didn't know, or didn't care, what would fly and what would flop. On which note, J.K. Rowling, when in her twenties, wrote two novels for adults which have never found a publisher, and only then began *Harry Potter* which itself underwent numerous rewrites. And isn't this rather like the world's best baseball players who only manage to hit the ball on four out of ten tries, meaning that more often than not they're missing? History shows how very many high-achievers rely on this same brand of tenacious productivity to eventually make some celebrated progress. Their most prized accomplishments are invariably surrounded by a vast number of missed shots. For every golden egg, there's a whole flock of turkeys.

We can, then, counter the scourge of perfectionism by making it our goal to be as *productive* as possible, not as *perfect* as possible, in the sure knowledge of what we might call the "Shakespeare Principle": through high productivity we can still hope to create the occasional gem.

This isn't a charter for mediocrity. Quite the opposite, for perfectionism doesn't mean doing an excellent job. Perfectionism means rarely starting because we fear not reaching our idealized standards. Or it means rarely finishing because we never feel things are good enough yet. Or it means investing far more resources of time, money and energy than the task ever warrants, resulting in a large net loss. By releasing us from such self-defeating behaviours, rejecting perfectionism sets us free to be truly productive and creative – and perhaps, every once in a while, to produce something really exceptional.

Why bother to get really good at something?

Everything we've learned in this chapter so far has confirmed that each of us has the potential to get really good at something. But we've also seen that gaining expertise requires many hours of creative and dynamic boundary-pushing practice – and of course that practice may involve sacrifices in terms of the intimate personal relationships that make our lives so fulfilling. If expertise requires so much of us, why should we bother?

The short answer is this: being good at something is far more enjoyable than being bad at it. As discussed in Chapter 1, we seem to be hardwired by our evolutionary history to want to improve our "relationship with life". Evolution has made this relationship our priority because it's our best chance of surviving and thriving. As a consequence, it brings us profoundly satisfying feelings to get to know something really well, becoming intimate with all its dimensions, whether that be a skill, a place or a person.

We also gain a wonderful sense of confidence in our future from knowing how to get good at something. It reassures us that things can and do progress, and that life gets better if we work at it.

What's more, we're going to have to do something to make our way in life, so we can either get really good at something we'd dearly like to do, or we can let the world randomly allocate us to wherever it wants. If we have a skill, if we've something rare and valuable to trade in return for our livelihood, this might well give us the power to make some choices about what, where and with whom we wind up living and working.

The Matthew Effect

It's well worth our while getting good at something, if only on account of the "Matthew Effect", whereby an initial success in something tends to lead to even greater success, while an early failure means we're likely to become even less successful in the future. In short, it seems that success or failure will grow as fast as wild lavender, whichever gets the upper hand first. The effect derives its name from a passage in the Gospel of St Matthew, 25:29. "To everyone who has, will more be given, and he will have abundance. But from him who has not, even what he has will be taken away."

This phenomenon operates in every arena of life you care to think of, (whether in dating, sport or business), and for institutions just as much as for individuals. For example, individuals who positively stand out by taking a lead in something (it could be receiving more offers to dance, or receiving more work commissions) will begin to accrue ever more offers as a knock-on effect of their glowing reputation, while at the same time their actual skills will also improve dramatically on account of their fast-accumulating real-life experience. In short, a good reputation and useful experience will work together in an upwards spiral, so that eventually the successful individuals are attracting a vastly disproportionate amount of the best offers available.

That's the Matthew Effect: success snowballs, but so does failure, so we need to get our ball rolling in the right direction.

Finally, let's not forget that getting really good at something can result in a far higher income. And that in itself could well make us feel much better about our lives, as we are about to see.

More money can help

The mantra "money can't buy you happiness" is repeated in almost every popular guide to happiness and well-being. The accepted wisdom is that once an individual is above the poverty line, any extra income brings only a fraction more happiness.

This opinion is over-reliant on a couple of preliminary but nevertheless much-cited studies that accidentally set the low standards of proof adopted by subsequent research in the field. In fairness to the investigators (both of whom were deeply courageous pioneers in "happiness research" during the decades when it was angrily disapproved of by university psychology departments), these two landmark studies were simply "pilots" to test the water, and were never designed to offer strong evidence. In the first, social psychologist Dr Philip Brickman speculated that lottery winners soon return to their previous levels of happiness; in the second, Professor Ed Diener of the University of Illinois at Urbana-Champaign speculated that billionaires tend to be not much happier than the average Joe. It's ludicrous that these two studies have become cornerstones of the belief that money can't make you happy, and that Dr Brickman's study in particular has been cited as providing "dramatic evidence" that people will acclimatize even to the most joy-bringing events. (Brickman referred to this phenomenon as "the hedonic treadmill" – hedonic being derived from the Ancient Greek for "pleasure" – and the phrase has been eagerly revived by Positive Psychology.) For on closer inspection they're both extremely weak foundations on which to build a theory.

Brickman was interested in individuals who'd received windfalls of millions of dollars through some form of lottery win. His research question was a fascinating one, but his methodology was fatally flawed: undergraduate psychologists telephoned a couple of dozen lottery winners one year after their windfall, and asked them over the phone in a brief questionnaire-style interview how much they were enjoying life compared to before the windfall. Turns out that most of the winners (the research paper neglected to say how many) claimed they'd pretty much returned to their pre-win levels of happiness. Unfortunately, it doesn't take a rocket scientist to imagine the problems with this form of inquiry: the gross inaccuracies due to memory distortion or image management by those million-dollar winners; the vagaries of the novice student phonecallers.

When Professor Diener wanted to know how happy billionaires were compared to the rest of us, he sent questionnaires to the one hundred people on *Forbes* magazine's rich list. As we'll see on pp.224–227, questionnairing people is a feeble way of finding things out about them, but Professor Diener's research was particularly slight. Only 49 of the billionaires replied to his questionnaire, far too low a number for us to place much faith in the representativeness of their replies. Who knows, maybe the other 51 folks were too busy being happy to write back.

Of course the feebleness of the evidence so far gathered in favour of the adage that money can't make us happy is not in itself proof that money *can* make us happy. But in the absence of compelling evidence to the contrary, we're free to listen to our common sense and our own experience. And these might tell us that, despite its bad press, it's very likely more money really can make a difference. The proviso is that how we earn it and spend it must not detract from the health of our essential relationships. If earning more money means spending cripplingly long hours in the office away from our loved ones, then the trade-off is probably too high. Equally, if we blow our hard-earned cash on booze or material possessions we know we'll soon tire of, then it'll all have been for nothing. But if we earn our money doing something we're really passionate about, and then invest that money in enriching ways – perhaps taking lessons in some warmly social activity, or trekking with a friend in faraway places to broaden our horizons – then it has the potential to greatly improve our well-being. More money, wisely earned and wisely spent, can enhance our relationships, just as much as any other well-channelled, well-invested resource such as beauty or brains or boldness.

Conclusions

The great legacy of all the research outlined in this chapter is that no child or adult of seemingly ordinary abilities need ever be discouraged from pursuing a longed-for career or extracurricular ambition because of a false belief that they lack some special gift for it. (Let's note, too, that intelligence – at least the logical intelligence measured by conventional IQ tests – is a very poor predictor of either career success or happiness. These prizes are open to all comers.)

The many in-depth, systematic and truly investigative studies of lives going well have shown how we can all help carve our own future. Our professional-level performance can be acquired through learning and is *not* reliant on our having some kind of inherited head start by way of innate gifts, special talents or aptitudes, call them what you will. Unless there are exceptional circumstances inhibiting us (perhaps some permanent damage through accident or illness), we can each and every one of us comfortably become a highly skilled contender in whatever field we choose. And it's all the more intriguing that good humour, playfulness and pure holidays play such a vital part in this.

8

Our environment

Our environment

Our cultural and physical surroundings

Does the environment in which you live bring out the best in you? Could you make changes to improve it, or should you think of upping sticks and moving somewhere more supportive of your happiness and all-round well-being?

When thinking about the effects our environment has on us we need to think both large and small. Our physical environment stretches from the largest scale – whether that be lush pastoral landscapes or towering urban terrains – down to the rooms we inhabit and whether they have oppressively low ceilings or a pleasant view. Meanwhile, our cultural environment comprises everything from the laws and attitudes of society at large through to what values are prioritized by our schools, workmates and social groups.

In this chapter we'll consider what effect the country in which we live can have on our happiness, as well as what we can do ourselves to improve the environment of the institutions in which we spend our days. We'll also think about how we can make the most of our physical surroundings, by spending more time among the healing powers of the natural world.

Somewhere over the rainbow...

Wouldn't it be good to know whether there's "somewhere over the rainbow" that could be a considerably better fit for us than wherever it is we're presently trying to live? This improvement could very plausibly be brought about by a blend of factors: the climate, the cost of living, the level of taxation, the employment situation, the landscape, how well people tend to treat each other, and the ways of life they deem important. In an attempt to find that rainbow's end, here are two headline-making attempts to compare the happiness levels of different countries. Postponing for the moment our critique of the way their research was conducted, let's first look at their aims and claims.

How much happiness per dollar earned?

The graph opposite, reproduced from Richard Layard's *Happiness: Lessons from a New Science*, seeks to plot countries' happiness levels against their average income. The happier you are, the further towards the top of the graph you appear; the richer you are, the further to the right.

There are many different ways of looking at a graph such as this. We might notice first that *all* the countries towards the rich right of the graph are pretty happy, whereas for poorer countries happiness seems to be far more uncertain. For example, Vietnam and Moldova both have a per capita income of around $2000 a year, but almost eighty percent of Vietnamese people surveyed rated themselves as happy or satisfied, compared to only forty percent of Moldovans.

From this we might conclude that money is a pretty good safety net against misery. However, the glass-half-empty folk might point out that greater wealth doesn't seem to garner as much extra happiness as we might expect. After all, according to the graph, comparatively "dollar-wealthy" populations such as the US, Norway and Switzerland are only a smidgen happier than some "dollar-poor" nations such as Indonesia, El Salvador, Colombia and Mexico.

Yet the conclusion most commonly drawn from this graph by social scientists and journalists – the one that makes the headlines – is even

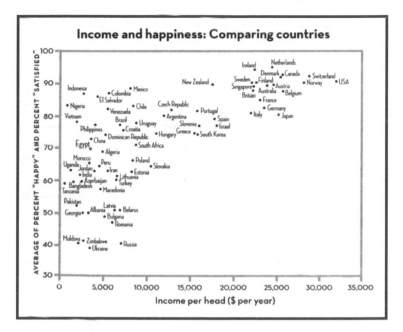

Income and happiness: Comparing countries

more surprising: that after a certain point more money doesn't seem to make us any happier at all. In the top right-hand corner of the graph there's no apparent correlation between wealth and happiness. The US is no happier than Sweden, despite its extra $10,000 or so per person per year. Such a conclusion would have very significant implications for

Close-knit and trusting communities

Research suggests that in the past fifty years there's been a ten-fold increase in depression among the seemingly cheerful population of the US. Intriguingly, that means depression is now a whopping ten times more common among the general population than it is among the 8000 or so people of the Old Order Amish community in the countryside near Philadelphia. Is the rarity of depressive illness among this community the result of their close-knit, un-modernized existence? Work done by Harvard's Professor Robert Putnam on how much we feel "a sense of trust" suggests this might well be the case. He found that in more neighbourly and trusting communities there was not only less malaise but also less crime, less tax evasion, greater educational attainment and greater physical health. Based upon the available evidence, such a "sense of trust" would seem to vary quite considerably between countries. The World Values Survey found that in Brazil, only 5 percent of people said they felt that other people could be trusted; in Norway the figure was 67 percent.

those who decide how such comparatively wealthy nations should be run, for if our dogged pursuit of yet more economic growth isn't making us a mite happier, then isn't it something of a blind alley?

How much happiness per eco-footprint?

Created in 2006, the Happy Planet Index sets out to see how efficiently each country converts the Earth's resources into two outcomes: life-satisfaction (i.e. an overall sense of happiness in general) and life expectancy (as a rough guide to health). This is a combination recommended by Dutch sociology professor Ruut Veenhoven as giving an overall picture of well-being.

The HPI's website (happyplanetindex.org) recognizes that it could more accurately be called the Unhappy Planet Index because of the damage to the planet that our behaviours are causing. The HPI is the brainchild of the New Economics Foundation, NEF, whose motto is "economics as if people and the planet mattered". It's a clever combination of two of today's buzzwords: "happiness" and "ecological footprint", and the index has understandably received the support of Friends of the Earth. NEF make it clear that the nations that top their 178-nation chart aren't the happiest places in the world, because the HPI measures how efficient countries are at generating happiness, rather than absolute happiness; nonetheless, they claim, those nations that score well show that achieving long and happy lives without over-stretching the planet's resources is an entirely feasible goal.

So which nations are using their resources most efficiently according to the HPI? The top three are:

1) Vanuatu (No, it's not off the Welsh coast. It's a collection of islands in the Pacific Ocean, far east of Australia out towards Fiji.)
2) Colombia
3) Costa Rica

Shamefully low down the list we find…

108) The United Kingdom
111) Canada
139) Australia
150) The United States

Overlooked by a beautiful banyan tree, three girls enjoy a game of volleyball on Tanna Island, Vanuatu. Vanuatu may be one of the world's poorest nations, but it's a peaceful country, with excellent levels of democracy. And islanders are surrounded by a rich and unspoilt natural environment. However, what's pushed this little-known country to the top of the HPI poll is that these benefits are achieved with minimal impact on the natural world: along with many island nations, Vanuatu's ecological footprint is unusually small.

It's notable that according to the HPI Germany has almost exactly the same well-being as the US, but because it achieves that longevity and happiness twice as efficiently in terms of its eco-footprint it ranks much higher, at 81st overall. The appearance of the famously happy, long-lived Swedes way down the rankings at 119th (because their well-being comes at a high price in terms of their use of the world's resources) is a reminder of how different things can look when we move the goalposts.

We should applaud the innovative intentions behind the HPI: a non-government organization boldly setting out to persuade governments to reconsider by what measures they gauge their country's progress – specifically to stop relying exclusively on economic growth as the exclusive indicator of national prosperity, and to start giving far more weight to their citizens' levels of life-satisfaction, and to Planet Earth's physical health. In the face of the threat of climate change, this is timely stuff.

Inadequate research methods

Both these studies raise important questions that go far beyond simple "who's the winner" rankings. They make us think about how we ought collectively to live our lives. Is economic growth not the best means to greater happiness after all? How should we balance our pursuit of greater well-being against the strain this puts on the planet? But the problem is that, on closer inspection, it becomes clear that in both cases their findings are based on such flimsy evidence that it's impossible to place much confidence in their conclusions. And, regrettably, that makes it all the easier for politicians – and the rest of us – to ignore their implications about what our priorities ought rightly to be.

The HPI, for example, makes some fundamental assumptions about well-being that deserve to be cross-examined. Is life expectancy a telling measure of health, particularly if the final few years might be racked with dementia or physical woes? Western medicine has added some fifteen years to life expectancy since World War II, yet arguably our quality of life has diminished (see the following chapter for more on this).

But the biggest problem with both these studies, and with many similar ones, is their over-reliance on well-being data gathered via mass surveys – either very superficial interviews or simply questionnaires. A country's position on the y-axis of the happiness vs. wealth graph on p.221 is based on responses to two happiness/satisfaction questions among a 250-item questionnaire administered via a face-to-face interview conducted by the World Values Survey. That same survey was the main source of data for the life-satisfaction component of the HPI calculation. And yet, as we're about to see, such surveys can give a badly blurred picture of what's really going on.

Why might these surveys be misleading?

The organizers of surveys and questionnaires come up against some tricky cultural problems when they attempt to make comparisons between countries. For example:

▶ **Different priorities:** A question about "your satisfaction with life" has very different connotations depending on where we are in the world. For instance, in community-oriented cultures such as Japan and China, the well-being of the group is held as far more important than any individual's happiness, which is a quite different approach from many Western countries in which the individual is the most important unit, not only to individuals but also to the state. So, right from the outset, an Easterner may be perplexed at the individual-oriented nature of the question. They might wonder why they are not being asked "How happy are your loved ones?" or "How happy is the community in which you live?"

▶ **Different taboos:** What may also be muddying the waters are the cultural taboos on various sorts of emotional expression. For instance, in Japan it's impolite to show "pained" or sad facial expressions in public; whereas in China it's not done to look too pleased with life, since painful emotions (such as loneliness or

Does the weather matter much?

Could it be that something as simple as better weather could make a new location a happier home for us? Certainly the many Brits who choose to emigrate to the sunny Mediterranean seem to think so. But the truth is we simply don't know what effect the weather might have on our mood.

Two world-leading psychologists in the field of decision-making and human judgement, David Schkade and Daniel Kahneman, have very often been quoted as having demonstrated that living in the reliably sunny climes of southern California does not make the residents any happier than rain-drenched New Englanders, for instance. But what is this popular claim actually based upon?

The professors published a research paper called "Does Living in California Make People Happy? A Focusing Illusion in Judgements of Life Satisfaction". Their paper recounts how they recruited 3500 undergraduates who were each paid around $10 a piece for filling in a one-hour self-report questionnaire asking about their job prospects, financial situation, personal safety, social life, outdoor activities, cultural opportunities… oh, and the effect of overall climate. The professors noted that people in colder, greyer places thought they'd be cheerier in warm ones, but they were apparently mistaken because their counterparts in sunny southern California didn't attribute much benefit to it.

In fairness to Schkade and Kahneman, the goal of their study was not to discover the effect of weather; it was to show that by asking questions in different ways that focus a participant's attention on one matter rather than another, you can induce people to give quite different answers (hence the subtitle of their paper). Nevertheless, over-zealous journalists and psychologists have often leapt on this research as "proof" that the weather doesn't matter to our sense of happiness. Maybe it doesn't, but only one thing is for sure: 3500 questionnaires can prove nothing on that point.

fear) are traditionally regarded as the norm. It's plausible, too, that unwritten cultural rules are subtly operating among Western countries and affecting the self-ratings of various nations. In South American countries and the US, people might think it's their duty, or will benefit them socially, to appear more cheerful than they feel. This "pressure to be perky" is perhaps less evident in northern Europe where being dour or pessimistic is not so frowned upon. Taken as a whole, it's more than likely that in answering survey questions, people are unthinkingly slanting their answers towards the ambient beliefs, practices and pressures of their wider culture, rather than offering an accurate and honest personal evaluation.

But there are also more general problems with using questionnaires to find out about how people think and feel. It might seem obvious to say it, but an unhelpful question can get an unhelpful answer. When researchers ask "Are you satisfied with your job?", a suspiciously high percentage of people claim "yes!" But when asked "Would you recommend your job to your son, daughter or best friend if they were interested in the field?" the numbers plummet. The discrepancy seems to occur because we're reluctant to admit to ourselves, let alone a researcher, that we're unhappy in our work but haven't done anything about it. It makes us feel feeble, so we fib instead. Questions need to be cleverly worded to nip around such natural defences. This is possible in an in-depth interview, where the questioner has the time and flexibility to test the waters with revealing questions. So, to find out how happy a person is, they might begin with an indirect question such as "What sorts of things would you like to improve in your life?", that's likely to elicit a much more considered and candid response than a more direct approach. But in a questionnaire or a rigidly scripted fifteen-minute phone interview this just isn't possible, and so researchers all too often fall back on that old chestnut, "On a scale of one to ten, how satisfied are you with your life in general?"

Why this over-reliance on questionnaires?

This over-reliance on questionnaires and other superficial means of quickly gathering data is a problem that dogs social science as a whole, not just comparisons of happiness between countries. The entire field is let down by a surfeit of questionnaire research and mass surveys, and a dire scarcity of more thorough and painstaking observations of how people lead their lives. Social science has too often seemed to be saying to itself "Why bother to go to the trouble of a thorough investigation, when we can just hand out a questionnaire?"

Let's draw an analogy: when a police detective wants to know if you murdered your neighbour, she doesn't ask you to circle whichever answer seems most accurate to you:

Did you murder Mrs Jones?
▶ Not at all
▶ Not really
▶ Maybe
▶ A little
▶ A lot

Nope. In their search for convincing evidence, the police will dig up the garden, rip up the floorboards and take DNA swabs. They will actively look for evidence that corroborates and contradicts the alibis and apparent explanations. So why is it when psychologists want to find out something as important as "How satisfied are you with your life in general?" they pretend to be satisfied with a self-report questionnaire or a fifteen-minute interview?

All around the world, university academics and government researchers are on a very tight budget and in a hurry to publish research papers in a bid to secure future funding or gain promotion. Since publicity makes both these goals more likely, it's very tempting for them to allow their studies to be over-interpreted by a story-hungry media, with the result that relatively weak levels of evidence are used to generate sweeping claims and front-page headlines which too often neglect to add the all-important detail about how the study was conducted that would have readers rolling their eyes in contempt. (See box on pp.98–99 for a dissection of a couple of much-publicized studies from the Positive Psychology fold.)

Social science's "inconvenient truth" is that there is no cheap, quick and easy way to find out what people really think or feel about their life. The kind of in-depth, holistic research that's needed may be too costly and time-consuming for cash-strapped university departments to consider, but the fact is that the alternative – rushed and superficial questionnaire-based research – may not be worth the paper it's written on.

More revealing ways to estimate well-being

If we want to know about the well-being of a single individual or a whole population, one of the best ways of discovering it is to see what they actually do. How do they spend their valuable time and hard-earned money? For instance, do they appear motivated to invest in their future, or do many of their activities seem to be aimed at anaesthetizing some underlying pain or fear? A detailed one- or two-hour interview could find out a lot about people's habits and activities. However, even such in-depth questioning has its problems. We have only the interviewee's words to go on and, however clever our questions, we'll never know for sure we've got an accurate picture of their day-to-day life. Relying on people's self-reporting is always risky, because they can be honestly but majorly mistaken in what they remember, they can be just too embarrassed to own up to things, or they can be downright duplicitous.

Let's take an analogy from close to home: if we want to know how much someone loves us we'd be wise to avoid direct questions such as "How much do you love me?", since a lot of baggage can get in the way of an accurate answer. It's much better to let the proof be in the pudding: if someone loves us, they will do a range of things that make that self-evidently clear and undeniable. Words are one thing; what we actually do in reality is, more often than not, quite another.

Applying this principle to our social research into well-being, it's no good simply asking people about their activities because they might, for any number of reasons, give us inaccurate or incomplete replies. We need hard evidence. Such evidence might sensibly include the following:

▶ **Physical indications:** levels of obesity; amount of physical activity per day as measured by a wrist-worn monitor
▶ **Psychological indications:** number of serious car accidents; level of personal debt; consumption of alcohol
▶ **Social indications:** time spent volunteering; dinner parties thrown per month; hours spent participating in social clubs and societies.

For all of the above indicators, we could readily imagine how we could obtain some quite accurate figures through close observation and objective tests (without having to rely on anyone's opinion at any stage), although this would of course be a painstaking exercise.

Note that when considering the state of a whole nation, it's not helpful to gauge malaise by looking at such things as alcoholism, because it only affects a small minority of any population and so is not a helpful indicator of what the great majority of social drinkers are feeling, thinking and doing. Likewise, murder and suicide rates are not a good indicator of the general state of affairs, because such figures reflect the actions of only a tiny and extreme fraction of the population. The Oscar-winning documentary *Bowling for Columbine* made it quite clear that suicide and murder rates are probably more indicative of the availability of firearms than they are of relative rates of depression (because firearms are so devastatingly effective at taking life, whereas a pills overdose, for instance, often fails to kill and so gives the depressed person a second chance).

Taken alone, any of the above "proxies" for well-being could be flawed or skewed, but together they are likely to give a fair indication of the all-round well-being of an individual or whole population. There are some exemplary studies out there which do corroborate in-depth interviews with such objective tests of how people actually live their lives (see box on pp.194–195 for a review of the famous Harvard Study and

The Indiana Jones of social science

Robert Biswas-Diener is a pioneering psychologist who thinks there are better ways to explore how people lead their lives than mass surveys and questionnaires. This affable young family man from Oregon has taken himself to be face-to-face with the Amish, the Maasai, Israeli peaceniks, young people in the streets and brothels of Calcutta, and seal hunters in the far north of Greenland. He interviews and observes remote groups of people who tend to get overlooked by desk-bound researchers armed with questionnaires.

"I have dedicated my life to the careful pursuit of happiness outside the research laboratory", he says. "I show up to a location ... deep in the Kenyan bush, for instance ... and stay for a month or so while I interview dozens, and sometimes hundreds, of men and women about their daily life events, the amount of positive and negative feelings they experience, their life satisfaction, and personal goals."

Despite such enterprising research, Robert has received only modest recognition from major academic institutions, compared to the honours they heap upon his tenured seniors. Could it be that some university professors are jealous of this Indiana Jones of life-quality research, lest their own questionnairing of undergraduates on campus seems lazy and anaemic by comparison to his painstaking investigations? But as that hero of the silver screen Professor Henry "Indiana" Jones sagely advises, "If you want to be a good archaeologist, you have to get out of the library." We might add "If you want to be a good *anything*, you have to get out of the library."

p.147 for details of Professor John Gottman's revolutionary "Love Lab"). But unfortunately, so far, nothing like this rigorous level of research is available when it comes to comparing happiness and well-being between countries. And so, for the moment, we simply do not know if one country is truly happier than another.

Of course, even if we did know one country's population was happier than that of the place where we currently live, that wouldn't necessarily imply we'd be better off there. So much depends on our own individual circumstances and personality: the direction and strength of our passions, our ability to rest and recuperate, our daring to explore. What's more, when we get off that boat, if we bump into someone "special" who fast becomes a soul buddy for highly physical outdoors and social adventures, then our experience of that El Dorado is likely to be transformed for the better, perhaps sufficient to compensate for an unenlightened political regime or dreary weather. In short, good fortune and "the right fit" can play a major role in how we take to our new home.

Improving our environment

In the absence of compelling evidence that the grass really is greener elsewhere, perhaps we'd be better off staying put, and taking a closer look at the cultural and social environment we already inhabit. What could be done to improve it? And who's responsible?

Should governments be doing more?

If happiness in one form or another is the right of all, does this mean that the state has a duty to provide it? Should parents or teachers or employers be legally required to ensure it for those in their care? Could it be added to the drinking water, like fluoride? Could it be part of the school curriculum, like citizenship, biology or physics?

If you just stop reading for a moment and listen carefully, you can hear the receding footfalls of government officials legging it off down the corridors of power… shouting back at us "This isn't my problem! I'm just responsible for health, education, low crime and high prosperity. No connection there at all with happiness, well-being or whatever the hell you call it!"

Famously, the former king of the isolated nation of Bhutan, Jigme Singye Wangchuck, attempted to rule his country in such a way as to maximize "Gross National Happiness" rather than Gross National Product. He didn't always back helpful initiatives (see p.193 for the disastrous results of his finally allowing television into the tiny country in 1999). And GNH is, as yet, more of a working philosophy than something actually measured. But the king has nevertheless become something of a figurehead for people worldwide who share his scepticism about the Western approach to development.

Some Western countries, notably Canada, have flirted with the idea of "Gross National Happiness" or some other alternative to GNP that takes a broader view of progress than mere economic growth. However, most governments still focus doggedly on wealth as their sole indicator of progress, and seemingly pay only lip service to the happiness, life-satisfaction or all-round well-being of their citizens.

Some governments now urge schools to nurture the well-being of their students, just as the law places a duty of care on employers as regards the welfare of their staff. But these requirements lack any real teeth. If a government really wanted to do something about their citizens' well-being, here are just a few things they could do for starters:

▶ **Introduce the study of well-being into every school**… and not crammed into just one hour every two weeks, which is all Personal, Social and Health Education is presently allocated in British schools. What's needed is an hour's class every day, so that the "study of lives that go well" – i.e. the close examination of how our society's much-admired individuals, past and present, have led their personal and professional lives – would be a central part of the curriculum, on a par with English and mathematics. Not hero worship, but rather a close analysis of the pros and cons of various ways of thinking and behaving in response to life's challenges. For instance, debating in class how the sickly and under-sized twelve year old from a very modest home went on to become Dame Kelly Holmes, winner of two Olympic athletics golds in 2004; or attempting to understand how the bullied, sorrowful teenager who was injured out of his

Our subconscious on the curriculum?

We educate our children about physical exercise, good nutritional habits, safe and natural sex, alcohol abuse and road safety. We screen them for hair nits, hearing problems and dyslexia, and inoculate them against various life-threatening diseases. Thinking back to Chapter 2, should a truly well-rounded curriculum also explicitly teach children about the workings of their subconscious minds?

Students could learn how to take good care of, and make good use of, their subconscious, how to harmonize its energies and defuse its misunderstandings. They might even learn to recognize in themselves and those around them the early signs of life-inhibiting emotional traumas, and ask for skilled help, just as we would wish them to do after a serious sports injury. Moreover, cunning advertisers already target the subconscious minds of our young people just as aggressively as they do those of adults. Better our education system own up to this, and discuss with the young how we can defend ourselves against such subliminal propaganda.

football career went on to become Gordon Ramsay, one of the world's most successful entrepreneur chefs.

▶ **Make good nutrition and vigorous physical activity a major part of every child's daily life.** We know beyond all reasonable doubt that all-in-one vitamin, mineral and omega-oil supplements will halve the incidence of anti-social behaviour among the most troubled teenagers; and that for all of us, sweat-breaking exercise for 45 minutes three times per week is by far the best prevention and cure for depression. Yet state education does next to nothing to act upon these facts. Children are still driven or bussed to school, when walking or jogging could absolutely transform for the better their physical health, their psychological mood, and their esprit de corps.

▶ **Free schools from competing so overwhelmingly on conventional subject grades.** Instead, schools could be judged by the progress their students make in their ability to generate their own good health and positive social involvement. A well-being-focused education like this promises far greater benefits for a nation's social and economic prosperity, and far fewer casualties in terms of psychological stress and physical sickness.

▶ **Require all employers to provide their staff with monthly well-being training** that benefits their personal and professional lives. Self-employed people and parents could have access to free places on publicly provided training courses at their local universities, colleges and schools. Our politicians go on and on about restructuring the health service and tinkering with agreements about the natural environment, while by contrast they totally sideline the educational measures that could prevent the vast majority of psychological, social, physical and environmental problems from fermenting in the first place.

▶ **Bring in tougher laws to tackle "social drinking".** Banning smoking in public places has shown what social innovations are possible, but why stop there when we consider that alcohol consumption is at least as costly and damaging to individual lives and families, the workforce and the healthcare system as smoking-induced cancer? (For more on the effects of drinking, see pp.194–196.)

▶ **Pass legislation to reduce the number of hours people spend at work**, perhaps by bringing in new laws about maximum working hours.

But do we even want such cultural change?

Our governments have shown themselves decidedly reluctant to make significant changes such as those listed above. The problem seems to be that governments, much like individuals, only make major changes when they're very highly motivated; for instance, *terrified* by TV master chef Jamie Oliver demanding better school dinners for every state school child in the UK. But how can we expect them to put our well-being first when we apparently don't? We give every indication that we want our leaders to continue to prioritize wealth above every other goal; governments' approval ratings rise and fall in line with the state of the economy, and tax increases are universally complained of, no matter whether the money is to be used for some unquestionable good, or the tax is intended to discourage unhealthy behaviours such as excessive drinking or polluting our planet.

When it comes to our individual actions, the story is much the same. In recent decades, there have been numerous attempts to re-define happiness and the good life, but it's the very small minority of people who act accordingly. Something just isn't sufficiently compelling to have us sell up and down-size so that we can halve our working hours and double our time in creative physical activities with loved ones. When we think of the rapid take-up of the Internet, mobile phones and portable music players, or of how the tide has turned as regards smoking in public or airport security, we begin to realize just how un-transforming all the hype and hoopla about well-being has so far shown itself to be.

Judging by how we spend our time and money, our good quality of life (perhaps measured by social warmth, shared physical activity and harmony with nature) is still rated as far less important than such criteria as academic A grades, our appearance, our earnings or our ownership of

Beware the "cult of the expert"

One reason we should perhaps be grateful that our politicians don't take a more active interest in our all-round well-being is that they're too often led astray by the "cult of the expert". Finding themselves in charge of government departments for which they have no relevant experience, politicians are all too eager to call in the "experts" to help them devise policy. But, as we're about to see, the experts don't always get it right.

In his book *In Defence of Food* (2006), Michael Pollan deftly critiques how government nutritional scientists dramatically changed our eating habits in the 1960s when they confidently declared that butter was bad for us and that we should all eat highly processed margarine instead. For a whole generation of eaters, highly processed foods claiming to be very low in fat became all the rage. Still are. Trouble is, the scientists have been proven quite wrong, and such fat-depleted processed food is likely to be far worse for us than its naturally healthy, wholesome counterparts.

Likewise, when it comes to alcohol consumption, it has recently been revealed that the "safe amounts" once recommended by the British Medical Association were figures plucked from mid-air because the specialist doctors didn't know what to advise, but wanted to say something that sounded authoritative.

Sometimes, brutal as it may sound to say it, the experts may not even want to tell us the full story. Cancer has created its own economy: the researching and treatment of cancer is a multi-billion-dollar business, providing lucrative livelihoods for scientific research groups in search of new anti-cancer drugs, for the huge pharmaceutical manufacturers who produce and sell these expensive drugs, and for the medical consultants who prescribe them and perform surgery. Yet, though we know that very many cancers could be prevented by healthy eating and frequent physical activity, barely a fraction of anti-cancer efforts are invested in prevention. Professor Richard Sullivan, for many years the research director of Cancer Research UK, says: "Though we should not ignore how some cancer research has undoubtedly helped, for instance in fighting childhood leukaemia, the field in particular, and medicine as a whole, has manifestly ignored prevention."

The same is true of every other healthcare field, from heart disease and dementia to depression and anxiety. Prevention is only a fraction of the experts' activities, because the system has evolved in such a way that it's in no one's clear interests to pursue it. Putting it another way, these "ill-health economies" literally rely on millions of people suffering with these problems. Prevention doesn't serve the

houses, cars and other symbols of "success". Investing in real life is still the poor relation to instant pleasures or virtual realities. And, perversely, we seem to be applying the same principle to our pursuit of happiness: we tend to use studies of happiness and well-being as a supplement to the Prozac approach, whereby "hints and tips for happiness" are something to reduce stress or anaesthetize us temporarily, rather than being considered as part of some great debate about the foundations of a better life and greater harmony with the planet.

industries' employees, because it is not how they're judged. They are paid to care for the sick people on their doorstep, not to devise long-term prevention plans.

Exacerbating this problem is the fact that such powerful preventative measures as healthy eating, adequate exercise, sound sleep and good friendships can't be owned or patented by an industry or group of experts. And hence there is little or no incentive for big business to invest in them.

By educating our children, teenagers and adults to take good care of themselves, we would within 25 years decimate the visible costs to our healthcare systems, as well as the hidden costs of people who don't end up in the consultant's surgery or hospital, but are nonetheless struggling through life only half as creative in their work, play and relationships as they could otherwise be. Yet so long as their incentives remain as they are, it's unlikely the industry experts will be recommending such a course of action to our politicians. As Professor Sullivan puts it, "Perhaps the key is to change our culture from the 'medicalization of disease' to a 'holism of health' paradigm, so that all-round good health becomes our goal, rather than the treatment of disease. This would take political courage at all levels, something we are in short supply of these days."

How we lead our daily lives requires vital personal choices that should not be left to the experts, because such groups are too often ill-equipped and ill-motivated to be given a monopoly on advising us. The bottom line is, we have to weigh things up for ourselves. So, next time so-called experts stir up a panic about some aspect of modern life, let's ask "What exactly is your evidence for this?", and let's think what they might have to gain from convincing us of their story.

Happiness and well-being are fast becoming the margarine of modern living: something highly processed and artificial that people are falling over themselves to sell us as a wonder cure. (By contrast, our painful emotions such as anger, shame, fear, regret and loneliness have been demonized, just like "the wrong type of fats" were from the 1960s onwards.) We should be wary of such over-hyped, over-packaged solutions for "maxing our happiness", whether it's new toys or gizmos, the latest wonder drug, or books that claim to have "found the answer" (something this Rough Guide emphatically does *not* do). And we should remember that there's much which can't be packaged, and which it's in no one's interest to tell us about, but which might be far better for us than these advertised quick fixes. On that point, this chapter concludes with something no one can patent: the natural world.

Changing the culture of your institution

Cultural change does happen: think of how our attitude to the environment has been transformed by the growing recognition of the reality of climate change. And so it's not impossible that ten years from now our societies and hence our governments could come to place a far higher value on our all-round well-being, instead of narrowly focusing on wealth or instant pleasures. In the meantime, there is much we can do, in the absence of legislation, to improve the environment of the institutions in which we spend our days. Mahatma Gandhi said "We have to be the change we want to see in the world." So we shouldn't wait for things to get better before changing what we do; we should first set in motion the changes because it's these that help things to get better.

Well-being in our workplace

Can we persuade our workplace to prioritize well-being as the foundation of its whole ethos? We could, for instance, ask our employer to arrange practical workshops in skills such as relaxation and imaginative rehearsal. Within our own department or team, we could talk about how work could be shared out so as to play to each individual's "signature strengths" (see p.89), so that everyone gets to do what they're best at rather than struggling with tasks that aren't a good fit. And we could talk to our HR department and others about balancing our personal and professional lives and how our institution could be more considerate of the wholeness of life.

If we encounter reluctance or scepticism, we would do well to point out that it's not just what happens between 9am and 5pm that shapes the person who turns up for work each day. Our personal relationships, our private passions, how we travel to and fro, and how we sleep at night will all have a bearing upon our performance. Helping employees develop a healthy and happy balance between the different aspects of their lives shouldn't be seen as a costly luxury, but rather as a vital endeavour that could reap a whole range of welcome rewards. Naysayers will argue that nothing can be done until there is an evidence-based action plan proving that one or more others have already done so successfully. This is a profoundly flawed argument, because no two organizations will be the same, no matter how apparently similar, so the only genuine way forward is for each to explore for itself what works where and when.

Supporting our schools

Though most of us would wish to foster our children's open-hearted, open-minded love of life, what is it in practice that schools too often prioritize? Exam answers and doing what we're told.

What a wasted opportunity this is, because schools can readily sow the seeds of a lifelong passion to thrive and flourish, so that the individual grows up expecting well-being to be the priority in every aspect of their life. Some schools, such as Wellington College (see box), are leading by example, pioneering an approach to education that has well-being firmly at its heart.

Prioritizing well-being at Wellington College

Wellington College in Berkshire, England, is a leading private school for girls and boys aged thirteen to eighteen. In 2006, under the mentorship of its new headteacher, Dr Anthony Seldon, it became a pioneer for prioritizing the principles of well-being in its whole school ethos and curriculum.

Dr Seldon argues that for too many years now, orthodox education has tried to maximize academic performance by focusing on the intellectual skills of reading, writing and logic, to the near total exclusion of all else. He reminds us that the word education derives from the Latin *ex duco*, meaning *to lead outwards*, yet for too long formal education has been "narrowing the student down". Working alongside Seldon is his Head of Philosophy and Well-being, Ian Morris, who also regrets the current direction of so much education: "Rather than equipping young people with the skills they need to be human, it's equipping them with the skills they need to be units of production in the workforce. Schools don't educate the whole child, they train children to sit exams, to become automata."

In defiance of such unwholesome trends, Wellington College aims to educate the whole child: not moulding children to fit a place in the workforce but "opening hearts and opening minds". In particular, it has introduced classes teaching "the skills of well-being" to students in years 10 and 11 (ages fourteen to sixteen). By studying lives that have gone particularly well, the pupils gain an understanding of what might help a life flourish. They learn about the importance of their relationships with others, as well as the benefits of good nutrition and exercise. And they learn techniques such as imaginative rehearsal, positively channelling emotional energy, and overcoming fears and unhelpful inhibitions. The summer after these classes were introduced, Wellington College students achieved the highest public examination grades in the school's distinguished history. That result is by no means proof of the worth of teaching well-being, but it is food for thought.

The top-down organization of the state-school curriculum means government support and commitment will probably be needed before state schools are able fully to embrace such a wholesome approach to education. However, here's one simple example of how we could be a catalyst for improved well-being in our schools, without needing the support or involvement of "decision-makers" at all. Our around-town transport systems are just one glaring example of how we and our governments have let the selfish application of technology ride roughshod over our community's best interests – physical and cultural. Push-bikes and motor vehicles self-evidently don't mix well (people get hurt), and understandably parents feel the urge to ferry their children to and fro. But rather than wait around helplessly for town planners to create proper dedicated cycle paths, how about school students (and their teachers) take the initiative and gently jog the few miles to school, then shower and change on site? After all, a posse of teenagers could easily keep each other company and cover three or four miles in forty-five minutes. From everything we know about the benefits of frequent exercise, we can be sure that their moods, learning abilities and bodies would all benefit enormously. With depression, substance abuse, bulimia and obesity threatening all of our young people, we'd be doing them a timely good turn by making such a school run *de rigueur*. And by rejecting the sedentary alternatives, they'd be striking at one of the root causes of "lifestyle overload".

The revitalizing power of nature

We all appreciate that getting closer to nature is good for us, from a sandwich in the park or a weekend hike to swimming in the sea or sleeping beneath the stars. But let's just remind ourselves of its full potential.

Alas, the evidence to date comes only from small-scale studies that have struggled to monitor the numerous factors that could affect a person's well-being. As discussed above, the problem with funding such research is who does it benefit, save the individuals who will get better because of it? No industry or group of experts can own nature or access to it, and many groups have cause to fear its effect on their own profits,

---

"Nature conquered!", boasts the professor

The following quotation is from *Happiness: Lessons from a New Science* (Penguin, 2006), written by Richard Layard. A professor emeritus at the London School of Economics, Layard is a leading British economist, and an adviser to the British government on a range of vital social issues including what type of psychotherapists should be trained, and what to teach children about depression.

> By using our brains, we have largely conquered nature. We have defeated most vertebrates and many insects and bacteria. In consequence, we have increased our numbers from a few thousand to a few billion in a very short time – an astonishing achievement. Much of our anxiety and depression is no longer necessary. The great challenge now is to use our mastery over nature to master ourselves and to give us more of the happiness we all want.

Layard's view of mankind's relationship with nature, and the absolute priority he attributes to "greater human happiness", are widespread within the dominant scientific and political circles.

In absolute opposition to this prevailing determination to "conquer nature", this Rough Guide believes it is exactly because we have tried to "domesticate or eradicate" rather than partner with nature's fauna and flora that we humans are in dire and perhaps terminal trouble. We have *too much* used our logical brains, and *too little* listened to our compassionate emotions and our physical bodies. The plague of humans represented by six billion people, many of whom are starving, is a manmade *disaster*, not an achievement. It seems more than likely that, rather than being no longer necessary, our internal "alarm systems" are quite rightly registering pandemic levels of anxiety and depression in an attempt to forestall the impending implosions of our species and planet. Our priority challenge now is to work *harmoniously* with the nature within us and all around us, so as to make genuine progress in our rapport with life

(Chapter 1 challenges the "cult of happiness" that has swept the West since World War II.)

---

i.e. the "ill-health economies" who benefit from selling us the well-being that the countryside offers freely.

Even so, what research does exist is heartening. In 1984, environmental psychologist Professor Roger Ulrich of Texas A&M University studied the post-surgery notes of 23 gall-bladder patients, each of whom had a room with a view of a small copse of trees. He then made a comparison with 23 very similar patients recovering in near-identical rooms in the same hospital, whose windows looked onto a brick wall. Ulrich discovered that those who had a room with a view were discharged on average one day earlier (after eight days rather than nine) and used considerably less of the powerful painkiller medication. These may only be modest improvements, but then again the view of the trees was equally limited

Earthy pleasures

French philosopher Jean-Jacques Rousseau observed in his 1750 *Discourse on the Arts and Sciences* that the liberalism of the Enlightenment had led to a pursuit of material luxury and pleasure that threatened quality of life in terms of community and family. He spoke of "reason without wisdom, and pleasure without happiness". Civilization was becoming frivolous, with no heart and soul. For him, happiness was most readily found in those moments when he was able to leave civilization behind and head out into the natural environment: "As soon as I am under the trees and surrounded by greenery, I feel as if I were in the earthly paradise and experience an inward pleasure as intense as if I were the happiest man."

for those fortunate patients who had one. This potential link between having a window looking onto nature and having improved physical and psychological health is equally relevant to families living in inner-city housing estates, and to prisoners in high-security cells. Professor Ulrich has also observed that open-heart-surgery patients recovering in rooms decorated by art depicting some form of natural water feature have lower post-operative anxiety than patients exposed to pictures of other natural scenes or simply no art at all. It's interesting, too, that the highest levels of patient anxiety were associated with abstract paintings.

Though these studies do not by any means demonstrate conclusively that views of nature improve well-being, they do begin to suggest it, and lend support to Pulitzer Prize-winning Harvard sociobiologist Edward O. Wilson, who coined the term "biophilia" for what he believes to be the in-born affinity that we humans feel for the living creatures around us and the Mother Earth we call home. It's interesting that NASA space projects and polar exploration teams both fully appreciate the morale-boosting quality of plant life for their personnel living in extreme environments, and consequently factor in the need for greenery in space vessels and polar outposts.

**Fish in the sea
you know how I feel,
River running free
you know how I feel,
Blossom in the tree
you know how I feel,
Dragonfly out in the sun
you know what I mean,
Butterflies all havin' fun
you know what I mean.
Sleep in peace
when day is done,
That's what I mean.**

Nina Simone's "Feelin' Good" captures the affinity we have for nature.

And not all countries are slow to act upon the health potential of the great outdoors. In 2007 the Netherlands had 600 "care farms" operating as a fully integrated part of their health service, and dedicated to restoring psychological health. So in Holland, if you're suffering from depression or anxiety, your doctor can prescribe you a couple of weeks on a farm where you'll help out full-time. (Britain, by comparison, has three times the population of the Netherlands, but fewer than a hundred care farms, very few of which are dedicated entirely to mental health.)

So how might the natural environment be achieving its calming and recuperative effects?

First of all, our attention is naturally drawn outwards to the fauna and flora around us, rather than ruminating introvertedly on our worries. We feel engrossed but in an undemanding way that apparently helps

Growing Well (growingwell.co.uk) is a six-acre organic market garden on the edge of the UK's Lake District. It involves local people recovering from mental health problems in the running of the business – from seed sowing and harvesting to financial management and administration. Participants build their confidence and skills through their involvement in the team.

rest and restore our thinking capacities. It also seems likely that we are subtly reminded of how life is seasonal and regenerative and that good things aren't always dead and gone, but might only be lying dormant and awaiting some nurturing sunshine. We can begin to understand why Nelson Mandela always relished gardening and fought for permission to create his own allotment on the prison colony of Robben Island. Of this, he wrote: "To plant a seed, watch it grow, to tend it and then harvest it, offered a simple but enduring satisfaction. The sense of being the custodian of this small patch of earth offered a small taste of freedom."

In respect of all the above, it behoves us to cultivate our very own series of experiments. Do we feel any better for a brisk walk around the park at lunchtime? Do we sleep any sounder for a half-hour stroll before bed? Does it noticeably enhance the month ahead if we go "walkabout in the outback" one weekend? And if we were to plan a wilderness adventure, what would be our chosen tonic: a seascape or the open savannah, the river bank or the mountain trail?

Honouring our inner wild

When was the last time you…

▶ **climbed a tree, or planted one?**
▶ **walked in the hills, hopefully with a map and compass?**
▶ **Wellington-booted through the country rain?**
▶ **slept out on a summer's night beneath the Milky Way?**
▶ **made love in a hayfield or a bluebell wood, with the sun streaming down?**
▶ **roasted dinner on an open wood fire?**
▶ **ate something you grew from seed?**
▶ **skinny-dipped from a river bank?**
▶ **stopped for a couple of minutes to stare bewildered at a sunset or snow falling?**
▶ **helped a bee, or a trapped bird, find an open window to freedom?**

Add up your score to find out if you're really alive, or simply a HoRe: a Homo-Replicant produced by TechWorld Products Incorporated, so as to serve the state machinery. Older models suffer hair loss and TV addiction, while younger models require constant re-booting via iPod earplugs.

The thing is, if we can't respect our *inner wild*, will we be able to respect the nature all around us? Our prehistoric ancestors were wild animals, but so-called civilization has domesticated us through its urban living and high-tech life. We put our well-being at peril if we discount the role of our underlying instincts. We are animal-beings first and foremost – our human-ness is only a specific breed of this. Let's try to appreciate, honour and fulfil our animal nature.

"Passionata!"

Legend has it, this is the name of an international secret society that emerged from Cambridge University during the Renaissance. Membership simply requires prospective candidates "to secretly make sexual love unto orgasm" in any building that is ferociously reserved for *intellectual* pursuits. Passionata! wish not in any way to desecrate the jealously protected venues in which they "pledge" themselves, but rather to bless these cerebral places with a sensational wave of sexual and emotional energy. Take, for instance, Cambridge's University Library, a fascistically designed building of authoritarian and bullying proportions, constructed in the 1930s as if on Hitler's personal command. That hard-faced, tight-lipped library would be a deserving contender for up-and-coming students of secretly shared orgasms. That said, Passionata! is open to *all* good souls bold enough to bring molten passion to any cold-hearted place where the hot blood of our human physique and shimmering emotions are in some sense outlawed. (One can only hope that Bill Clinton and Monica "Oval-teeny" Lewinsky can count themselves as fellows.)

This up-tight library is crying out for an orgasm.

In *The Shawshank Redemption* (1994, written and directed by Frank Darabont) Andy (played so touchingly by Tim Robbins) gains unauthorized access to the prison's loudspeaker system so as to play his fellow inmates an operatic aria. Inspired by this, and by the free-spirited mission of the Passionata! fellowship, we might all think how we can introduce a little passion and poetry into otherwise unwelcoming environments.

Wild-water swimming

Seaside, lagoon, river, lake or pond swimming is one of the great joys of living. Yet, somewhere between our TV screens and shopping malls, our theme parks and multiplex cinemas, we're prone to forget the sheer widescreen, full-colour surround-sound beauty of nature: the barn owl at dusk, hovering above its prey; the myriad shades of green across a summer canvas; the muted stillness of snow falling. *Wild Swimming*, a book by Daniel Start, reveals 150 hidden rivers, lakes and waterfalls in Great Britain that are ripe to be visited for the ancient pursuit of skinny-

Beautifully photographed by Daniel Start himself, Loch Beinn a Mheadhoin, in the north of Scotland, is one of *Wild Swimming*'s recommended sites for a spot of naked bathing. Natural refreshment for body and soul!

dipping, which, if approached wisely, is a most welcome alternative to the chemical chlorination and clamour of swimming pools.

It's not that rural life is intrinsically better than the town or city; but rather that we should retain for ourselves the ability and the habit of moving freely from one environment to another as our spirit calls, just as birds migrate with the seasons. Many cultures have a long history of fleeing their over-heated urban homes for several weeks of the year so as to recuperate and refresh themselves in the cooler mountain air or near rivers in the deep countryside. Let's not lose it.

The Kingdom of God is within you and all about you, not in buildings of wood and stone. When I am gone, split a piece of wood and I am there; lift a stone and you will find me.

The words of Jesus of Nazareth according to the Gospel of St Thomas offer a Christian message resonant with pantheism, the principle that "God is everywhere".

Conclusions

Human well-being needn't cost the Earth. On the contrary, our fortunes are intimately tied to that of our natural world. In respect of which, let's dare to wonder how else we might live. If we aspire to ways of living that we value passionately, we could emigrate to a country where teachers are well supported, where workaholism is treated as a symptom of distress, and where alcohol-free, highly social and outward-bound after-school and after-work activities are the widespread and welcome norm. We could even create such a wonderful world in our own back yard.

9

Saving our soul from technology

Saving our soul from technology

More faster easier isn't the way to well-being

Something is making us sick. Medical experts may be preoccupied with the threat of an imminent flu pandemic, fearing a repetition of the one that swept the world in 1918–19, killing at least twenty million people. But the truth is that a far more crippling pandemic is already at large. Modern, high-tech societies are displaying what we might call a "circle of symptoms", characterized by epidemics of the following:

▶ **Clinical depression and hyper-anxiety**
▶ **Obesity and bulimia**
▶ **Addiction to everything from alcohol and gambling to shopping, sex, pornography, TV, the Internet, mobiles and emails**
▶ **Excessive debt and over-spending**
▶ **Allergic reactions and hyper-sensitivities**
▶ **Workaholism and perfectionism**
▶ **Obsession with physical appearance and clothing brands**
▶ **Violence, road rage, child abuse and self-harm.**

We probably all have one or more of these symptoms, or know someone dear to us who does. The maladies on this list (and far more ills besides) appear to be symptoms of the same root cause. We speculate that there's a root cause, because if we reduce the smoking statistics (halved in the past 25 years) obesity seems to take its place (quadrupled over the same period). If we reduce drink-driving, then road rage replaces it. In psychotherapy, we call this "symptom substitution".

What on earth is wrong with us?

An emotional climate change

The behavioural symptoms listed above indicate that something's wrong with life in general. They are all attempts to kill pain by distracting or anaesthetizing ourselves. They are temporary and desperate measures in response to a single key emotion, which seems to lie at the centre of this circle of symptoms. That painful emotion is fear.

Homo sapiens have always been scared; we're hard-wired that way. That's one of the reasons we got to be top of the evolutionary ladder: we're the nerdy, neurotic, workaholic animal, always looking over our shoulder, or straining to see ahead into the darkness. We've always been jumpy. But it's a matter of degree, and we're getting increasingly anxious.

We fear crime (far more than we ought to, according to the police). We fear that we're being poisoned by nasties in our food, that our kids will have a terrible accident if we don't wrap them in cotton wool. We fear being overwhelmed by the demands of daily life, being abandoned by the folks most dear to us. We're profoundly social animals, and fear of rejection, of isolation, of loneliness is a paramount driver for us. Most of all, though, it seems we fear the future.

More than ever before, it seems we have a deep-seated feeling that the future is uncertain, and that our lives are out

A soul in jeopardy

It's telling that the 2008 Oscar for best film went to *No Country for Old Men*, in which a Texan sheriff played by Tommy Lee Jones withdraws from the opera of twenty-first-century life by hanging up his badge and retiring. He feels the future has taken a very dark turn, represented by a pathological killer who's perpetrating a string of cold-blooded crimes across the county. The sheriff hasn't the heart to pit himself against this new foe, because "A man would have to put his soul at hazard. He'd have to say OK, I'll be part of this world."

of our control. Some commentators have speculated that dropping birth rates in the developed world signal a profound uneasiness about what the future might hold for future generations (see box below). But even at a purely monetary level, it seems we're reluctant to invest in what looks like an increasingly uncertain future. As John Gray of the London School of Economics puts it, "none but the incorrigibly feckless any longer believe in taking the long view … Saving is gambling; careers and pensions are high-level punts." Of course, our faith in financial institutions has been rattled in recent years. We've seen that it takes only one rogue share-trader or financial terrorist to destroy a bank or shake an economy through billion-dollar losses, as was demonstrated by the French banking giant Société Générale in 2007. That same year the sub-prime property market collapsed in the US, leading to the first run on a British bank (Northern Rock) since Victorian times. But even before these shocks, it was clear the majority of us were much keener to spend than to save for the future. Our cavalier attitude to mounting personal debts and

Why are we no longer choosing to be parents?

Parenthood is becoming rarer among the populations of Japan, Italy, Germany and Britain, which are all levelling out at their present size, and will soon decline, because many educated adults are choosing not to become parents. Instead, they are prioritizing their professions, their passive leisure time and their personal adult relationships, seemingly in that order. It's generally assumed this is just another result of our materialist culture, with potential parents baulking at the loss of spending power and leisure time that a child would entail. But is there something else going on?

One proposed explanation is that modern adults are less inclined to become parents because, coming from broken homes as more than half of young adults now do, they had childhoods in which they were requisitioned as "parent-substitutes" to their younger siblings, and to some extent had to care for their lonely parent still remaining. In short, it's thought that the parenting instincts of an entire generation were "triggered" far too early, and now they have nothing left with which to start their own families.

However, it's also been argued that like other mammals, particularly other primates, we are reacting to the stress of over-crowding and uncertainty in our daily lives by not wanting to breed. We might intellectualize our behaviour a hundred different ways, but our wanting sexual intimacy without procreation could be a direct, instinctive reaction to the plague proportions of the human population and the natural fear and aggression this engenders. In other words, at a subconscious level, we are living for today and forgetting about tomorrow and future generations because somewhere deep down we don't believe there will be much of a tomorrow to live in.

Financial market computer screens are like the legs of an alien spider terrifying the scurrying humans – which is pretty much how it was in the second half of 2008. Who saw the crash coming – and what else can't the experts predict? (See pp.101–106 for Nassim Nicholas Taleb's devastating critique of our human need for a false sense of control and predictability.)

our increasing reluctance to save for our retirement seems to indicate a mentality of "live for the short term, damn the long term", as if deep down we suspect the long term is so uncertain it's not worth thinking about or preparing for.

It seems we're right to be afraid; certainly some of our most eminent scientists think so (see box opposite). But what is it about our modern age that's made the future such a terrifying and uncertain prospect? One answer seems to be technology. Whether it be climate change or nuclear war, genetically modified foods or rogue nanobots, many of the new threats – real or imagined – that haunt us are the result of the relentless advance of technology. What's more, our sense of impending techno-logical doom is exacerbated by an underlying climate of stress in which the demands of our daily lives are exceeding our emotional resources. And what's making our lives so demanding? Ironically, it seems to be those very technologies that we co-opted to make our lives easier. In short, our high-tech lifestyle is overwhelming us. And not only does it stress us out and make us sick, it damages us in many other ways too, as we're about to see.

Are we right to be afraid?

The future is defiantly unknowable stuff. Even the so-called experts have a pretty poor track record of prediction, as exemplified by the US National Academy of Sciences which, in 1937, made its own set of predictions about the future. Not only did this A-team of experts fail to predict penicillin, computers, jet engines, space rocketry, nuclear fuels and nuclear weapons, they even failed to foresee World War II, which lay just 24 months ahead of them.

So it pays to take any future forecasting with a hefty pinch of salt. Still, the visions of today's experts make for sobering reading. Take the following quote, for example: "I think the odds are no better than 50/50 that our present civilization on Earth will survive to the end of the present century without a serious setback." This uncompromising statement comes early in a slim paperback, *Our Final Century*, written by Professor Lord Martin Rees, President of the Royal Society, Astronomer Royal and Master of Trinity College, Cambridge. In short, this international leader in the field of science thinks there's a good chance we won't make it out of the twenty-first century alive.

Professor Rees notes that "the danger of nuclear devastation still looms, but threats stemming from new science are even more intractable". Here are some of the calamitous possibilities he identifies:

▶ **Airborne killer-viruses that could be spread on the four winds**

▶ **Fungi attacking plant life, causing world starvation**

▶ **Rogue nanomachines that could self-replicate like a flu virus or a swarm of killer bees** (A nanometre Is one billionth of a metre, so these are almost unimaginably small gizmos that can only be made and seen beneath powerful microscopes.)

▶ **Super-intelligent computers as fast and capable as the human brain, which might take a severe disliking to us.**

What's really changed the game, says Professor Rees, is technology's ability to put devastating power into the hands of one or a very few individuals, which simply wasn't the case even 25 years ago. To attract attention to the catalogue of catastrophes that threaten us, Professor Rees has placed a $1000 bet that "by the year 2020 an instance of bio-error or bio-terror will have killed a million people".

What sets apart the predictions of Professor Rees and others in the twenty-first century is a new awareness that the human race is not necessarily a permanent fixture on the Earth. Professor John Gray of the London School of Economics is uncompromising in his insistence on the possibility of a post-human future: "Long after the last traces of the human animal have disappeared, many of the species it is bent on destroying will still be around, along with others that have yet to spring up. The Earth will forget mankind. The play of life will go on." This – perhaps even more than our own individual mortality – is a concept that takes some getting used to.

The trouble with technology

"Why does this magnificent applied science, which saves work and makes life easier, bring us little happiness? The simple answer runs: because we have not yet learned to make sensible use of it." Albert Einstein

Sixty years on, this observation still holds true: we humans have a stunning ability to develop technologies – combustion engines, TV, medicines, phones, the Internet – which we then vastly over-use to the extent that they ruin our quality of life and threaten not only our own existence but that of the whole planet. The law of unintended consequences has been hard at work. We hoped our technologies would liberate us, but they have accidentally enslaved us:

▶ **Rather than ease our burden, they exhaust us.**
▶ **Rather than deepening our experience of life, they have diluted our all-important relationships.**
▶ **By providing so much to consume, they have atrophied our ability to create.**
▶ **By increasing the speed at which we live, they have made us forget how to savour.**

In short, with our fabulous capacity for invention, we have invented poisons. Our misuse of technology has struck at the heart of our human soul.

Technology could reasonably be defined as any device, system or approach that increases human abilities. Technology isn't new: it was in the region we now call Iran, circa 3200 BC, that wheeled transportation was first used, and early hieroglyphic writing systems were developed. It is the sheer *speed* of change in the twentieth century that is unprecedented in all of recorded human history. We entered the century riding horses and penny-farthing bicycles, and left it on rockets that can carry a human towards the moon at 25,000 miles per hour. Across the millennia, we have gone from trusting the gods to guide us to trusting the Church, then the state, and now we're trusting science and technology in all its myriad forms. From the moment we're woken unnaturally early and abruptly by the sound of our alarm clock, we're in the hands of technology in all its myriad forms. We rely on it for every aspect of our increasingly artificial lives: for getting up too early and going to bed too late; for transportation and communication; for how we spend our leisure time; for dealing with our illness.

This chapter argues that the tail of technology is wagging the dog; and that our technologies – whether they be for information, transport, cosmetic surgery, pharmaceuticals or communication – are playing

Mary Shelley (1797–1851) was still in her teens when she began to write her novel *Frankenstein*, in which the scientist Dr Frankenstein creates a man that becomes a monster. First published in 1818, this universally recognized story is striking in the way it so foreshadowed how man's machinery would come to run amok. The book's numerous film adaptations (such as this one from 1931 starring Boris Karloff) are evidence that Shelley's fiction continues to speak to us loud and clear as a powerful warning against the threat of technology.

ever more upon our vulnerabilities. Rather than supporting our human nature, technology dominates it, and Mother Nature is increasingly disapproved of as messy, inadequate, harmful and shameful. We're told that our foods need processing, and that our world generally needs sterilizing before it's safe for habitation.

The trouble is we're addicted to these technologies, and to the artificial short cuts to feeling good that they can provide. In quantities quite unprecedented, technology permits us to eat, booze, charge things to our plastic, download pornography, watch TV, and consume our planet's limited resources. And we've been all too eager to take advantage of this, no matter the cost to our own physical, psychological and social health, and the wider health of our planet.

Technology traps us in a vicious downward spiral of self-defeating behaviours. We over-work, compromising our social life and loving relationships, so we can afford ever more technology-fuelled quick fixes, and so buy our way to temporary happiness. But rather than bringing us genuine satisfaction, technology only exhausts, isolates and demoralizes us further, leaving us even more vulnerable to its lure. Let's take a closer look at how the technology trap reels us in, and how we can break free.

Technology isolates us from each other

If it's the activities we're addicted to that reveal what's troubling us, then what do the following say about us?

▶ **The constant texting and mobile phoning and checking our emails dozens of times per day; anything and everything to communicate, no matter how trivial**
▶ **The ever-growing popularity of Internet dating agencies, chat rooms, blogs and social networking sites**
▶ **The insatiable male appetite for pornographic images and videos that account for nearly half of all Internet traffic.**

What the above appetites seem to be saying is that we're terrified of being sidelined, left out or left behind: we're longing to join up, to be intimate, to touch and be touched, and we're reaching for whatever substitute technology can provide. Only none of these technologies seems capable of quenching our thirst, because what we really need to do is spend face-to-face time holding hands with someone special to us. Instead, we're sitting in front of one sort of screen or another, and squeezing people in around our work schedules. In our over-crowded cities, many of us can't find someone to live with, let alone a lover.

Fame is fake friendship

Aristotle wrote that "the unexamined life is not worth living", a sentiment echoed perhaps by Descartes' "I think therefore I am". Increasingly, the twenty-first-century update of those philosophies appears to be "The unrecorded life is not worth living. I'm *famous* therefore I am."

But are we really reassured because more people know our face or name, or refer to us as their friend? This is one of the great promises of technology: more will mean better. More contacts, more networking. We're particularly vulnerable to these technologies that claim to connect us because we are highly social animals and hard-wired to want to share, to belong and run with a herd, and to increase our status among our tribe. But it's arguable that technology only gives the illusion of satisfying these instincts, while in fact drawing our energies away from more fulfilling relationships.

It exhausts us and dilutes our relationships

We tend to sleep two hours less a night than our grandparents' generation. This is because we're checking emails, surfing the net, watching TV, working too hard, and generally trying to do more than we can healthily manage. As we saw on pp.114–116, sleep deprivation harms us in so many ways, from triggering unhelpful cravings for food to dangerously reducing our decision-making abilities. But most insidious of all is that sleep deprivation erodes even our closest emotional bonds, which is why it's still the favourite method for "breaking" enemy agents. Unless we get enough sleep, we really don't care about anything or anyone, and we'll sell them and ourselves down the river.

All the symptoms described in this chapter are caused by the demands of our daily life outreaching and overwhelming our personal resources. This painful imbalance is itself very largely caused by our misuse and over-use of technology: too much over-long commuting, too many virtual realities, late nights and premature mornings. We are both profoundly exhausted and dangerously diluted, and this toxic combination results in the severe erosion of our most personal and treasured companionships – the companionships which would normally be one of the mainstays of our all-round well-being. As was argued in Chapter 1, beautiful partnerships are what allow profound progress in our relationship with life. But developing and sustaining such partnerships needs full engagement, which in turn requires from time to time our undivided attention. Even when we do get together face to face, too often there's a TV on in the corner, everyone's got their mobiles on, and too many people have popped some sort of pill or are busy getting drunk, so the quality of the relationship is depreciated. We spread ourselves far too thin in twenty-first-century life. We end up having fast and frothy cappuccino relationships rather than living life deeply. A dear old friend calls up saying "Hey, it must be two years since we last met! I'm on a stop-over, so what you say we meet for coffee and a catch-up?" They don't hear our heart sinking.

Technology renders us passive

If we were to summarize modern consumerist society's take on happiness, it'd probably be that life's all about *feeling* better, and there's really no need to *do* better. We've lost our respect for creative and exploratory real-life action, and prefer instead to sit and consume – whether that be fatty foods and alcoholic drinks, or words and images via books, TV and movies. As sociologist Robert Putnam (see p.162) dared put it, "we don't make friends, we watch friends". He could equally have said that we don't play football, we watch football – in fact, we'd rather not bother to do anything creative at all when we can watch others do it on cookery programmes, DIY shows and reality-TV dancing competitions. We are increasingly voyeuristic, distancing ourselves from reality by means of a flickering screen. And, of course, it's technology that's made all this possible.

The dot.com revolution brought us the likes of Google and Wikipedia, which encourage us to spend even more time sitting flabby in front of a screen and soaking it all up. We feel sure we're getting cleverer with every click of the mouse, even though we couldn't prove

When was the last time you made something with as much love?

that it does us a jot of good when it comes to *doing* anything or simply being comfortable in the company of real people. We put our faith too much in knowledge that can be gathered in lorry loads from the Internet. But knowledge isn't wisdom... the wisdom of what to do, when, and with whom.

Compared to our grandparents' generation, the great majority of us spend less time with our family and friends, move our bodies far less and create far less of anything personal: less home-made music, fewer home-made meals, less home-grown food. We prefer instead to consume ready-made, off-the-shelf versions of everything possible. This new

Re-engaging with reality

The problem with all this passive consumption is that the only way we make progress in our relationship with life is by engaging with reality. Reading doesn't change our lives, nor watching a film, nor even a fabulous conversation. These totally sedentary and entirely cerebral activities can only be a catalyst, an inspiration. It's creative action that progresses a life. It's *doing* that makes each of us distinctive – and makes a difference – by engaging us with the world around us.

We need to revive our appetite for adventuring for ourselves on foot, first-hand, up to our ears in reality. Exploring other cultures, other terrains – the ones out there beyond the textbook, the computer screen and the TV documentaries. Real progress is found in the act of actually doing, of innovating, of trying things out, and by teaming up in real life, not in the pages of a book, no matter how learned. Clever, courageous, kind isn't what we think or feel, it's how we behave. Living isn't what happens to us. It's what we do in response to what happens to us.

ratio of nine parts consumption to one part creative action seems to be hurting many of us, if our physical ills, psychological disturbances and fear and loneliness are anything to go by.

Technology erodes our self-control

By constantly offering to do things for us, technology starves us of the benefits we gain from using our faculties to their fullest capacity: working our bodies, our intellects and our passions in real-life scenarios. Over-used technology stops our physique and personality and social partnerships from growing strong through having to do things for themselves. Why bother? We are increasingly taking drugs to change our mood, and we look to cosmetic surgery to change our appearance. The age of slave-technology increasingly persuades us that we shouldn't have to make much of an effort to feel or look one way or another. Instant meals and pre-packed snacks make home cooking seem too laborious, ecstasy tablets and alcopops artificially lift our mood or help overcome our shyness, while the simple act of downloading pornography makes a real-life sexual relationship seem unnecessary. Technology offers instant gratification with no immediate cost. "Have now, pay later" seems to have become the motto of the age.

We humans are in danger of wilting through lack of effort, because we're not using our physical muscles or our free will to push ourselves forward or hold ourselves back. Compare the following list with what your grandparents would have done in 1950:

▶ **When we're a tad hungry or thirsty, we want to eat or drink immediately.**

▶ **When we're lonely, we text or email and demand a reply within hours.**

▶ **When we want something, we buy it on credit.**

▶ **When we're tired or challenged, we throw in the towel and look for an easy way out.**

▶ **When we're anxious or depressed we ask our doctor for something to swallow that will take the feeling away.**

▶ **When we're irritated we road rage, we argue, we divorce.**

Can you resist temptation?

Self-control and self-expression go hand in hand because self-control lets us behave according to our deepest principles and in the best interests of our most treasured goals. Far from being limiting, the skill of self-discipline helps us achieve our heart-felt desires, rather than being a slave to the dictates of temporary appetites.

And the younger we start, the better. A landmark study begun by Dr Walter Mischel at Stanford University playfully challenged some four-year-olds to sit alone and make themselves wait fifteen minutes before eating a marshmallow. Their reward would be a second one.

Some of the children covered their eyes, while others sang songs to distract themselves; but some gave in almost immediately. When researchers revisited these tiny research participants as teenagers some fourteen years later, those who had held out for the second marshmallow were significantly more self-confident, self-motivated and better able to deal with life's frustrations than the ones who had been more impulsive as pre-schoolers. Not surprisingly, these characteristics were strongly reflected in their academic achievements: if you didn't know how to resist a marshmallow at age four, it seemed you were unlikely to know how to study for an exam at age eighteen.

And the ability to delay our gratification pays off well beyond the classroom. The Harvard Study of Adult Development (see pp.194–195) concluded that one of the five life-coping strategies which characterized the most healthy, happy and accomplished individuals was that they didn't act impulsively, but rather dealt with things when and how it suited their best long-term interests. They were able to resist present pleasures for a greater net gain further down the road.

Sound a bit of a harsh indictment? When was the last time you went a month without an alcoholic drink? Or a fortnight without television? Or two days without sending or receiving text or email messages? Or fasted for 24 hours without food? The fact is, we have too little self-control. We're poor at resisting pain or dealing with discomfort of any sort – we don't learn to cope or to ride it. We want fries with everything.

Living real life is a highly demanding and uncertain challenge, and many of us humans seem less and less willing to accept that. We want satisfaction to come easily, to come now, and to come for sure. We need to rediscover our grit, our resilience, our sticking power, the pioneer spirit that says "sure it hurts, but so what? I'm not made of butter, so I won't melt."

Technology undermines our sense of mission

We lack self-control because we have no sense of mission, of something worth striving for.

John F. Kennedy declared in 1962: "We chose to go to the moon in this decade and chose to do other things, not because they are easy, but because they are hard, because the goal will serve to organize and measure the best of our energies and skills." He was on to something: we grow well when striving for a mission, a journey, a *raison d'être*, of which we can be proud, and which is worthy of our resources. We tend to do well when we have something to be self-controlled for – some goal to get up in the morning for, keep well for, team up for, stay sober for, and sleep deeply for. It's so much easier to ignore distractions and temptations when we're focused on something worthy of our attentions.

It's sad, then, that of late it seems many of us, whole nations in fact, lack a sense of mission. Perhaps it's because high-tech living has taken all the challenge out of life, creating, in John Gray's words, "a population which – though it is busier than ever before – secretly suspects that it is useless". Perhaps it's because the pervading climate of stress we read about earlier has undermined our faith that there'll be a future in which to see our goals realized. Whatever the reason, it seems we're no longer sure what there is in life that's worth fighting for.

Without a heart-felt mission to strive towards, what are we left with? Judging by how we behave, our answer seems to be "How pleasurable

Restoring our sense of mission

A heart-felt sense of mission can be such a powerful focus for our lives that it is well worth reflecting on what we personally feel is worth striving for, and how we can make this a central driver of our everyday life. Chapter 5 will be helpful in thinking about this. We might also take inspiration from the following two extraordinary lives, which show that even when the future is bleak and we feel powerless it is possible to live our lives with a sense of mission.

In 1943 the extraordinary young German **Sophie Scholl** (see below) was guillotined at the age of just 21 by the Nazi courts for distributing anti-war literature to her fellow students at Munich University. The 2005 film which bears her name (directed by Marc Rothemund) is faithful to the transcripts of the interrogations that she endured. Under relentless pressure, Sophie spoke out both passionately and articulately against the senseless killing of yet more young soldiers like her brother and his friends who had already served on the Eastern Front. The court offered to commute her death sentence to imprisonment if she renounced her actions, but Sophie refused: "Someone has to be the first to say it. What we said and wrote was thought by many. They just didn't dare say it aloud."

A twice-divorced mother of three young children, **Erin Brockovich** surprised herself and everyone else when she squared up to a vast corporation that had been negligently poisoning the water supply of a local community. (Her story was made famous by Steven Soderbergh's 2000 film starring Julia Roberts.) Despite being on the breadline and juggling bills and babysitters, Erin took on the bad guys, the self-reliant wile and grit she had acquired in her demanding home life standing her in good stead when it came to detective work and legal skirmishing. Deeply admirable for daring to have a go, Erin reminds us of the personal resources that can lay dormant within each of us until we set ourselves a worthy challenge.

In the light of such moving accounts, we might well ask: what might I have done… and what action can I embark upon now that is true to my values, no matter how modest and faltering my first step?

can life *feel*?" We may not truly believe it's a worthy goal, but maybe it seems like our last resort.

Saving our soul from technology

The world-leading technologist Professor Lord Alec Broers of Cambridge University was right to title his series of magnificent Reith Lectures in 2005 "The Triumph of Technology". But that triumph needn't be at the expense of our well-being. We need to put technology back in its place, as a tool to be used with discretion, rather than the over-riding addiction it has lately become.

We need to reconsider the benefits of using, and not using, technology. We need to find ways to better harness its advantages, so that it fosters rather than hinders our fundamental human bonds and our progress in life. And sometimes we need to remind ourselves that we can simply say no. When technology says "Sit back, I'll do it for you", we can say "No, I'd like to do it for myself." We can exercise our ability to walk, run or ride our bike; go see someone rather than send an email; play an instrument or sing aloud rather than have our iPod do it for us. And when technology says "Here, have some more", we can say "I don't want any at all. I don't want to have my Blackberry with me when I'm out with friends and family. What I want is to be disconnected from the blabbering digital world, so I can focus on who I'm with in the here and now."

Cherishing our human senses

In our greed for speed and quantity, our abuse of technology pays little respect to the human senses, which have evolved for far more subtle relationships. "MORE!… FASTER!" is the dominant motto of our technological age. People send us reminder emails if we've not got back to them within 24 hours. "I've had trouble with my server – did you receive my request this morning???" But they're fibbing. They want what they want NOW! They hate to wait. How can we counter the headlong rush of technology, which hurries us along with its promises that "you can have more, faster, and you've not even got to be there, let alone make any effort"? We could try living deeper and broader, rather than longer and faster. Doing so will give our senses time to savour, space to breathe.

Fasting

Fasting – going without – is one way to reawaken our senses. Deliberately going without food is something very few of us have ever contemplated, and the nearest we've come to it is accidentally missing a meal while having a busy day. Yet missing a whole day's meals, by going without food and only drinking water from 8pm until 8am 36 hours later, can be a helpful reminder of how resilient we are, and how we really don't need nearly as many snacks and pick-me-ups as we tell ourselves, or are told by advertisers. Of course fasting needn't be all about food: we could fast from computers for a week, or television for a month. In fact, it can be a salutary experience to fast from anything we've come to rely upon or take for granted: alcohol, text messaging and emails, for instance. We could walk rather than sit, talk rather than write, sleep rather than watch. Fasting is one way to reassure ourselves that appetites can be resisted if we develop the ability to say no to ourselves as well as to others. We might also find ourselves curious to know what feelings, thoughts and actions will fill the gaps made possible by fasting.

Caught on camera versus living off the record

Are we in danger of over-doing the photo-taking and cam-recording of our everyday lives?

We might wonder why, when our human brain has had several million years to develop a flawless memory, it so clearly hasn't. There's no such thing as a photographic memory, and when it comes to recollection, what we come up with is something far more creative that we make there and then like baking a cake. This creative process of messily recording and then messily recollecting might actually serve a very healthy purpose, because this built-in malleability allows us by one means or another to reconcile ourselves with the past and move on. Is there a danger, then, that our insatiable appetite for digital mementos might do something akin to sealing our past in plastic and, by doing so, diminish our ability to digest it?

Of course, another reason for leaving the camera in its case is that to get the best from something, we need to immerse ourselves in the moment, even if this means we have it once only and there's no rewind button.

Slowing

Having begun fasting, we could also begin slowing.

We are too often like that White Rabbit who appears, briefly, in *Alice in Wonderland*. He's late and is going all to pieces because of it.

One of the underlying messages emerging from "well-being" approaches to life is not to let ourselves be swept along in a "rush and hurry, cash and carry, greed for speed" existence. Whether we're kissing or conversing, eating or driving, teaching or learning, let's try doing it gently and with greater depth. Slower motion for more profound progress is a strategy as old as the hare and tortoise fable, but it still applies. Let's not push life, let's lead it.

By simply taking sufficient time, we allow our senses to savour. When did we last stroll somewhere and pause and ponder the world around us, rather than power-walking our way to some destination seemingly more important? How slowly can we eat, speak or breathe, yet not lose these activities' essential flow? If this idea appeals, rather than telling ourselves to slow down, like the voice of an anxious mum, we'll respond better if we encourage ourselves to "turn on the slow motion", because trying actively to do something is usually far easier than trying not to.

The Slow Movement

With hundreds of thousands of adherents worldwide, but no particular HQ or centre, the Slow Movement originated in Rome in the 1980s as a protest against the opening of a McDonald's branch at the foot of the Spanish Steps. That protest inspired the founding of a "slow food" movement promoting locally grown, organic produce, biodiversity, traditional foods and eco-friendly, fair-trade values (see terramadre.info and slowfood.com). Since then, the benefits of living life slowly have inspired the concepts of slow travel (slowmovement.com/slow_travel.php) and slow cities (cittaslow.org.uk), among others. These emerging campaigns are united by their striving to re-establish socially oriented living whereby mealtimes, work schedules, commuting and other activities are sympathetic to the human need for savouring and companionship.

A commentator on these deeply appealing ideas, the University of Oslo emeritus professor of philosophy Guttorm Fløistad, explains: "The only thing for certain is that everything changes. The rate of change increases. 'If you want to hang on you better speed up.' That is the message of today. It could, however, be useful to remind everyone that our basic needs never change. The need to be seen and appreciated! It is the need to belong. The need for nearness and care, and for a little love! This is given only through slowness in human relations. In order to master changes, we have to recover slowness, reflection and togetherness. There we will find real renewal."

An added bonus is that taking an automatic skill, such as speaking, and doing it in slow motion renders the activity more accessible to our conscious mind (rather than the automatic pilot of our subconscious), and so presents an opportunity to re-craft even deeply ingrained habits.

A final strength of going slow is that we will often find far more joy and satisfaction in investing in a good journey, in the experiences en route, than in compromising our travels for the sake of some jackpot at our final destination. On this point, elite athletes often recount how, if they allow themselves to be distracted from the job in hand by imagining the moment of their impending victory, that's when the game can suddenly slip away.

Face to face

The communications giants are quick to claim that we will be better connected by their equipment. What the technology companies neglect to tell us is that more communication doesn't necessarily make for a better relationship, just as more information doesn't necessarily make us any wiser. It seems far more likely that there's some magical ingredient at work when we're in someone's company, face to face, hand to hand: we either hit it off, or realize we don't. We sense things that spoken or written words don't tell us. And the very fact that we're making time to be with one another is proof in itself of the worth we place upon the possibility of our getting on. So let's not be fooled into believing we can survive on a fast-food diet of phone calls, text messages and emails. Such heart-numbing "busyness" is deeply unsatisfying.

Our communication technologies would also have us believe we can keep up with the dozen or more people who've left town this past year or two. Instead of losing one friend and making another, we're tempted to keep both relationships spinning. But there's a high price to pay for this, not least because of three inherent problems.

First, the sheer speed and plague proportions of phone calls and emails has totally devalued them as a means of connection. Compare their impact to the message sent by a handwritten letter laid down in ink from a fountain pen. Such a rarity shows the recipient that we care enough to bother; that they matter.

Second, a virtual relationship may have little to do with the one we can sustain when face to face. Emails and calls cannot replace the shared adventures that are the lifeblood of a healthy relationship. We

Are we living too long?

John Steinbeck, author of *Of Mice and Men* and *The Grapes of Wrath*, won the Nobel Prize for Literature in 1962, and died three years later at the age of 66. In 1961, in *Travels with Charlie: In Search of America*, Steinbeck spoke out against the greed for longevity that even back then he felt was running riot: "I am not willing to trade quality for quantity. I see too many men delay their exits with a sickly, slow reluctance to leave the stage. It's bad theatre as well as bad living."

It's the limit on things that makes them valuable. Thankfully, our days of life are themselves numbered, and the simple lack of a guarantee can help bring us the courage to engage and savour.

can kid ourselves we're still together, but *being there* is the truly wholesome way to be a part of someone's life.

Third, the time and energy we invest in those dozen or so high-tech correspondences with absent friends jeopardizes our relationships with the folks we see every day in our face-to-face life. We end up shuffling along immersed in our mobile, or texting while we're with other people as if our present companions or real surroundings are somehow insufficient for us.

Such a state of affairs needn't be a *fait accompli*. We could say to an absent loved one: "I shan't be writing or phoning or texting. Not because I don't love you, but because I do. I don't wish to dilute what we have. I'll wait to share everything with you when I make time to spend a long weekend in your good company."

Quietly

Noise – unwanted sound – is one of the most insidious but under-recognized taxes on our well-being. School classrooms, open-plan offices, motorway driving and city living can all be so damn noisy. People with lawnmowers and strimmers and leaf-blowers, police helicopters and ambulance sirens and car alarms, tannoy announcements, other people's music and television drivel. Our travel-fatigue when flying may have more to do with that white hum of noise for several hours than with the dehydration and time-zone differences. Disposable wax earplugs that mould to fit the opening of the ear canal can help enormously with all of this. Makes conversations more interesting, too, because you have to guess what your companion might be saying to you.

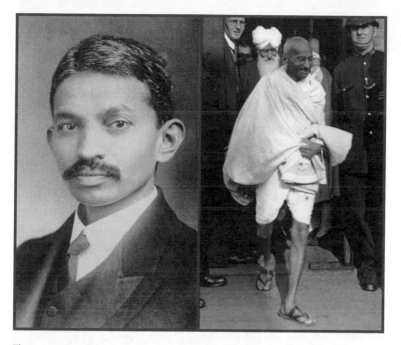

The young Gandhi (1869–1948) graduated from University College London and was called to the English bar as a barrister-at-law. Yet it was when dressed simply as an Indian fakir in homespun cloth that "Mahatma" ("great-souled") Gandhi had perhaps his most inspiring influence upon the world. One might say his progress was made possible by rediscovering the essential fundamentals. Might our relationship with technology have something to learn from this?

Naturally scented

Our sense of smell is such a source of delight – a freshly peeled fruit, wood smoke, the pages of a book, a loved one's hair – and it's such sensitivity that makes us vulnerable to technological bullying. We can only wonder at how our own natural body scent and that of those around us are distorted by the array of soaps, shampoos and artificial deodorants that we're persuaded to wear or forced to inhale. What is their effect on our social relationships, let alone on our sense of taste which so relies on our nose?

In all its guises, the seductive promise of technology is "more, faster, easier – life distilled – life concentrated". But that's not how life works; it wants to be wholesome not distilled, and savoured, not gulped. Life needs its natural form.

Conclusions

In Plato's *Charmides*, he recounts the teachings of Socrates from circa 390 BC: "One should not go about curing the body without also curing the soul. And this is exactly why most ailments are beyond the capabilities of Greek doctors, because they neglect the whole when that is what they should be paying attention to, because if the whole is in a bad state it is impossible for any part of it to be in a good state."

Socrates' words are a powerful reminder of the "wholeness" of our mind–body system, of the soul's centrality to our all-round well-being. Technology's assault on our soul is one of the greatest challenges to our happiness. But putting technology back in its place, to serve as a tool rather than ruling us through addiction, will require us to remind ourselves what it is we hold most dear. For it's this that we will fast for, go slow for, fall silent for, be present for. It's the who or what that makes our life worth living that will give us the strength to say no to the distortions and illusions of technology, so as to fully engage with the on-going journey of a life more beautiful.

10

Exploring the possibilities

Exploring the possibilities

What now, and where to start?

What have the voices and images brought together in this Rough Guide been trying to tell us? How might we act helpfully upon whatever may have moved us? This final chapter takes a last look at some of this book's recurring themes, and endeavours to suggest some practical ways to get started with creating a more wholesomely happy life.

Proving we prioritize well-being

Nullius in verba is the motto of the Royal Society of London: *nothing in words*. Words can be a good beginning, and perhaps a fitting end, but they're not the stuff in the middle. Words need action to give them weight. An idea isn't made whole until we've done something about it.

So, let's not be like the scared student who spends twenty hours reading (consuming other people's ideas) for every hour invested in creating their own explanations, and discussing out loud, and doing things for real. Let's not watch TV while promising ourselves all the places we'll go, and the friends we'll make. Let's act immediately to set ourselves rolling forward.

The measure of us is what we do *now* – not what we say, not what we plan, not even what we've done already. And what we do, how we behave, actively builds muscles, so it becomes not just the measure of us, but the making of us. Whether or not we succeed, our trying isn't wasted.

We'll never know enough to guarantee the outcomes. Life doesn't trade in certainties. The very essence of living is not knowing what's around the next bend. So let's follow our best hunch, our rules of thumb, and make a move anyway, no matter the pains and perils en route. As Shakespeare wrote in *Troilus and Cressida*, "Joy's soul lies

In *Breakfast at Tiffany's* Audrey Hepburn embodies a bold-spirited willingness to embrace adventure as she sings Johnny Mercer and Henry Mancini's "Moon River":

"Moon River, wider than a mile,
I'm crossing you in style some day.
Oh, dream maker, you heart breaker,
Wherever you're going I'm going your way."

in the doing". We are living creatures, so let's create. Rather than listen to music, let's play music. Rather than watch sports, let's take part. And rather than watch the news, let's try to be good news for the local world in which we live. If our endeavours feel a bit amateurish at first, then that's all for the better. The word *amateur* comes from the Latin *amare*, meaning "to love". We embrace the unknown *for the love of it*.

Nietzsche was on to something when he wrote "Active, successful natures act not according to the dictum 'know thyself', but as if there hovered before them the commandment: *will* a self and thou shalt *become* a self."

This Rough Guide's philosophy at a glance

From its very first pages, this handbook has proposed that profound happiness is brought about by improving our rapport with life. This endeavour seems to benefit from the coming together of at least six raw ingredients, however we choose to create them within our everyday lives. Our mission is to be ingenious in how we interpret and apply these qualities to our particular circumstances:

1 Well-rounded: Lasting improvements come from embracing a good range of dimensions, perspectives and activities that honour *all* of our passions and callings, needs and abilities. Such a broad-ranging approach also creates synergies whereby the rich mixture of ingredients serve to enhance each other's benefits.

2 Well-balanced: Life makes many demands upon us which will naturally pull us uncomfortably off balance unless we actively compensate with complementary activities that rekindle and restore us (rather than temporarily anaesthetizing our discomforts by eating, alcohol, TV or other such distractions which only lead to more problems further down the line). The better we can balance ourselves, the further we can reach in our personal and professional lives. And the fuller the stretch, the better it will feel, as long as we're in balance. Using all of ourselves at full capacity feels great. That's flow: where the demands of the task are well matched to our capacities and hungers at the time.

To be well-rounded and well-balanced is to be wholesome, and this quality is caused by and creates a passion-led, lion-hearted, nature-loving rapport with life.

3 Passion-led: Let's make our heart-felt vocations our guiding compass and our motivating energy. Our intellectual cleverness and physical skills should help our passions, not hinder them. Our passion may come from great joy, deep gratitude, sheer desperation or a ferocious desire for revenge, *but passion we must have.*

4 Lion-hearted: Let's undertake our journeys with a spirit of highly adventurous exploration and experimentation that stretches us to our furthest capacities by being risk-taking, rule-breaking, mistake-making, varied, playful and surprising. It's these good-natured and gregarious characteristics which time and again appear to be the well-springs for many of the most satisfying and accomplished lifetimes.

5 Nature-loving: Let's be actively respectful, considerate and compassionate of all that's natural and wild within us, as well as around us. Not least because we need to better balance the artificial and excessive demands made by technology in all its forms, which can be so dismissive of our human needs and our natural environment.

6 Rapport with life: Let's make our life rich in close and creative partnerships

Inner and outer wild

If we don't honour our own wildness and nature, we are less likely to honour the nature and wildness around us. Maybe it's this that's holding humans back from a really whole-hearted embrace of the environmental movement.

with people, places and skills, in which the synergies are such that we achieve far more together than we ever could alone.

Weaving these six themes together is the idea that life feels so much better when we join it all up, rather than allowing ourselves and what we do to be separated or broken down into bits and pieces. Ever bought a new pair of shoes and then realized you actually need a whole new outfit to go with them?

Harnessing the wind in their sail and working together to balance the boat by putting themselves at full stretch – these lucky youngsters are learning lessons fundamental to life, and loving every moment.

What could this mean for our daily life?

Opening the preface to this book was a story about how baby elephants can become big elephants who don't think to explore what's possible. So let's just remind ourselves what the "Universal Exploration of Well-being" proposed at the end of Chapter 1 might mean in our everyday lives.

It could mean taking everything we do from the moment we wake up to the moment we fall asleep, and reconsidering how we could make the activity more fully rounded, and how the different elements could better balance each other. How, too, could each activity be more respectful of our heart-felt passions, of our inner and outer nature, of a mission worthy of our abilities, and of our need for close relationships? In a breath: how could we lead a more beautiful life?

▶ **When we awake first thing:** We could take five full minutes to relax our body and breathing so as to better consider our passions: who or what makes our life worth living, and what can we actively do about it today? What mission could we set ourselves that would be so self-motivating that it would persuade us to go to bed an hour earlier each night, so we could pursue it each morning? That is, going to bed early enough so we can sleep eight full hours yet wake refreshed in time to pursue our passion for a full sixty minutes or more, whether it be running, horse riding, book writing, music playing or planning a round-the-world trip. Think what it might mean to set out on our day's work knowing we've already honoured such an important part of ourselves.

▶ **A nutritious breakfast:** We could slowly eat just a very small portion of a much wider variety of foods, since a naturally colourful plate of ingredients usually indicates a good range of nutrients.

▶ **Our morning commute:** Can we make it far more physically active and open to the elements of daylight and fresh air, perhaps striding, running or cycling at least part of the way? Or can we introduce some reading or thinking that is a good balance to what the rest of the day demands of us?

▶ **Working well:** Is our work fully exercising us – satisfyingly stretching us – in our four core dimensions: emotional, intellectual, physical and social? What could we do to improve this situation? Are we responsible for completing whole tasks, A to Z, or just some fraction of a job? And once our task is set, do we have a satisfying sense of choosing how we go about it in ways that get the best from us, or do we feel bullied by a method imposed upon us? Does our work as a whole faithfully reflect our sense of what's important in life, or is it our means to a worthy end?

▶ **Putting technology in its place:** How about we check our emails only after lunch, so that our morning is entirely proactive – a reflection of what we deem important rather than simply a reaction to all the harrying emails that claim to need a reply straight away or sooner. For exactly the same reason, we might turn off our phone and simply check messages in the afternoon. Focusing all of ourselves on our appointed tasks can make a major difference to our productivity and quality of work.

▶ **Rekindling ourselves over lunch:** Let's try some slow-motion gentle breathing, body stretches and relaxation before arranging for a meal whose most nourishing ingredients include fresh air, daylight, natural surroundings and good companionship. Sandwiches in the park anyone?

▶ **Back to work:** When trying to go the extra mile, let's ask ourselves: i) How can we better relax, because relaxation helps our mind and body stretch further and faster? ii) What arts, sciences, faiths, philosophies and therapies might shed new light on our endeavours? iii) Who inspires us, because even Einstein worked with his heroes peering down on him from the pictures he'd hung above his desk?

▶ **Come the evening, how can we actively unwind?** How can we actively re-balance the demands of the day? We have a tendency to try to anaesthetize our aches and frustrations by consuming – alcohol, TV, food and so forth – whereas an equally fast but infinitely more rewarding strategy is to very actively do something; i.e. actively create rather than passively consume. If our day's been rather verbal, sedentary, polite and emotionally self-restrained, then we'll benefit enormously from an activity that is non-verbal, emotionally expressive, physically active and social for its own sake. These ingredients are to be found in singing, jiujitsu, dancing, and far more besides.

▶ **All-round exercise:** Rather than just working our bums and tums, or slogging away on a running machine in the gym, we could use our whole body in a variety of ways to exercise a fuller range of muscles in a fuller range of movements.

▶ **Giving all of ourselves to whoever we're with:** Let's turn off the mobile phone once we come in from work, so we can be in the moment with our loved ones and share some face-to-face mini-adventure together: from cooking dinner to playing games. How about having a rule that we don't discuss work for anything more than a fifteen-minute de-brief? This way, the job isn't allowed to dominate our personal relationships so that our home life can be a restorative sanctuary, and so be beneficial to our working life. Let's not forget that the principle of balance tells us that if we want to improve our professional life, we need to improve our personal life; and if we want to work better we need to learn to play better.

▶ **And when we're tucked up in bed again...** With no emails to check, calls to take or TV to watch, we might actually get to bed in time to have a full cycle of sleep: around eight hours. We might read a cheering novel, as we slow-motion breathe and relax our body to ease ourselves down from the day and put our subconscious in a comfortable state of mind. We can ask ourselves "What three things happened today that I can be grateful for?" And by doing so, we set our mind to a train of pleasing thought that can enhance our whole night's sleep.

The common theme to all of the above is boldly exploring how we can make every activity more wholesome. A good place to start is just doing things differently, so as to get us off "automatic pilot". So, at the supermarket, we could walk around the opposite way from usual, and buy a whole week's worth of entirely different items. We could put the phone to our other ear, and try a day when we don't use emails or the mobile at all. One day at the weekend could be set aside to explore a quite different dimension of life. We could put away the TV for a month so as to invest in real people and real activities. We could slow down and deeply relax not only our speech but our eating, our going to the loo, our bedtime reading and our making love. We could sign up for an evening class that we've not previously considered. Unexpected part-

Time to earn your wings: consider the peaceful grace of a glider flight that relies on your skill for appreciating and channelling the natural resources all around you – a lot like life. You'll recall from Chapter 1 that it takes just fifteen hours for most folks to fly solo for the first time. Getting ourselves airborne – in a glider and in life – needn't take for ever.

Notes on a "healthy partnership"

The healthy partnership is one in which we each explore, create and achieve far more than we could alone. We feel bolder, more considerate, more open-minded. The reason we can go beyond ourselves is that the other person inspires our passions, but also balances us, and by doing so allows us to stretch further. Together, we spiral upwards. And when we turn ourselves jointly to something, the magic of the relationship has far greater power than the sum of its parts on account of the synergy between us. In romance, friendship or work, such are the characteristics of a really healthy partnership.

nerships – odd couples – are often the most creative. Variety in the sorts of personalities we know is always a healthy thing.

The aim of all of this is to shake ourselves out of any ruts so we're able to make a fresh appraisal of the values by which we're living.

What's holding us back?

The Nobel Prize-winning physicist Richard Feynman once told a graduating class of students "The first principle is that you must not fool yourself – and you are the easiest person to fool. So you have to be very careful about that." The point being that our enthusiasm to be right, or our reluctance to face the problems, can easily get the better of us. If we are to make progress in our life we mustn't kid ourselves – we need to keep things as real and face-to-face as we can bear. We need to keep at bay all those things that blur or distance reality: our temptation to lie, exaggerate, fantasize, drink or take pills. And when life hurts, rather than anaesthetize ourselves, we'd do better to wonder instead what the pain is telling us and where it could carry us if we could only learn – or dare – to ride it.

Any persistent failure to progress in our relationships, our work or our physical health is no accident. We saw in Chapter 2 how traumatic pains or even traumatic pleasures are quite capable of trapping us in a cycle of unhelpful behaviours. To move on, we need to understand what hidden beliefs, fears or rewards are tethering us in place, or causing us to self-sabotage. Only then can we lessen or prevent the sort of civil war between our conscious and subconscious mind that can result in physical ills (from migraines and IBS to sleepless nights and ME), as

It's not our age, it's our attitude

Why should we feel it's too late to make progress in our life? There's no such thing as "too old". Youthfulness, at its best, is not an age, but an attitude: it is the passion to progress rather than be stagnant. It is curious and inquiring rather than blinkered and closed. It is flexible and adaptable rather than rigid and backward-looking. Rather than being pompous, youthfulness makes its point with playfulness and humour. And it's a skill we learn by trial and error, just as we have to learn maturity. For all of these reasons, youthfulness is beautiful; but neither youth nor beauty pay heed to age, just as wisdom is not the exclusive preserve of the old.

well as psychological impediments to our progress in life (from phobias and flashbacks to self-limiting relationship roles). There are at least three common causes of our subconsciously fuelled problems:

▶ **An inadequate balance between our four fundamental dimensions (our emotions, thoughts, body and social relationships)**
▶ **Not honouring our heart-felt passions**
▶ **Emotional trauma from an incident or relationship in our recent or distant past**

If you suspect subconscious distress may be causing you problems, turn back to Chapter 2 for a reminder of how we can gently invite our subconscious mind to declare its hidden motivations and consider some more helpful ways of dealing with life. Progress will usually follow. A crucial benefit of promoting our internal harmony like this is that the better relationship we have with ourselves, the better relationships we can create with those around us. Also take a look at the following chapter, "Working with a Therapist", because professional help is vital in helping us tackle such emotional trauma.

Learning to relax helps everything

If there is one theme that's recurred time and again throughout the preceding chapters, it's that there is no part of our life that cannot greatly benefit from the skill of relaxation: our work, play and loving; our eating, thinking and talking; our dancing, singing, sex and falling asleep. In short: our rapport with life is profoundly improved by relaxing into things.

Thank goodness, this skill can be learned.

"Relaxed" needn't mean doing things slowly. Slow can still be tension-bound, as with the perfectionist who is painfully slow because he's so extremely tense, worrying he won't be good enough. Relaxed, on the other hand, reveals itself in being fluent and fluid, no matter it be fast or slow. Relaxed is not bothered about the outcome, but is fully engaged by the journey. Relaxed helps us be well-rounded because it helps us be supple and versatile enough to try new things. Relaxed helps us be well-balanced because it's centred rather than being pulled tensely in one direction or the other. Relaxed allows us to balance better and stretch further because we make faster and more sensitive adjustments. Relaxed helps us boldly explore because it's not rigid or rule-bound.

▶ **Physical relaxation** is embodied in the fluidity of dancing or singing.
▶ **Intellectual relaxation** is the solution suggesting itself when we're not straining to think about it.
▶ **Emotional relaxation** means we can move easily and unencumbered from one feeling to another.
▶ **Social relaxation** allows us to explore some rapport with another person, without fretting about where it's all leading or whether they will like us or not.

It's not that tension is the enemy: tension is the complementary opposite of relaxation, its necessary companion. For instance, feeling passionately called to a mission is the polar opposite of deep relaxation; and we need them both to make progress. However, our everyday lives do tend to be tension-rich and relaxation-poor. That seems to be the way most of us are wired, the result of our evolutionary history in which our ancestors had to keep always one step ahead of ferocious predators and harsh environments.

Our ineptness at relaxation causes us all sorts of problems: because we are prone of late to lead narrow and imbalanced lives that don't naturally embody relaxation, we tend to be lonely (because we're not good at rapport), irritable and aggressive (because we're tired and frustrated), tense and depressed (because we're stuck rigid in a negative view of the world). In an attempt at self-medication, we resort to things that first excite us and then slump us into a superficial level of relaxation, such as excessive use of alcohol or food or frightening films. Technology exacerbates this unhelpful cycle because of the "More, Now, Faster, Faster!" mentality with which we tend to apply it. Technology too often disrespects our *journey* in favour of the *outcome*. It tends to be objective-focused. It gets us there by bus or car, but only by bullying along the road, noisy and disrespectful, whereas a horse or bicycle or running would have required so much more relaxation and rapport.

What, then, can we do to relax in healthy ways?

We could try moving our body, our emotions, our intellect and our relationships, indeed our whole life, *the other way* from whichever way we're presently being over-pulled, so as to stretch ourselves in re-balancing directions. We could also seek improvements in the flow of our mind–body energy system by learning how to work "energetically" with our meridians and chakras as suggested on pp.130–134.

Explore and experiment

Self-evidently these past few millennia since we've been making notes, no silver bullets or formulas for life have presented themselves. The principle which suggests itself is "explore what works and when!" This is akin to "find a good fit … the right niche", an idea which is itself related to synergy, and to the notion of the "beautiful partnership" (discussed in Chapter 1).

We do best to explore for ourselves not only because no ready-made answers present themselves, but because we learn so much better that way. So many times in this book we've come across the idea that we

Even exploration needs its opposite

Our emotions and intellect, like our body and social relationships, will adapt to what we ask them to do most often. The more challenging situations we put ourselves in, the more capable we'll become. But there's a caveat: in our hunger for improvement, let's not forget that exploration as much as any other activity needs to be balanced – balanced by times of stillness and tranquillity; times in which we rest easy, we recuperate, we relish and savour and sleep deep; times in which we reconnoitre possible journeys and potential travelling companions. Our abilities to consolidate, to play and to restore our spirits are crucial allies in our attempts to make lasting progress.

A time for everything

In the Bible's Old Testament, Ecclesiastes 3 seems to support the whole idea of discovering what works and when:

To every thing there is a season, and a time to every purpose under the heaven:
A time to be born, and a time to die; a time to plant, and a time to pluck up that which is planted;
A time to kill, and a time to heal; a time to break down, and a time to build up;
A time to weep, and a time to laugh; a time to mourn, and a time to dance;
A time to cast away stones, and a time to gather stones together; a time to embrace, and a time to refrain from embracing;
A time to get, and a time to lose; a time to keep, and a time to cast away;
A time to rend, and a time to sew; a time to keep silence, and a time to speak;
A time to love, and a time to hate; a time of war, and a time of peace.

learn best not from books and theory, but from getting into the thick of things, fully inhabiting the moment and engaging with and exploring complex, messy, real life. What's more, we are creative and expressive beings, and we need to create things for ourselves, not follow steps prescribed by others. It's perhaps no accident that many world-inspiring pioneers are self-taught (see the box overleaf on Philippe Petit), in the sense that they learned by doing things for themselves, and by observing a range of "master practitioners" around them, rather than swallowing a particular syllabus. Life itself is the most important skill of all, and everything we've read in this Rough Guide suggests that getting stuck in, exploring and creating solutions for ourselves, is the best route to getting really good at living, just as it is for any other skill.

Daring is beautiful

No matter it's a musical piece or a gymnastic performance, an arthouse film or a human face, whichever one attempts the more daring composition is the one most likely to win first prize and capture our hearts.

Why does such daring appear more beautiful to us? The more daringly something is balanced, the further it can reach, and by doing so it discovers things and surprises us. If we can bring disparate elements

It only appears impossible

In the summer of 1974, the 24-year-old Frenchman Philippe Petit walked across a 43-metre length of steel wire stretched between the 417-metre-high rooftops of the newly built Twin Towers in Manhattan. He did so not once, but eight times. No parachute. No safety harness. No permission. Simply the passion of a six-year dream, impeccable planning, some good (and bad) luck, and the indispensable help of loving friends. All of that, and a great deal of highly realistic practice which began a long summer nine years before when he first taught himself the wire-walker's "art of balance".

The audacious mission seemed impossible until Petit, together with his girl-friend Annie Allix and his long-time friend and accomplice in adventure Jean-Louis Blondeau, began to explore the impossibilities. Solutions began to emerge. For instance, they fired an arrow from one rooftop to the other that bore a fine filament of fishing wire – this led to a thicker cord, then a rope and eventually, several hours later, 200kg of steel cable. (What a wonderful metaphor for how our grandest ambitions can be achieved from the slimmest of beginnings!)

Before taking on the Twin Towers adventure, Petit had performed wire-walks on the Sydney Harbour Bridge, the Eiffel Tower and the towers of Notre Dame. He had also practised tirelessly with the sorts of high winds, rain and treacherously bouncing wire that he might encounter on the day.

This exuberant and audacious joining together of the Twin Towers was certainly rule-breaking, but very importantly Petit took great care to do no harm. Here was a wholly benign and deeply inspiring act of creativity. Petit was on the wire for 45 minutes: dancing, kneeling in salute to his audience and the seagull above him, and lying outstretched on the wire. New Yorkers declared themselves grateful for the gift, the magnificent display, the sense of freshness and wonder that it brought to their lives, and the feat was recounted on newspaper front pages around the world. Rising to the occasion, the authorities charged Petit only with trespass and causing a public disturbance; and even these charges were dropped in return for his giving a more pedestrian performance for the city's children.

Beyond the teamwork, ingenuity, resolve and engineering expertise, this wasn't simply a display of balletic prowess. Much of its awesome beauty came from its inherent danger. It was daylight robbery, and what Petit got clean away with was his life. Though his preparations were superb, even so he confessed "Death is very close … but to die in the exercise of your passion: what a beautiful death."

When asked *why*, Petit said "there is no why". He was simply defying the fear and bullying of the seemingly impossible, and honouring the beauty of those towers. We need to know our limits, but should not restrict our dreams. "You must exercise rebellion!" says Petit.

together successfully, and still have them balance each other, then something very wonderful can be created.

So often the special moments in life – no matter they be ideas, melodies, games, sex, stories, solutions or relationships – are the ones that take delightfully unexpected turns. But there's a price to pay. Exploring

Perhaps some of the magic of Petit's mid-air stroll is that it stands as a metaphor for how all of us can traverse seemingly impossible divides between where we are now and where we aspire to be. Petit describes himself as half engineer and half poet but, above all, an explorer. For sure, his actions embodied rounded balance, and a passion-led, nature-loving, lion-hearted rapport with life.

(Petit's adventure is recounted in his captivating memoir *To Reach the Clouds*, and in the documentary film *Man on Wire*.)

the "beautifully unexpected" can't really be done without getting our knees grazed and our hands muddy. Exploration is messy stuff, but our life is often making most progress when things are messy (or maybe things get messy when life's making progress). Nor is uncertainty a reason to do nothing. Progress, as with walking or running, is only made possible by losing balance so we can move forward. The greater our ability to tolerate such uncertainty, the further we can venture. It's like reaching out our hand to life and saying "We don't yet know each other, but do you care to dance?"

And finally...

Though our explorations will be a journey, we should not expect "arrival", because it seems the natural state of life is to be a work in progress. William Blake wrote:

> He who binds to himself a joy
> Does the winged life destroy.
> But he who kisses the joy as it flies
> Lives in eternity's sunrise.

So let's not demand that things stand still or be permanent. It seems our experience of life is meant to be worn loosely, and flows better that way. To live is to journey, which is why the measure and the making of us is not how far we've already come, but rather…

▶ **The journeys we are now inspired to set out on**
▶ **The spirit in which we travel**
▶ **The loving companionships and rapport that we dare to create en route.**

Thank you for reading. And in pursuit of the beautiful journey, let me wish you "Bon voyage!"

Nick Baylis
Well-being explorer

Appendix:

Working well with a therapist

Working well with a therapist

Seeking guidance from experienced practitioners

The fundamental message running throughout the pages of this book is that there is very much we can do ourselves to prevent and alleviate psychological problems, and develop our strengths and passions. However, sometimes it is wise to partner up with a professional therapist or coach for the additional insights and encouragement they can provide. In earlier chapters we've learned about many of the techniques a professional guide might use. As a complement to that information, this chapter describes what to look for in a therapist or coach, and what to expect from your relationship with them. It also puts the spotlight on the two commonest psychological ills – depression and anxiety – and describes how working with a skilled and sympathetic practitioner can help enormously with both of these.

Some starting principles

Becoming depressed or hyper-anxious about daily life, or feeling badly affected by incidents or relationships from the past, is all part and parcel of living. None of us avoids these pains, any more than we could or should avoid cuts and bruises when we're out for a hike in the wilds.

That said, we can do a great deal to help ourselves to heal by paying ourselves the respect of exploring what works best for us and when – a theme which has proved itself to be the founding motto of this book.

A reasonable rule of thumb is that if some of what we think or feel or do is getting in the way of our everyday life, or limiting the best of our heart-felt ambitions, then it's time to seek professional support. After all, we see specialists to heal or improve our teeth, eyes, hair and every other part of our body, so it makes good simple sense to see someone who has made a full-time profession out of understanding the roots of problems and of enjoyment in life. One phone call can be the catalyst to wonderful changes.

Here are some further thoughts to bear in mind when considering seeking support from a professional.

▶ **It's well worth facing up to things.** The skills we learn in owning up to and tackling our problems will stand us in extremely good stead in every other arena of our daily lives. For instance, in our most personal relationships and our working life, we will find ourselves more exploratory, keen to be well-informed, ready to challenge so-called expert opinions, and more able to keep ourselves going in the face of life's inevitable setbacks. By working through our problems, our personality grows stronger, deeper and more richly coloured. That's good for us, and good for those closest to us. We owe it to ourselves and those we care for.

▶ **Team up with a healthy range of well-proven professionals** for the encouragement, fresh ideas and different perspectives they can provide. The temptation is to soldier on alone, or see the topic as taboo, or feel as if we're whingeing. Everyone, but everyone, has experience of some really troubling problems, so we're not the odd one out. However, no one is going to be nearly as interested in solving our problem as we are, so it's we who must set the pace of progress.

▶ **Research what's known about the problem.** It helps if we make ourselves an expert on the problem, by checking it out on the Internet and finding out about the very latest book. If we're to make headway, we need to be prepared to experiment and to broaden our horizons.

▶ **Be world-class.** We should tenaciously seek advice from specialists in quite different fields until we find someone who can help us beat the thing. In this search, let's bear in mind that the approach taken by British or North American practitioners might be quite different from standard practice by medical practitioners in Germany (who can choose to prescribe the herb St John's Wort to lift depression), in the Netherlands (who can send stressed and depressed patients to therapeutic farms), or in Japan (who use magnets in mattresses or worn on the body to relieve chronic pain). So let's be a truly world-class explorer when we're seeking improvements. (If we're discerning about the quality of websites, the Internet can be a help in this.)

▶ **Take multiple approaches at the same time.** As this book has repeatedly argued, there are no silver bullets that work all the time or for everyone, and most problems require a combination of powerful measures that when taken together are sufficient to overcome the inertia and improve things, thanks to the positive synergy between them.

▶ **Therapy and coaching go hand in hand.** Effective coaching requires us to address problems that may be holding us back, while effective therapy requires us to build upon our existing strengths and skills. Hence, therapy and coaching can be seen as complementary endeavours that merge into one another.

▶ **We're never average.** Science and medicine tend to be interested in averages, i.e. what works for the average Joe and for the majority. As individuals, though, we very often fall far outside the statistical average, and so we need to explore and experiment to find out what works for us personally.

▶ **Keep cheerful.** We should take mini holidays from fighting the problem, and do whatever else it takes to keep ourselves in good spirits. This will enable us to recover in the face of set-backs, and to be resourceful in weaving around obstacles.

How to find a good therapist

Your medical practitioner can be a good source of information on reliable therapists who have proven themselves able to help people back to good health. Alternatively, a well-run complementary health clinic that has a range of associates practising different crafts is worth visiting to find out what's available. The peer pressure and collegiate atmosphere of such a dedicated health centre can help keep standards high and minds open and versatile.

A recommendation from one of our own friends is also a starting point for choosing a therapist, but it's important to remember that our needs might be very different from theirs. A good fit between our needs and personality and the particular skills and personality of whoever we end up working with is arguably the single most important factor in a successful client–therapist partnership.

Qualifications are no substitute for well-proven, well-respected experience. Unfortunately, membership of a particular professional organization offers little guarantee that a therapist is as keen as they were when they qualified, is any good for our particular sorts of problems, or will work well with us. Training courses in professions of the same name (counsellor, clinical psychologist, psychoanalyst) are rarely standardized, and many of the job titles listed below are not protected by law in some countries, so for instance in the UK anyone at all can put a brass plate up calling themselves a hypnotherapist or psychoanalyst or psychotherapist, without so much as a minute of training. So-called "master practitioners" in a host of therapies may have received little more than a week's training course. Diplomas may have been earned in just one weekend rather than a whole year.

It recently came to light that prime-time TV nutritionist "Dr" Gillian McKeith had acquired her doctorate – a PhD, not a medical doctorate – via a correspondence course from a non-accredited distance-learning college. McKeith agreed to stop using the title "Dr" in her advertising when the Advertising Standards Authority deemed it could be misleading to the general public. At the very same time, no less an eminent figure than the NHS consultant psychiatrist and Professor for the Public Understanding of Psychiatry Raj Persaud, who had been constantly in the media advising the public on mental health issues, was found guilty of passing off other people's work as his own, and so "bringing the profession into disrepute". He was suspended for three months. Such revelations left us wondering how many other "experts" have professional qualifications that might not tell the whole story.

It is because such uncertainties exist at all levels of the healthcare marketplace that word of mouth from trustworthy sources is all the more helpful to us. We have to be a good detective and make some calls to find out about the person we'd like to work with. A confident therapist will happily give us the email or phone number of an organization or fellow practitioner who can vouch for them. Thereafter, nothing beats being prepared to try a couple of sessions and either stick at it or move on to another therapist, depending on how much confidence we have in the emerging relationship.

Some common job titles

Here are just some of the many therapeutic approaches available. In the UK, most can be found in the state healthcare system, and all of them can be found in private practice. In the US, some would be covered by your health insurance; for others you would have to pay privately.

▶ **A well-being therapist** takes a decidedly holistic, fully rounded and highly exploratory approach to life improvement (akin to what this Rough Guide strongly advocates), looking for dynamic measures to improve the balance and harmony between our physical, intellectual, emotional and social dimensions. Their approach is both remedial (i.e. addressing problems as would a therapist) and developmental (i.e. positively developing existing strengths as would a coach).

▶ **A psychotherapist** is a very general term for any specialist who attempts to improve their client's psychological health. They may use one or a whole range of techniques (but never prescription drugs of any kind; that is the preserve of a psychiatrist).

▶ **A counsellor** may or may not have quite the same depth of training as a psychotherapist when it comes to particularly serious psychological problems.

▶ **A Cognitive Behavioural Therapist (CBT therapist)** uses CBT (see pp.82–85), an approach widely favoured by state-provided psychological healthcare in the UK and US, and may not have training or experience in other complementary approaches.

▶ **A psychologist** is the general term for someone in the field with a psychology qualification beyond undergraduate level, but he or she may not be a therapist; they may instead have specialized in research or lecturing. However, the terms "clinical psychologist" or "counselling psychologist" clearly indicate that the individual has specialized in therapeutic practices, though the range and type of their approaches is by no means standard.

▶ **A psychoanalyst** is a psychotherapist who uses an approach largely grounded in some form of Freudian or Jungian theory and practice (see pp.63–64). Such analysis can often be intended as a long-term therapy with weekly meetings over many months or years, unless the analyst specifically practises a shortened form.

▶ **A psychiatrist** is a medically qualified and state-licensed doctor who has specialized in psychological problems and is trained and licensed in using prescription drugs to tackle those problems. They also have some training in talk-therapy techniques.

▶ **An energy therapist** conceives of the human mind–body system as having subtle energies that can be beneficially affected by a range of techniques such as Thought Field Therapy or Emotional Freedom Technique (EFT) (see pp.130–133). They may or may not have a background training in psychotherapy. (A well-being therapist or psychotherapist might use an energy therapy technique, or hypnotherapy, as one part of a whole range of approaches.)

▶ **A hypnotherapist** uses hypnotic techniques (see pp.65–73) to help improve our physical, psychological or social health. They may or may not have a background training in psychotherapy. The same goes for NLP therapists (see p.72), since NLP is largely derived from the principles of hypnosis.

▶ **A life coach** may or may not have a therapeutic background, but is a specialist in "performance improvement" rather than remedial work. They may have business or sporting credentials relevant to their approach and clientele.

The costs and benefits of therapy

The most pertinent question here is: can we afford not to? Consider what our problem might be costing us financially in terms of days off work, or delayed promotion, or the money we spend distracting ourselves from the problem (perhaps through binge shopping, extravagant holidays or other anaesthetics that ease the emotional pain temporarily). We might then look at what matters far more, which is the cost in terms of our close personal relationships and our quality of life in general. Can we afford not to face up to what problems are chasing us, or holding us back?

An effective course of therapeutic training can often require fewer than a dozen weekly one-hour, ninety-minute or two-hour training sessions, (depending on how the therapist prefers to work and what pace suits us), plus some daily homework assignments. With the help of a good professional, we'll soon learn skills that build back our psychological, physical and social confidence, in much the same way that specific physical exercises help us regain the full use of a muscle after we've suffered an injury, or sports or music coaching will help us stride ahead. It's well worth the effort so as to lead our life the way we want to.

There are no standard fee rates, but in the private health sector it would be very unusual to pay less than £50 ($100) for an hour's session; £100 ($200) would be the middle range, and £250 ($500) for a meeting of between one and two hours is by no means excessive for a high-profile professional in popular demand. Bear in mind that a good therapist must consider your notes before you arrive and make further notes when you leave, and will need to take themselves on expensive training courses to keep at the top of their game. And if they don't work from an office at their home (the ambience of which is particularly conducive to such personal one-to-one work), they will have office rent and secretarial charges to cover. The reality is, therapists are rarely matching the annual income of other similarly qualified professionals, yet they are making vital judgements on what course of action to recommend to their client.

What to expect from a good partnership

Knowing what makes for a good therapeutic relationship – and what we ourselves need to bring to that partnership – will allow us to get the very best out of our training sessions.

A sense of rapport

Expect rapport to develop between you – i.e. a considerate and compassionate appreciation of and responsiveness to each other. We need to feel comfortable with the person we'll be working with, and feel that they have our best interests at heart. We need to feel that they rather like us, and that they certainly respect us for making an effort to improve our situation. They should also radiate a powerful positive energy, and be optimistic yet realistic in their plans about helping us make major strides.

If, for whatever personal reasons of their own, our therapist is just going through the motions with us, or there's a sense of rush or weariness on their part, then even the most capable practitioner will still give

A good rapport between you and your therapist will make all the difference to how well you progress. In *Good Will Hunting*, therapist Robin Williams provides just the right mixture of hard-talking home truths and irreverent good humour to help Matt Damon release himself from the self-destructive anger that has haunted him since childhood. This film also captures very well how therapy isn't neat and gradual and linear. More often than not, we tend to make breakthroughs towards the end of a session, or after a couple of static weeks in which our problem may have seemed particularly resistant, even belligerent.

second-rate service, and we're best to move on to someone who's at the top of their game and passionate about helping us.

As in any other relationship, a healthy partnership is one in which you spiral upwards together, bringing out good things in each other that far outweigh the irritations and drawbacks.

An active collaboration

Life-changing therapy is a highly collaborative process and requires our highly active participation. We and our therapist are allies, just like a hill-walker teaming up with a native guide for help through some unfamiliar and difficult terrain. We don't want a "You doctor, me patient" sort of relationship. That's why we should bring a notepad and pen to our meetings, because good therapy requires us to be very active in our listening, thinking and explaining. To draw a comparison with making physical improvements, psychotherapy is like having a sweat-breaking work-out with an instructor at our side guiding and encouraging our activities. It is not at all like having a massage or visiting our dentist whereby we just turn up, sit back and let it happen, with little effort required from us.

Putting it into practice

Improvement relies on a potent combination of revealing talk and dynamic action. We might practise role plays so as to rehearse different ways of dealing with tricky situations; and there will be homework tasks for between sessions, ranging from reading a book or watching a particular film through to joining a couple of social clubs or taking a day in the countryside. This homework is important because getting better is something we have to do every day. If we're not making time for this, then getting better isn't a priority for some part of us, conscious or subconscious. Our reluctance to invest in ourselves needs to be challenged.

Discussing the problem and doing imaginative rehearsals and role plays once per week is no substitute for actually leading our life differently. It's vital to do things differently so as to derail our unwanted behaviour, thought or emotion. So, if we want to relieve our stress and depression, then we're going to have to become far more physically and socially active in a wide variety of rewarding ways. This will perhaps hurt at first, because we'll be exercising unused or barely existing muscles; but our capacities will build. Only frequent and regular exercise will develop the skill of asking someone to dance or actually dancing with them quite comfortably, just as learning to speak well in public is half a matter of background confidence and half a matter of real-life practice. Understanding and confidence alone won't build our physical muscles, helpful habits and lovely companionships. There's no avoiding the sheer mess and mistakes and perspiration of everyday reality, not if we want to live well. They're our stepping stones.

Challenging questions

Your therapist will probably challenge you in quite uncomfortable ways. Because they are on your side, from time to time they are going to question your behaviour or deliberately provoke what might be your unhelpful responses so that you can both see how you're coping. This might involve questions such as:

▶ **If there was emotional energy driving this problem, take a guess at what emotion that would be.** For example, the emotion might be "I hate myself", "I want to punish so-and-so", "I don't deserve to live well", "I was bullied when younger and got scared of life".

▶ **When *don't* you have problem symptoms?** Under what circumstances do you spontaneously and dramatically improve?

▶ **What will your life be like when this problem is behind you?** Why will it feel so much better?

▶ **What, paradoxically, might be the downsides of you getting over this problem?** What might be the hidden benefits of being held back by this?

The more honest, clear and revealing we can be in our explanations of our present problem and our hopes for the future, the better chance we have of progress. Our therapist will be looking for patterns in our behaviour, and our track record in health matters, work and personal relationships, that might help reveal the dynamics of our inner and outer life. At some point, it would be unusual if our therapist didn't explain and discuss with us the workings of our subconscious mind and how that relates to our conscious decisions and behaviours.

Finding the root cause

Our goals in therapy benefit from being highly flexible. Though it's natural and even helpful to have clear goals to start with (for example, I want to feel far less anxious), we should be prepared to change course en route, because what seems to be the source of all our problems (perhaps our IBS or depression) often turns out to be merely a symptom of some underlying cause or combination of causes, perhaps incidents or relationships that we as yet only half acknowledge are a problem.

We will find, too, that our problems are rarely singular; they tend to have multiple aspects. For instance, perhaps I was traumatized by an incident of bullying twenty years ago, when I was thirteen. I may presume that it is only fear that grips me. But when I find myself thinking about it, I won't just feel fear, I might consciously or subconsciously feel shame at myself for being too weak to prevent it, anger towards those responsible, and deep sadness or loneliness for having been abandoned to such pain like that. So a range of left-over emotions may hinder my confidence and ability to concentrate on my studies or work, and to engage in healthy social relationships. Likewise, my emotions will be reflected in my body, perhaps affecting how my stomach and guts feel and function, where my eyes look or daren't look, how my speech and voice sounds, how comfortable I am with human touch, how much I sweat, and how deeply I sleep. It is because of the inter-woven nature of our mind–body system that we need to consider the whole problem and its effects on every aspect of our lives. All of those left-over emotions will need to be addressed in therapy.

(As we saw on p.56, there are excellent techniques to neutralize traumas from our past, which do not require us to recount the initial incident; so we shouldn't worry that effective therapy need entail any upsetting blow-by-blow disclosures of painful past experiences.)

Taking a break

Be prepared to take a break from your therapist. You may have worked together twice weekly or at least fortnightly (because frequent and regular sessions make it easier for both of you to maintain momentum). Perhaps after twelve sessions, though, you could at least consider moving on to a new therapist for a while, because whatever helpful "muscles" (psychological, physical and social) have been developing, they will need rest and recuperation time, just as an athlete needs rest at the end of the season. Other muscles can then be focused on. If you've worked with a CBT therapist, perhaps now's the time to explore energy therapy; if you've worked with an Ericksonian hypnotherapist, why not explore so-called eco-therapy (working on the land for a week or more, to allow the break and the natural surroundings to heal stress or depression).

Depression and anxiety

Depression and anxiety – the commonest of psychological ills – most often travel together. It seems that if we are anxious we all too easily become depressed about it; and if we're depressed, we're prone to fret about every aspect of it. Such is the vicious circle.

It is very possible that some form of emotional trauma (a negative incident or episode in our lives, whether four weeks or forty years ago) is driving our depression or anxiety. Identifying and dealing with such trauma is discussed in detail on pp.51–62 of Chapter 2, "Our Subconscious"; though, as is emphasized there, the support of an experienced therapist will be very important to us in this.

Identifying depression

The likelihood is that someone we know well is quite depressed, even though they might be hiding it. It's estimated that one in four of us will become seriously depressed at some point in our lives, and the average age for someone to have a first major depression is now just fourteen. Back in the 1960s, an individual would be nearer thirty when depression first hit them. This is no longer just a problem of over-worked executives or parents. It seems that everyday modern life is rather more demanding and less nurturing than it once was. (Reasons for this are suggested in Chapter 9, "Saving our Soul from Technology".)

Depression is a much over-used word, but we might usefully describe a psychological depression as when everything in life feels lacklustre and miserable. Not just one arena, but everything; and it won't lift even after a few days. As well as being characterized by low moods, it can show itself in irritability, sleep problems and lack of appetite for food, friendship, sex and all of life's other fundamental callings. As a rule of thumb, we are depressed if for two or more consecutive weeks our once enjoyable activities fail to bring us pleasure, and we've been resoundingly down in the dumps with life feeling like one long grind.

It's estimated that only a quarter of individuals who suffer this very debilitating state actually seek help for it, not least because depression is characterized by a lack of motivation and a pessimistic outlook. It's because of those feelings that a sufferer will tend to drop out of psychotherapy within a couple of sessions because their dark moods persuade them that their situation is hopeless. Yet the reality is that no matter the cause of our depression – and there can be many – if we practise a good range of well-proven approaches, we've every chance of initiating a full recovery.

Some possible approaches to depression

Depression is not simply a result of something that happens to us, because it's not uncommon for someone to lose their job, or to lose a loved one, and yet they do not necessarily become depressed. Depression is our *reaction* to something, and this means it lies within our power to change that reaction by generating positive thoughts and activities. So, rather than reaching for a quick fix to numb the pain by one means or another (alcohol, TV, too many cakes, or trying to buy our way out of the blues with spending sprees), we would do far better to apply nature's own-brand remedies. For instance, just as depression can have physical, psychological and social symptoms, its remedies can likewise be physical, psychological and social:

▶ **Let's take care of our bodies.** A depressed and hyper-anxious person will benefit greatly from a good range of frequent and vigorous physical activity, broad daylight an hour every day, a rich variety of fresh and nutritious foods, and adequate sleep and naps (see Chapter 4, "Our Bodies", for more detail on all of these).

▶ **Let's reconsider our goals.** Randolph Nesse, a pioneering professor of psychiatry at Michigan University, argues that depression can sometimes serve the strongly beneficial purpose of telling us to stop our activities and reconsider. He proposes that depression could be a healthy response to our unhelpful tendency to set ourselves goals that are too large and too distant. All the evidence suggests that many of us derive far more satisfaction from pursuing highly manageable, shorter-term goals, indeed multiple goals so long as they are all pulling in compatible directions that are truly in line with our values and passions.

▶ **Let's improve our social life.** Building a better social life of rewarding personal relationships is probably the strongest and most reliable means of improving our physical and psychological health.

We are highly social animals and thrive in the company of others, whereas loneliness can lead to rumination and looking inwards. Joining a local club, voluntary society or neighbourhood group can introduce us to a healthy variety of new personalities and points of view (see pp.162–164).

The advice and encouragement of a sympathetic therapist will be very helpful to us as we aim to make positive changes in our lives in ways such as these; but at least some of these changes are so simple and straightforward that we can make great progress all on our own.

Identifying anxiety disorders

Feeling stressed, anxious, scared, terrified? Everyday worries are one thing, but anxiety disorders are a very uncomfortable state of unease which prevents us enjoying and progressing in our everyday lives. Such disorders can come in several different forms. See if any of the following resemble what you've been suffering:

▶ **Generalized Anxiety Disorder** is a condition in which most of our day, every day, for week after week, is filled with a sense of worry and anxiousness. We're jittery, on edge, tense and nervous, and this state is likely to leave us tired, irritable and sleeping poorly.

▶ **A phobia** is an unreasonable and excessive fear of quite particular things such as the dark, spiders, cats, crowds, heights, flying or being home alone.

▶ **Social phobia** is an excessive fear of feeling humiliation or embarrassment in public. (For children this might mean a phobia about how their peers will judge them.) This is strongly related to shyness and even perfectionism and the fear of making mistakes.

▶ **Obsessive-Compulsive Disorder (OCD)** is characterized by repetitive thoughts, images or impulses that we find very hard to resist. These might include repetitive washing or cleaning, or checking that taps are turned off, or thinking a negative thought. As a sufferer, we might know that the frequency of such thoughts or behaviours is excessive and quite unreasonable, but we are unable to stop them intruding much of the time. The purpose being served for our subconscious by these compulsive rituals of mind or body is to reduce our sense of anxiety, though this underlying goal might not always be obvious to us.

▶ **A panic attack** is an overwhelming fear that some catastrophe will befall us. There's a range of physical symptoms such as an alarming shortness of breath, dizziness, racing heart, chest pains, chest tightness, nausea or a cold sweat. We fear that we might die of suffocation, or lose control of our mind or body in some way. We might also fear we are suffering from some severe medical problem, perhaps having a heart attack or a stroke. The attack begins abruptly, peaks within about ten minutes, and then subsides gradually. Afterwards we're prone to live in real terror of another attack.

▶ **Agoraphobia** (from the Ancient Greek meaning "fear of the marketplace") can often develop after panic attacks, but might also be unrelated. We become irrationally but overwhelmingly afraid that, while out and about in some public space where we would be helpless, we will somehow fall ill or need help or be caught short. Physical symptoms of agoraphobia might include dizziness, nausea and fainting.

Some possible approaches to anxiety

No matter which brand of anxiety we're suffering from, in the great majority of cases psychological measures are better than drug therapy by a considerable distance, very largely because people treated with drug therapies are far more prone to relapse soon after they cease taking the medication (see box overleaf). Here are some quite different approaches that a therapist might explore:

▶ **Slow-motion breathing.** Everyday anxiety, such as run-of-the-mill worries and apprehensions, responds very well to gentle, slow breathing for twenty minutes, twice per day; perhaps when we're in the car, in the bath or at our desk. (Such breathing is fully described on p.74.) This is because our rate of breathing affects our brain state, i.e. relaxed or tense. An anxious individual will often have relatively fast breathing as if slightly out of breath, even when they're sleeping. (No one's subconscious mind sleeps; it keeps watch; but some more anxiously than others.)

▶ **"Gradual desensitization"**, whereby you, step by step, achieve a comfortableness with the once-feared stimulus, would usually go hand in hand with this sort of breathing. Such desensitization is described on pp.53–56.

Considering prescription medicines

When we're addressing our depressive and hyper-anxious symptoms, we owe it to ourselves to thoroughly discuss the pros and cons of prescription medications with one or more trusted physicians. Such medications can obviously be dangerous, can have a range of unpleasant side-effects, and can be addictive. Yet they can also work swiftly and well for some of those who use them, correcting a brain chemistry imbalance that psychotherapy or other lifestyle techniques cannot remedy sufficiently or fast enough. For these reasons and more, the effects of such medication for each and every one of us need to be frequently and thoroughly monitored by the medical practitioner who prescribes them to us. Unfortunately, medications have too often been over-prescribed and their usefulness to the individual patient has been inadequately monitored by some over-burdened medical professionals. What well-respected studies also seem to show is that depression recurs far more often after medication than it does after non-drug psychotherapy. This means that for many of us, medication might be appropriate for short-term and medium-term symptom relief over several months, but we should be very cautious of automatically accepting its longer-term use. In any event, such medication should not be seen as a seemingly easier solution for our emotional discomforts than learning to use our social relationships, thoughts, feelings and bodies in far more helpful and satisfying ways. Medication should only be one of a whole complement of dynamic approaches, as outlined in this chapter, and the rest of the book.

▶ **Subtle energy therapies.** As we saw on pp.130–134, these therapies are thought to tap into our mind–body energy circuits known as meridians. With names like Thought Field Therapy, EFT and Tapas Acupressure Technique, they bring together two different approaches: using our fingertips to stimulate our acupressure points while simultaneously focusing our conscious attention on whatever is troubling us, whether the problem be emotional, intellectual, physical or social. When applied in conjunction with all-round dynamic change to our daily lifestyle, they are perhaps the most promising yet least known innovation among all of the complementary therapies. With the guidance of a really experienced practitioner (there are still too few of these), many of us will find that even long-standing emotional traumas, depression, specific phobias, panic attacks and general anxiety can all be dealt with in just a handful of sessions. Moreover, our demoralizing physical symptoms will quickly alleviate once the root mind–body cause is remedied.

▶ **Paradoxical Intention** (PI) is a therapeutic technique devised originally by Dr Viktor Frankl, whereby we do the very thing we've been trying not to. So let's say we often feel an anxious compulsion to repeatedly check that the front door is locked. Our therapist would encourage us to very deliberately check it time after time, no matter it be 150 times one after the other, until we're quite sick of doing so and grind to an angry halt. Or, if we're prone to lie in bed at night worrying, instead we very deliberately try to stay awake and do lots of disagreeable chores. The idea is that our mind (conscious and subconscious) soon gets the message that the negative habit which has been bullying us is most unwelcome. Paradoxical Intention allows the energy that's driving the bullying symptom to trip over itself in its own eagerness to bully us. Rather than try to stop it, we accelerate it out of control till it tumbles in on itself. PI uses a mixture of known antidotes: it confronts the symptom, laughs at it, exaggerates it beyond all possibilities, surprises it, and by so doing derails it.

Conclusions

The bottom line is, if our problem is interfering with our everyday life, we should see a specialist professional. All the above insights and ideas – indeed this very handbook you're holding – are intended as complementary approaches to the tailor-made personal guidance we should seek out from a highly recommended therapist with whom we can quickly establish a good rapport. What we don't want to do with any form of depression, anxiety or other distressing symptom is to permit the problem to distort our life any longer, while we postpone facing up to it. With the help of a good therapist, we could begin to make major improvements in just a handful of sessions, even with some very long-standing, quite debilitating and seemingly insoluble problems. From then, our sense of progress will be its own reward and will help re-energize every aspect of our life.

Most people don't dare seek help in the first place, don't persist tenaciously in the face of inevitable setbacks, or don't vary their approach so as to keep progressing. Let's not be one of them. Finally, let's remember: what works for one person won't work for another, and what helped six months ago might not take us any further. Look around enthusiastically. Stick at it. The future's ours for the making.

Where now?

Where now?

Courses, books and films to inspire well-being

I f you feel inspired to continue your exploration of some of the themes raised in this book, here are a handful of training courses, books and films that might provide a helpful next step. You'll see I've been very selective, and this is for three reasons:

▶ I wanted to vouch for each suggestion from my own personal experience.
▶ I wanted to present a manageable number of suggestions rather than swamp you with choices.
▶ Each of the following have something to say about the whole of life, rather than focusing on one aspect in isolation. Such wholesomeness is rare.

Training courses

Rather than being bound by one school of thought, these highly practical training courses benefit from being free to draw upon a range of approaches. They have the added bonus of being open to all members of the general public, with no previous experience necessary.

One-day Workshop in Applying the Skills of Well-being
Putting into practice the themes of this Rough Guide, this friendly and encouraging day is designed to help a wide range of adults foster profound improvements in their personal and professional lives, and the lives of those they care

for. It is suitable for individuals and partners, parents and teachers, healthcare professionals and personnel managers, university students and retired folk. Taught by Dr Nick Baylis at soul-inspiring locations in Cambridge, England; or on-site at your workplace anywhere in the world. Visit nickbaylis.com.

Practitioner's Diploma in Teaching the Skills of Well-being
(in schools, healthcare and business settings)
This course of circa six intensive days equips you to teach and apply these well-being principles with confidence in your workplace. The diploma is designed, tutored and examined by Dr Nick Baylis, leading a team of some of the world's foremost practitioners. It is hosted at beautiful venues in Cambridge and London, and cities in the US, Canada, Australia and Europe. Visit nickbaylis.com.

Practitioner's Diploma and Masters in Human Givens Psychotherapy
Mindfields College
For those interested in psychotherapy practitioner training, the Human Givens approach offers a broad-ranging and well-taught programme affiliated to Nottingham Trent University, England, that is popular with some National Health Service departments. The diploma requires attendance at several introductory days, plus eight full-day workshops and eight full-day seminars, followed by a two-week intensive course commonly held in London, York or Bristol. The masters programme requires a substantial supervised research and written thesis component, in addition to the diploma requirements. Visit mindfields.org.uk.

Three books to follow up

Each of these books gives a sense of confiding in the reader with a very personal perspective on living life that is nonetheless grounded in some of the world's most compelling evidence. As a set of three, they would nicely complement each other.

Learning from Wonderful Lives
Dr Nick Baylis (2006, Cambridge Well-Being Books. Only available by mail order via nicksbook.com)
Here are gathered the lessons from the study of well-being, brought to life on every page by the personal stories of some much-admired individuals. From Oprah Winfrey to Lance Armstrong, Kate Adie to Ellen Degeneres, J.K. Rowling to Bill Bryson, Nelson Mandela to Mahatma Gandhi, fifty profoundly inspiring lives illustrate every point with poignant moments and good humour.

Philosophy for Polar Explorers: What They Don't Teach You in School
Erling Kagge (2006, Pushkin Press)

In 1994, at the age of thirty, Norwegian Erling Kagge became the very first human in recorded history to have taken himself (unassisted by dogs, skidoos or aircraft) to Planet Earth's three poles: the North Pole, the South Pole and the summit of Everest. Fifteen years on, he is a father of three, as well as an acclaimed publisher and collector of contemporary art. This is a deeply personal and beautifully illustrated celebration of the possibilities for exploration in our everyday life, inspired by a whirlwind tour of art, philosophy, science and culture in the good company of this Renaissance-spirited family man.

Ageing Well: Surprising Guideposts to a Happier Life from the Landmark Harvard Study of Adult Development
Professor George E. Vaillant (2002, Little, Brown)

This is a tender summary of some key lessons about nurturing our mind, body and social relationships, drawn from what is widely regarded as the finest study of evolving lifetimes. Written by leading psychiatrist George E. Vaillant, who directed the Harvard Study for 35 years of its 65-year duration, it reads like a fine novel and proffers powerful insights for adults of all ages, not just those aged 50-plus upon whom it focuses.

Further reading

We all sigh heavily at those recommended reading lists that seem to go on over the page and into the distance. With this in mind, none of the following have been added lightly. Each would more than repay its privileged place on your bedside table, and may well become a treasured friend.

My Voice Will Go With You: The Teaching Tales of Milton H. Erickson
edited by Sidney Rosen (1991, W.W. Norton)

The original words of one of America's most influential therapists, full of vivid insights into developing our everyday rapport with our subconscious mind.

Man's Search for Meaning
Viktor Frankl (1959, Beacon Press)

Dr Frankl recounts what philosophies of life helped him survive years in the Nazi death camps and the loss of his family.

The Seven Principles for Making Marriage Work
John Gottman (1999, Crown)

For many years this well-respected psychologist has taken the trouble to closely observe partnerships-in-motion.

Straw Dogs
John Gray (2002, Granta)

Written with succinct and accessible clarity, this is a fabulous all-in-one critique of our religious, philosophical and political thinking these past few thousand years.

Genius Explained
Michael J.A. Howe (1999, Cambridge University Press)

An intriguing protest against the all-too-common belief that you need to be born with special genes or abilities to get really good at something.

Psychoanalytic Energy Psychotherapy
Phil Mollon (2008, Karnac)

A lucid, up-to-the-moment overview of the theory and practice of subtle energy techniques and their unifying mind–body approach to improving well-being.

All Quiet on the Western Front
Erich Maria Remarque (1929, Vintage)

A heart-rending, life-cherishing tale of a young man speaking up for a whole generation of youth misled into bloody war.

Join-Up: Horse Sense for People
Monty Roberts (2000, HarperCollins)

This is a clear guide for parents and those working with young people, advocating gentleness between living creatures, by the man they call the "horse whisperer".

The Black Swan
Nicholas Nassim Taleb (2007, Penguin)

Is it possible that good luck and ill fortune play a far greater role in every aspect of our lives than we dare admit? Taleb presents some stunning possibilities.

Adaptation to Life
George E. Vaillant (1977, Harvard University Press)

A compassionate and vivid account of how a closely followed group of male Harvard graduates fared in their personal and professional lives in the next forty years.

YoungLivesUK.com
This website for young people and educators brings together life-advice from a range of highly accomplished individuals.

Inspiring biographies

We each of us know of folks whose lives inspire us to do better with our own, and we should consider ourselves very fortunate if we can learn from their first-hand accounts of how they managed things. Here are four wonderfully different individuals whose personal stories help illustrate that there is no one way to live life beautifully.

The Autobiography of Eleanor Roosevelt
Eleanor Roosevelt (1961, Da Capo Press)

A deeply spirited account by America's best-loved first lady, who in mid-life reinvented herself as a world-leading philanthropist.

Long Walk to Freedom
Nelson Mandela (1994, Little, Brown)

From childhood to protest against apartheid, and eventually winning his freedom from 27 years of incarceration, here is the life of this Nobel Peace laureate and first black president of South Africa.

An Autobiography: Or the Story of My Experiments with Truth
Mahatma Gandhi (1927, Penguin)

From early childhood and training as a British barrister through to his eventual return to India, here are the personal philosophies of one of history's greatest advocates of non-violent protest against oppression and injustice.

In the Footsteps of Churchill
Richard Holmes (2005, BBC Books)

A well-balanced and compelling explanation for the great strengths and flaws, victories and defeats, that carved and coloured the lifetime of Britain's most admired leader.

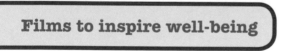

Films to inspire well-being

Each of these is a delight, and for very different reasons. But at the heart of each is a celebration of life's possibilities no matter the pains that befall us.

Into the Arms of Strangers: Stories of the Kindertransport
2000, dir Mark Jonathan Harris

This Oscar-winning documentary tells the story of the German-Jewish children who were evacuated to Britain from Nazi Germany at the eleventh hour in 1939. The evacuees, now elderly men and women, recall their experiences in a series of moving interviews.

American Beauty
1999, dir Sam Mendes

A portrayal as painful as it is humorous, of how parents and their teenagers alike face personal crises in their lives.

Little Miss Sunshine
2006, dir Jonathan Dayton and Valerie Faris

The story of a floridly turbulent family who nonetheless hold each other together.

Ferris Bueller's Day Off
1987, dir John Hughes

A delightful madcap comedy that reminds us, young and old, to take time to savour life.

It's a Wonderful Life
1947, dir Frank Capra

The story of someone in the depths of despair who questions whether their whole life has really changed anything for the better, at which point their guardian angel steps in to offer some alternative perspectives.

Credits

v Dr Alejandra Gardiol; 1 AFP/Getty Images; 6 Pat LaCroix/Getty Images; 15 MGM/Warner Bros/Ronald Grant Archive; 17 NASA; 21 MGM/Loew's/Warner Bros/Moviestore; 23 Mike Powell/Getty Images; 24 Paul Maze; 25 FilmMagic/Getty Images; 42 Working Title/Relativity Media/Studio Canal/Universal Pictures/Focus Features/Kobal; 44 © Reuters/Corbis; 61 © Christian Schmidt/zefa/Corbis; 69 Courtesy of the Milton Erickson Foundation, www.erickson-foundation.org; 73 © Mary Evans Picture Library/Alamy; 84 Liberty Films/RKO Radio Pictures/M&A Alexander Productions/Republic Pictures Home Video/Artisan Entertainment/Moviestore; 89 © Chris Lee; 102 © Mindaugas Urbonas; 104 akg-images/Erich Lessing; 113 © Kevin Galvin/Alamy; 122 Paul McCormick/Getty Images; 128 © Stuart Forster/Alamy; 133 © Kelly-Mooney Photography/Corbis; 140 DreamWorks/Jinks/Cohen Company/United International Pictures/Kobal; 145 Image courtesy of Monty and Pat Roberts Inc.; 152 The Metropolitan Museum of Art, Arthur Hoppock Hearn Fund, 1916 (16.53). Image © The Metropolitan Museum of Art; 153 The Metropolitan Museum of Art, Bequest of Hamilton Fish, 1894 (94.9.3). Image © The Metropolitan Museum of Art; 156 Alberta Film Entertainment/Focus Features/Good Machine/Paramount Pictures/River Road Entertainment/Kobal; 162 Bavaria Film/Radiant Film GmbH/Süddeutscher Rundfunk/Twin Bros Productions/Westdeutscher Rundfunk/Columbia Pictures/Ronald Grant Archive; 165 Photo Researchers/Science Photo Library; 167 National Geographic/Getty Images; 168 BAHA, photograph by Drum Social Histories; 175 Amblin Entertainment/Canal+/Carolco Pictures/Lightstorm Entertainment/Pacific Western/T2 Productions/TriStar Pictures/Artisan Entertainment/Live Home Video/Moviestore; 189 © Craig Tuttle/Corbis; 193 © Lynsey Addario/Corbis; 199 © Austrian Archives/Corbis; 201 The Art Archive/National Gallery London/John Webb; 207 Getty Images; 211 Getty Images; 221 "Income and happiness: Comparing countries" (p.32) from Happiness by Richard Layard (Penguin Books, 2005). Copyright © Richard Layard 2005. Reproduced by permission of Penguin Books Ltd.; 223 James Strachan/Getty Images; 241 Reproduced courtesy of NCFI; 243 © Nick Baylis; 244 © Daniel Start. Reproduced courtesy of Punk Publishing; 252 © Joseph Sohm; Visions of America/Corbis; 259 © H. Armstrong Roberts/ClassicStock/Corbis; 269 (l) © Bettmann/CORBIS; 269 (r) Popperfoto/Getty Images; 255 Universal Pictures/Moviestore; 274 Jurow-Shepherd/Paramount Pictures/Kobal; 277 © Onne van der Wal/Corbis; 280 Reproduced by permission of Ronald Richardson; 287 Jean Louis Blondeau/Polaris/eyevine; 298 Be Gentlemen Limited Partnership/Lawrence Bender Productions/Miramax Films/Buena Vista International/Moviestore.

Index